ENCYCLOPEDIA OF GRAFFITI

ENCYCLOPEDIA OF GRAFFITI

Robert Reisner
and
Lorraine Wechsler

Galahad Books • New York City

Published in 1980 by
Galahad Books
95 Madison Avenue
New York, New York 10016
By arrangement with Macmillan Publishing Co., Inc.

Library of Congress Catalog Card Number: 74-16045
ISBN: 0-88365-443-1

Printed in the United States of America

INTRODUCTION

Graffiti—Inscriptions of figures, designs, or words on rocks or walls or sidewalks or the like, or on artifacts made of plaster, stone, or clay. The singular form is graffito.

[Italian diminutive of *graffio,* a scratch (of a stylus); Latin *graphi* (*um*); Greek *graph-ein*, to write]

Sometimes the humblest and the most pervasive activities are most important in the study of mankind, yet they are often overlooked. Graffiti have been with us since prehistoric man placed his hand on a cave wall and traced the outlines of his fingers with pigment. It was his way of saying "I exist."

Messages have been left by man in every age. The graffitist engages in political views and satire, comedy, homemade philosophy and advice to the lovelorn. From the stylus of Pompeii to the spray paint on New York subway cars, graffiti tell us something about ourselves. Graffiti represent man's desire to communicate. When written, his feelings—hopes, desires, fears—give him a certain satisfaction. Perhaps the wall becomes his therapist. On its surface he hurls his hostilities, expresses his fantasies, communicates his triumphs, vents his frustrations, proclaims his rebellion, declares his propaganda.

Graffiti are the voice of the common man. We are used to taking our history from aristocrats and statesmen and their paid scribes. But through graffiti we discover evidence of another version of history, characterized by oppression and opposition to the official point of view. Topics too sensitive, too bigoted, too outrageous for the official version are the natural province.

At least nine-tenths of wall writing is insignificant, banal, and sheer defacement. But that other small percentage that interests the collector justifies wading through all the triteness. It seems that almost everyone has had certain profound experiences that bring out in him something literary, if only a single line. A thought occurs to someone and, virtually simultaneously, there is a compulsion to express it. Graffitists are people who do not have any other outlet for their thoughts. They are not in the media; they do not express themselves before the public in any way. One might also surmise that they don't have any family or friends to exchange thoughts with.

For this collection, the widest sources of graffiti have been considered: writing and pictographs on walls, tracings in dust on a windowpane, diamond scratchings on glass, messages written on signs and posters, chalk doodlings on sidewalks and streets, love letters in the sand, and even the very ephemeral sky writing.

Most of the graffiti in this book were gathered by the author, who visited various locations and jotted down the writings, noting the place and date. Another portion was gleaned from the memories of individuals, thus accounting for the incomplete citations in many cases. Letters concerning graffiti have arrived from all over the world. They usually begin something like this: "I also am fascinated by wall writing. Have you ever seen the one which said . . . ?"

Helpful scholars provided leads that pointed the way to manuscripts in which graffiti had been collected by certain imaginative individuals. Such little bonanzas account for the erratic chronology. One has to work with what is preserved. Nature's freakishness preserved the Pompeiian inscriptions. Hurlo Thrumbo, an enterprising English publisher, put together a book of graffiti from eighteenth-century England by appealing to his countrymen to send him their findings. A group of German sociologists published their findings in public toilets around the turn of the century. Wetti Himmlisch, a female bathroom attendant who was proud of the intellectual caliber of her clients, recorded some of their wall-writing efforts. These appeared in her autobiography. The Kinsey researchers, assiduously studying and recording the sex habits of men and women, kept numerous examples of intimate wall messages. Another group of inscriptions was provided by Dr. Allen Walker Read's pioneering investigation of traditional and raunchy remarks by the common folk of Western North America. All such sources helped make this encyclopedia of graffiti easier to compile.

Certain special interest groups may find that the study of graffiti can provide new insights into their fields of study. For sociologists graffiti represent first-hand evidence of social change and unrest. For psychologists and psychiatrists the messages that indicate wish-fulfillment, fantasy, loneliness, may provide insights useful in diagnosis. For politicians graffiti are the secret ballot box providing clues about what constituents really want, because those who feel that the formal avenues for requests are useless may still write their gripes and needs on a wall. Political scientists and statesmen can gain a sympathetic edge in understanding and relating to particular groups of people by exploring their graffiti, which usually reveal a preoccupation with certain topics. For entertainers and lecturers graffiti provide a most quotable range of subtle wit and blatant burlesque. And for the intellectually curious graffiti should provide them with bittersweet feelings as they ponder these fragments of dialogue in the *comédie humaine*.

This work is only a jumping-off place for those interested in doing further research in graffiti. The book's omissions are as important as its inclusions. A collection of graffiti that is amusing, interesting, and significant to the general readers perforce ignores the dullest and most repetitive graffiti, which may be of value to professionals working on particular projects. The repetition of names hundreds of times may not be interesting to most people, but such a phenomenon could provide vital information for investigations of the breakdown of discipline and order, or into the workings of the moronic or ego-starved or bored mind.

Graffiti are serious business, but one should not approach them solemnly. The views herein expressed do not necessarily reflect those of the author, editor, publisher or the reader. A good portion of the material is, of course, highly iconoclastic. Everything we are cautioned about not saying before a microphone or at a dinner party—assaults upon morality and sexual "normality" and patriotism—is said here. Statistically, graffiti may be difficult to evaluate (though all persistent messages bear investigation) because one cannot always be sure whether they indicate social trends or social problems, or merely the hangups of some individuals. A mass neurosis is difficult to identify. But beyond their diagnostic usefulness, graffiti do tend to become a blow for liberty for the disgruntled minority, the deviant, and the supercynical. Obscene language, a salubrious tool for the release of tension, is also unshackled.

The walls have traditionally played an important role in politics. Stark statements of defiance or exhortation have been boldly written on them in times of turmoil, hardship, and revolution. Some persons who have no specific gripes that they are able to (or care to) define, but who are generally discontented with things as they are, write graffiti to express this feeling. Some have declared on the walls their desire for the demise of the existing government, or even the existing world. If one were to describe the last decade, it could very well be called the "Decade of Protest." The emphasis on activism and political involvement has stirred up many graffiti writers. But instead of writing on the walls out of despair and hopelessness, in a kind of weak and painful cry into a miserable and disinterested world, these graffitists clearly state their messages. Perhaps this attitude has come about, in part, because today we are told that everyone is important, that anyone can tip the balance, and that the government's eye is on every sparrow. The list of causes and groups promoted by individuals is long and varied. Pacifists, civil rightists, homosexuals, proabortionists, atheists, feminists, pot-smokers, antivivisectionists are only a few of the groups who now write on walls.

What type of individual writes graffiti? The answer depends on the nature of the message, how and on what it is written, the spirit of the times, and the region or country where it is written. Not very much is known about people who write on walls, since the spirit of the activity is anonymous. Graphologists might deduce certain characteristics from the handwriting; other conclusions have to be drawn from the content.

Sometimes the reason for writing on a wall may be sheer boredom. To one sitting in a bathroom with nothing to read, the bare walls may present a challenge. It may also be that these bare walls offer a limited sensory stimulation that makes the person more aware of his internal conflicts and more aware of sensual feelings; thus, he writes something about his thoughts. A major force behind the graffiti of inmates of sanitoriums and prisons is to counter the sameness of the environment and the day-to-day boredom.

Psychiatrists have called graffiti that contain raw sexual messages and obscene drawings a form of psychic masturbation, of exhibitionism. An exhibitionist is driven by some unrelenting anxiety to expose his own sexual organs in public in order to relieve that anxiety. The exhibitionist once-removed draws or describes imaginary genitals, usually in an exaggerated manner.

There are many better-adjusted persons who write what are often classified as "dirty" words on walls. The psychoanalyst Sandor Ferenczi has written some fascinating observations about obscenity and its role in the developing psyche:

> In the fourth or fifth year of life, and considerably earlier with precocious children . . . a period is interpolated between the relinquishing of the infantile modes of gratification and the beginning of the true latency period, one characterized by the impulse to utter, write up, and listen to obscene words.

Ferenczi further states:

> It is the suppression of these sexual phantasies and actions, manifested in the weakened form of speech, that really connotes the beginning of the latency period proper, that period in which [and he quotes Freud] "the mental counterforce against infantile sexuality, namely, disgust, shame, and morality are formed" and the child's interest is turned in the direction of social activities [desire for knowledge].

The repression of obscene verbal images is usually not absolute in the normal individual. During everyday life the latency is broken through often enough so that what has been repressed is looked at from a different point of view.

Dirty words serve as a pressure release, a safety valve for pent-up emotions, sexual or otherwise. When tension mounts, the writing of these words seems to alleviate it. These words may also signify love, joy, and sorrow as well as boredom, despair, or hatred. Cursing one's enemy is a substitute for batting him around physically. Writing an obscenity on a wall may be a substitute for more violent action. As with most slang words, the precise meaning gives way to broader and broader meanings. The word *fuck,* for example, does not necessarily always pertain to the sexual act but to many levels and states of emotion. In certain circles *mother-fucker* may be used affectionately.

A pleasant aspect of graffiti is its humor. The person writing amusing statements on a wall is likely to be either one who is struck by an original funny thought and unselfishly writes it to share with the world, or the compulsive joke teller who must repeat something funny he has seen or heard.

Sometimes a person will feel an urge to *reply* to a particularly striking graffito. He may see a statement that appears so outrageous or disagreeable or incorrect that he feels compelled to write a comment underneath. His reply may even inspire another and thus set off a whole chain of dialogue. This type of "conversational graffiti," owing to its spontaneity and inspiration, is often the most successful sort of wall writing.

On the other hand, there is the recent phenomenon of the spray-can artists. These graffitists set out in groups to do their writing, having decided in advance what and where they will write. When graffiti becomes self-conscious, is produced without spontaneity, it loses both its strength and its quirky, madcap quality. It becomes what might be termed a "communal graffiti," in which content becomes relatively unimportant and defiance and lawlessness and peer competition are the main purposes of the exercise. The art itself becomes the message.

The art of graffiti will continue to wax and wane, reflecting the shifting conditions of life. As people sense they are becoming more computerized and their lives open punch cards, the graffitist, especially the solitary variety, will probably strive to counterbalance the trend toward depersonalization with a fascinating range of personal statements that all say, "I write, therefore I am."

A

AARDVARK

Kiss the ass of an Aardvark.

(Kettle of Fish Bar & Restaurant, New York City)

ABORTION

Abortion on demand is murder by request.
The Devil says: legalize abortion, pot, homosexuality.

(IRT subway, New York City)

I am a mistake—legalize abortion.

Student Abortion Agency.
You rape 'em, we scrape 'em.
No fetus can beat us.
Babies are our business.
Her womb is its tomb.

(Men's room, Princeton University, 1970)

Protect your local abortionist.

ADLER, RENATA (1938–   )

Renata Adler is smarter than Susan Sontag.

ADOLESCENCE, see YOUTH

ADULTERY

Clarinda lay here
With a young Cavalier;
With her Heart full of Fear,
For her Husband was near.
L.L. Feb. 2. 1728.

UNDERNEATH

'Tis very true; for we saw Rem-in-Re through the Key-Hole.
S.M.)
J.M.) Feb. 3. 1728.
R.H.)

UNDERNEATH

If the Husband had come,
And had seen his Wife's B—m,
He'd a known by her Looks,
She'd been playing ——
At Hoy Gammer Cooks.
S.B. March 3. 1728.

(On a window, Red Lion Inn, Southwell, England)

Gene M is married—but only his wife thinks so.

(Ladies' room, Greenwich Village, New York City)

I just fucked my governor's missus.

(Men's room, railroad station at Woking, England, 1965)

I'm a different kind of librarian. I'm a young adulteress.

(Library staff lounge, cited in American Library Association Bulletin, *January 1969)*

On a Gentleman's saying he had calculated his Son's Nativity, the Boy being then about nine Days old:
Lavinia brought to Bed, her Husband looks
To know the Bantling's Fortune in his Books.
Wiser he'd been, he look'd backward rather,
And seen for certain, who had been its Father.

(On a window, Bath, England)

Sir— was chosen our Recorder,
Hoping he'd put our Wrongs in Order.

But, in Truth, the young Gentleman prov'd such a Rake,
That he kiss'd all our Wives, and make all our Heads ake.

(On a window, Yorkshire, England)

Suburbia Today: Bookmobiles are out; wifemobiles are in.

(Arlington County Public Library, Va.—cited in American Library Association Bulletin, *April, 1969)*

Whilst Lady Mary slept at Ease,
Secure from Jealousy and Fleas,
Her Lord with vig'rous Love inclin'd,
To kiss her Maid, and ease his Mind:
The Maiden did not long resist,
But gently yielded to be kist;
And in the Dance of Lovers move,
With sprightly Bounds to shew her Love:
When in the Height of am'rous Fire,
She cry'd, my Lord, I've one Desire,
Tell me, my Peer, tell me, my Lord,
Tell me, my Life, upon your Word,
Who does it best, my Dame or me?
And then she fell in Extasy.
My Lord in Fire of his Love,
Call'd her his Minion, Turtle Dove;
You have the only Art to please,
All this he swore upon his Knees;
Your Dame is like a Log of Wood,
Her Love is never half so good.
My Lord says she, all that I know;
For all the World has told me so.
S—d—rs, April, 1717.

(On a wainscoat at the Crown at Harlow, England)

AGING

As a man grows old his balls grow cold.

(Iowa State Teachers College Library, 1925)

At Home Miss Molly's scarce fifteen,
  Mamma says she's no more;
But if the Parish-Book says true,
  Miss Molly's thirty four.
          Poor Miss Molly!

(Tuns in Cambridge, England)

The difference between "stick-up" and "hold-up" is age.

Do retiring volkswagens go to the "old volks home"?

I am getting old and have almost reached my barrier,
What used to be my magic wand is just my water carrier.

I look back to the beautiful time when all joints were flexible—but one. But those times are over and all the joints became stiff except one.

(Men's room, Germany)

Is Molly Fr— immortal?—No,
She is; and I will prove her so.
She's fifteen now, and was, I know,
Fifteen, full fifteen Years ago.

(Tuns in Cambridge, England)

Jack and Jill are over the hill.

Old golfers never die, they merely lose their balls.

Old postmen never die, they merely lose their zip.

Pushing but coming.

(On a truck, Mexico)

There's Nothing sure can vex a Woman more
Than to hear the Feats of Love, and be Threescore.

(On a window, Rumford, England)

'Tis hard! 'tis wonderous hard!
  That the Life of a Man
  Should be but a Span,
And that of a Woman a Yard!

(In the Angel Tavern, London)

This is the menopause that refreshes.

When Phillis wore her brightest Face,
All Men rejoic'd in every Grace:
Her Patch, her Mein, her forward Chin,
Cry'd, Gentlemen, Pray who'll come in:
But now her Wrinkles are come on her,
All Men who ever were upon her,
Cry out, a Fart upon her Honour.
C.M.

(Temple Bar, England)

When the hair turns grey,
and the cock turns blue,
and you can no longer piss in arcs,
These for sure are three bad marks.

(Men's toilet, Leipzig, 1882)

On two old Maids:
Why are Doll's Teeth so white, and Susan's black?
The Reason soon is known.
Doll buys her Teeth which she doth lack,
But Susan wears her own.

(In the Pump Room, Bath, England)

AGNEW, SPIRO (1918–)

Beware the Spirochete.
[An order of bacteria including those causing syphilis.]

Dick and Spiro add up to zero.

(Men's room, Bates College, Me.)

Effete snob for peace.

(On various walls shortly after a November, 1969, speech by Vice President Agnew in which he referred to certain peace demonstrators as effete snobs, also on a button)

Gag a goat.
Frig a pig.
Spear a steer.
Ball a wall.
Bang an orangutang.
Assault a Renault.
Rape an ape.
Intercourse a horse . . . of course.
Jog a dog.
Plug a bug.
Bump a stump.
Tool a mule.
Shaft a giraffe.
Screw Agnew.

(Men's room, University of Maryland, 1972)

Let us beat Spiro into ploughshares.

Mickey Mouse is wearing a Spiro Agnew watch.

(Vietnam, 1971—cited in Playboy, *August, 1971)*

Nixon is the first president to have an ass-hole for a vice president.

UNDERNEATH

No, Eisenhower was.

(University of Michigan, 1970)

No news is agnews.

(University of Michigan)

A pox Agnew.

(Subway, New York City)

Richard Nixon will have two cabinets—one to hide Spiro Agnew.

Spiro Agnew has hoof-in-mouth disease.

(University of Michigan, 1970)

Spiro Agnew: The human edsel.

(University of Michigan, 1970)

Spiro is our hero.

Spiro, peel me a grape.

(Men's room, Harvard University)

Spiro-Zorba the Beak Geek.

(Men's room, Harvard University)

Willy Brandt: don't give Nixon or Agnew political asylum in Germany.

(New York City, 1970)

AIR POLLUTION

Air pollution is a mist demeanor.

Caution: breathing may be hazardous to your health.

(Various walls, also on a button)

Clean air smells funny.

The following was written on a poster that said:
"Did you make New York dirty today?":
New York makes ME dirty every day.

Fight smog, buy a horse.

Fly the fetid skies of New Jersey.

Henry Ford invented emphysema.
UNDERNEATH
That's Edsel, dummy.
UNDERNEATH
Death anyway you spell it.

(Men's room, Princeton University)

Not only are you getting cancer you're polluting MY air.
—Mr. American Tobacco Co.
UNDERNEATH
Cancer, emphazema [sic], yellow teeth, death.
UNDERNEATH
Yes, but we're helping ease the population explosion.

(IND subway, New York City, 1971)

Of course I smoke it's safer than breathing.

The pollution you breathe may be your own.

(University of Michigan, 1970)

Stop air pollution—quit breathing.

Whatever happened to the good old days when sex was dirty and the air clean?

ALCOHOL

Absinthe makes the heart grow fonder.

Alcohol and tobacco do away with half of
mankind but without alcohol and tobacco
the other half would die.

(Men's room, Germany)

Alcohol is your enemy!

UNDERNEATH

The Bible says: Love thy enemy.

(Helsinki, 1970)

Alcohol kills. Take L.S.D.

(Nanterre University, May, 1968)

Drunk at Comb-Abbey, horrid drunk;
Hither I came, and met my fav'rite punk.
But she as well might have embrac'd a log,
All night I snor'd and grunted like a hog,
Then was not I a sad confounded dog?

(On a window, Star of Coventry, England)

A Hog, a Monkey, and an Ass,
Were here last Night to drink a Glass,
When all at length it came to pass,
That the Hog and the Monkey,
Grew so drunkey,
That both were ready to kiss the A–se
of Tom. Dingle.
April 17. 1710.

(Greyhound, Maidenhead, England)

How shall the Man e'er turn to dust
Who daily wets his Clay.

UNDERNEATH

In Dust he may fly
As Fools gallop by,
And no body can say Nay.

(On a window, Rumford, England)

Hullo, we're wineskins.

(Pompeii, 79 A.D.)

Hurrah for Korsakov's psychosis.
[This is the technical term for the D.T.'s.]

I don't drink water because fish fuck in it.

(Men's room, Gleason's Tavern, New York City, 1969—this message is really the brainchild of W. C. Fields.)

I'll never get drunk again,
For my head's full of pain,
And it grieves me to think,
that by dint of good drink,
I should lie with my Phillis in vain.

(On a window, Star of Coventry, England, 1712)

Like Mars I'll fight,
like Antony I'll love,
I'll drink like Bacchus,
and I'll whore like Jove.

(Common graffito in early 18th-century England)

Old Granddad is dead but his spirits live on.

The only thing that can cure love is the glass of forgetfullness.

(Ellis Island, N.Y., written in Greek, 1953)

Passerby, may you taste bread at Pompeii but drink at Nuceria—Nuceria!

(Pompeii, 79 A.D.)

Sterno is back.

Three Bottles of Burgundy, and a brisk Lass,
With a thousand of Grigs, should it e'er come to pass,
Would make me behave my self just like an Ass.
M. of Oxon, 1709.

(In the Catherine Wheel, Henley, England)

Anagram:
A Toast is like a Sot,
Or what is most
Comparable—a Sot,
—Is like a Toast;
For When their Substance
In the Liquor sink,
Both properly are said
To be in Drink.

(England, mid-18th century)

Who's been here,
The Devil I fear;
For he's left the Bottles clear.
(R. Eft—n, 1710.

UNDERNEATH

'Twas so; for nothing so like the Devil as an empty Bottle.
G.S. 1711.

(Swan at Uxbridge, England)

With booze you lose, with dope you hope.

(Men's room, Holly Tavern, Bellingham, Wash., 1970)

You don't buy beer here, you just rent it.

(Men's room, The Oasis Bar, Palo Alto, Calif.)

You fight and die but can't drink at 18.

(On various walls, 1968)

ALI, MUHAMMED (1942–)

Cassius Clay is really Al Jolson.

(Cited by Jim Murray, sports columnist, Los Angeles Times*)*

ALLAH

Allah
~~God~~ is dead.

Allah is the Ground of Being.

(Columbia University)

Allah was here!

UNDERNEATH

But he's dead now.

(Subway, New York City)

Curb your God
i.e. curb Allah
i.e. curb caballah.

UNDERNEATH

i.e. curb Cat Ballou.

(The Forum Coffee House, New York City)

AMBITION

Do something big—fuck a giant.

A go-getter, in some offices, is the fellow they send for coffee.

(Midtown New York construction fence)

Goyim are shiftless.

(Men's room, New York University)

I'd rather write than be President.

Nothing sucks like success.

Remember, even if you win the rat race—you're still a rat.

Some people carve careers, others chisel them.

The trouble with the world today is that there are too many nobodies trying to be Everybody!

(Lion's Head, New York City)

You've had eight jobs; now it only remains for you to double the list and make it sixteen. You've been a pub-waiter, you've made pottery, you've dealt in salted fish, you've done bakery, you've been a farmer, you've made small bronze oddments, you've been a street hawker now you make little flasks. If you only suck up to women, you'll have run the full gamut.

(Pompeii, 79 A.D.)

ANARCHISM

Anarchism now!

(Café Figaro, New York City, 1965)

Anarchists of the world unite, you have nothing to lose but your decentralized principles.

(Paradox Restaurant, New York City)

Anarchist please learn to flush.

(Co-ed toilet, Alternate University, New York City)

Anarchists unite!

(On various walls, and also on a button)

Anarchy is against the law.

(Co-ed toilet, Alternate University, New York City)

Anarchy is I.

(Nanterre, May, 1968)

Bakunin was right.

Everything is Dada.

(Paris, May, 1968)

Nihilism should commence with oneself.

(Paris, May, 1968)

Program = private property of the future.

(Sorbonne, May, 1968)

Silence: nihilists at work.

(Men's room, Princeton University, 1970)

The State is each one of us.

(Paris, May, 1968)

Vote anarchist.

Whoever sleeps with the same one twice already belongs to the establishment.

(Men's room, Germany)

ANATOMY

Add up the spinal column and get a disc count.

Ashes to ashes
  Dust to dust
What is a sweater
  Without a bust!

(Mainz, 1907)

Honey Greenhill has a 42″ bust. Confucius say: "Honey who wear falsies make mountains out of Greenhill."

(Ladies' room, Barnard College)

Hormones are a big bust.

I'd give my right arm to be ambidextrous.

If time heals all wounds, how come the belly button stays the same?

(Men's room, University of California at Berkeley)

In the asshole it is dark,
In the asshole it is dark.
Why shouldn't it be dark in the asshole?
No sun or moon shines here.

(Men's room, Germany)

How many men will not fuck with me because I am flat chested. Help!

UNDERNEATH

Thank god, honey—I am busty and that's all they want from me. It's a real problem, besides you don't have to wear a bra—while it would be truly uncomfortable and dangerous for me not to.

(Ladies' room, New York University, 1971)

Think how you look to your pinworms.
[These are little parasites around the rectum.]

(Doctors' bathroom, Bellevue Hospital, New York City)

My heavens, where did I leave my crotch?

Nudists are people who wear one-button suits!

Why do you kiss the cheeks
  of your bride?
Kiss her asshole,—
  it is the same skin after all!

The world is flat.
  —Class of 1491.

UNDERNEATH

All the girls in our world are flat.
  —Class of 1973.

(Men's room, Princeton University, 1970)

ANGER

Anger may glance into the Breast of wise Men:
  But it rests in the Bosom of Fools.

(On a Window at Christ Church, Oxford University)

Rail at your Father, rail at your Mother,
Rail at your Sister, rail at your Brother,
Rail on, my Boys, and rail at one another.

UNDERNEATH

Rail as you say, and you'll be all railed in.

(Crown at Harlow, England)

ANTI-SEMITISM

All Jews and Niggers are one and the same.

(Men's room, Rutgers University, 1969)

Christianity will live as long as there's anti-Semitism.

(Rutgers University, 1971)

Communism is Jewish.

(Union Terminal Railroad station, two blocks from JFK assassination site, Dallas)

The following was written on an ad for *The New York Times:*
Coons read kike N.Y. Post.

(Subway, New York City)

If you meet Jews while they are shitting, cover them with your own shit.

(Breslau—cited in Anthropophyteia, *Vol. 6, 1909)*

In the year '38 there was a shortage of eggs
that's why they cut the eggs out of the Jews testicles.

(Men's room, Germany)

Jew is nigger turned inside out.

The Jews are a gas.—A. Hitler.

(Ladies' room, Limelight Restaurant, New York City)

Jews are the biggest pigs, therefore kill them without remorse.

(Breslau—cited in Anthropophyteia, *Vol. 6, 1909)*

Jews: Eat molten death.

(IND subway, New York City, 1971)

Jews out!

UNDERNEATH

Nazis remain here.

(Toilet, Germany—during Hitler regime)

Only the Jew and the Protestant will shit on the rim.

(Breslau—cited in Anthropophyteia, *Vol. 6, 1909)*

Ruby was a fuckin' Jew queer.

(Toilet, Dallas)

Stop Zionist aggression [*sic*].

(Subway, New York City)

There will be a meeting of all non-Jewish students in the telephone booth.

(Boston University)

卐
These Nazis never learn.

(Gene and Bunny's Bar, New York City)

This rest room is reviewed in the 1969 edition of "The Protocols of the Elders of Zion."

UNDERNEATH

Which is why the Jewish Defense League is always on your ass.

(Co-ed toilet, East Village Other, *1970)*

Why are Jews so loud and obnoxious? They really are. Is it cultural or genetic or what? They repulse.

UNDERNEATH

Because you're a fucking, prejudiced, arrogant bastard who is probably a self-centered, ignorant, egotistical pig—then drop dead.

UNDERNEATH

Typical Jewish response, language of the gutter—defensive and coarse. Don't be ashamed of it, it's just the way you are.

UNDERNEATH

Why spread hate and prejudice?

(Ladies' room, New York University)

Why does everyone hate Jews, homosexuals and blacks?

UNDERNEATH

Were you ever circumsized, blown or mugged?

(Men's room, Hunter College, New York City, 1972)

APATHY

Sock it to me with apathy.

Tomorrow will be cancelled due to lack of interest.

Who gives a damn about apathy.

ARCHIMEDES (287–212 B.C.)

Archimedes had no principles!

ARCHITECTURE, *see* BUILDINGS

ARMED FORCES

Abolish the draft.

(On various walls, also on a button)

At this moment you are the only man in the Air Force who knows what he's doing.

(Men's room, Westover Air Force Base, Mass.)

Don't draft married men, all the fight's out of them.

Draft beer, not men.

(Ladies' room, West End Bar & Restaurant, New York City)

Draft the beat.

God is not dead,
he's just trying to avoid the draft.

(Subway, Boston)

Heaven is where the entire U.S. Navy stands in line with pricks hanging out.

(Men's room, IRT subway, New York City, 1940)

If God had wanted us in the Army, he would have given us green baggy skin.

(San Francisco, 1971)

If you are a lifer I hate you.

UNDERNEATH

I am a lifer and I know who wrote this.

(Men's room, Vietnam, 1972)

Join the Marines, intervene in the country of *your* choice.

Loyal — Lazy
Intelligent — Inefficient
Fearless — Fuck off
Energetic — Expecting
Responsible — Retirement

(Vietnam, 1971)

Make boys! Avoid the draft!

Marine Corps builds Oswalds.

The Marine Corps thanks the USAF.

UNDERNEATH

Your [*sic*] welcome, jarhead.

(Vietnam, 1966)

Navy dupes eat millionaires' shit.

UNDERNEATH

The U.S. Navy protects you long hairs too!

(Limelight Restaurant, New York City)

The Navy is a prime example of the *incompetent* heading the *unwilling* to do the *unnecessary* for the *ungrateful.*

The following was written on a Navy poster:
Navy sux.

(New York City)

The Official Army Teaching Code:
The inept teaching the indifferent.

(Army men's room, 1970)

Old soldiers never die. Young ones do.

(IRT subway, New York City)

On the 8th day God created the Army. After doing so, he saw he made a mistake, and he created the 7 day week.

(San Francisco, 1971)

The following replies were written on a sign on an elevator in the Princeton Library that said: "Out of service indefinitely for major repairs."

UNDERNEATH

Well tell Major Repairs that General Use wants this damn thing back in service immediately!

UNDERNEATH

Sorry, Major Repairs is out with Private Parts.

(Princeton University, 1970)

Resist the army.

ROTC builds men.

UNDERNEATH

Into what?

UNDERNEATH

Out of what?

(University of Michigan, 1970)

ROTC-NAZI

(Cornell University)

Sleep well tonight, the National Guard is.

(San Francisco, 1971)

There are two kinds of people in the Army. Them that gets articles 15's and them that gives article 15's.
(*Note:* Article 15 refers to military punishment not awarded by a court-martial.)

UFO's are for real: the Air Force doesn't exist.

(University of Michigan)

The United States Army;
194 years of proud service,
unhampered by progress.

(Army men's room, 1970)

We shall overkill.

(On various walls, also on a button)

ARMY, *see* ARMED FORCES

ART

Ars Longa, Vita Herring.

(Lion's Head, New York City)

Art is an academic neurosis.

(Paris, May, 1968)

Art is dead, don't eat its corpse.

(Paris, May, 1968)

Art is dead. Godard can't do a thing about it.

(Sorbonne, May, 1968)

Art is dead; let us liberate our daily life.

(Sorbonne, May, 1968)

Art is Love is God.

(Engagé Coffee House, New York City)

Art is shit.

(Paris, May, 1968)

Art: the living corpse of Western Civilization.

(New York University, 1969)

An artist without ideas is a mendicant, barren he goes begging among the hours.

(Florida State University)

Artists are misunderstood. Not by people, but by themselves.

Come hither, Heralds, view this Coat,
'Twill bear Examination,
'Tis ancient, and derives its Note
From the first Pair's Creation.

The Field is Luna, Mars a Pale,
Within an Orle of Saturn;
Charg'd with two Pellets at the Tail:
Pray take it for a Pattern.

UNDERNEATH

I don't see your Luna, nor Saturn, nor Mars,
But I see her—plain, and I see his bare A–se.

(On the wall, under a curious piece of drawing, in one of the summer houses in Gray's-Inn Walks, England)

Dada saves!

(Lion's Head, New York City)

Everything is Dada.

(Paris, May, 1968)

Fuck all queer avant gardes.

(Le Metro Caffe Espresso, Second Avenue, New York City)

Up art's jazz.

What is art?—To hold on to a tree and run around it so fast that you fuck yourself in the ass.

(Germany, 1908)

ASSIGNATIONS

I wait for you. Are you as hard up as I am?

(Men's room, Germany)

If you are an intellectual truck driver with a 7 and ⅜ cock, be here on Friday 4 o'clock Sept. 23, 1949.

(Men's room, New York City, 1949)

PE 4-084—Please! no cranks.

ATHEISM

God is an atheist.

I am an atheist. I don't believe in Zeus.

(Construction wall, Philadelphia, 1969)

Pray for the success of atheism.

(On various walls, also on buttons and stickers)

Sacred cows make great hamburgers.

Poster: "Worship Together This Week."

UNDERNEATH

Is it your business?
Don't advertise religion.
Keep our God free of churches.
Just a universal conspiracy for idiots.

ATHLETICS, *see* SPORTS

ATOMIC POWER

Ban the bomb.

UNDERNEATH

And homework.

Ban the bomb, save the world for conventional warfare.

Due to a lack of tomorrows interest has been cancelled.

(Men's room, Princeton University, 1970)

Eat, drink and be merry for tomorrow you may be radioactive.

The Fat Jap will never forget Nagasaki.

In case of atomic attack . . .
1. Put your hands over your ears.
2. Put your head between your legs.
3. Kiss your ass goodbye. You've had it.

In case of atomic attack,
the federal ruling against prayer in schools
will be temporarily suspended.

(On a fence—quoted by Norton Mockridge)

Ring around a neutron
A pocket full of protons
A fission, a fission
We all fall down.

(Construction wall, Philadelphia, 1969)

AUTOMATION, *see also* COMPUTERS

Lie down I want to automate.

(Free Library of Philadelphia)

We have an electric eraser. What have you done for automation, lately?

(Library staff lounge—cited in American Library Association Bulletin, *January, 1969)*

The following replies were written on a poster that said: "What will you do when this circuit learns your job?":

Buy a circuit breaker.
Pull out the plug.
Buy two and retire.
Go on relief, stupid!
Make one that can do yours.
Marry it, of course.

When an automatic machine is wrong, it's automatically wrong.

(San Francisco State College, 1970)

AUTOMOBILES

Drive defensively, buy a tank.

Help send VW's back to Germany.

In a hurry? Go underneath. *(On a truck, Mexico)*

Pedestrians pressed. 

(On a dry-cleaning truck, Mexico)

Plymouth is out to run you over this year.

(This is a variation on the ad: "Plymouth is out to win you over this year," 1968)

Spare the rod and spoil the drag race.

(Library staff lounge, Fort Belvoir, Va.—cited in American Library Association Bulletin, *April, 1969)*

We want anti-gravity cars, the wheel is obsolete.

(IND subway, New York City, 1970)

B

BABA, MEHER (1894–1969)

We are all one in Baba's ocean of love.

(Goddard College, Vt., 1971)

BACH, JOHANN SEBASTIAN (1685–1750)

Back to Bach.

BACON, FRANCIS (1561–1626)

Shakespeare eats Bacon.

UNDERNEATH

It can't be Donne.

(Lion's Head, New York City)

BAKUNIN, MIKHAIL (1814–1876)

(Note: Russian anarchist who believed that anarchism, collectivism and atheism were requirements for human liberty)

Bakunin was right.

BALDWIN, JAMES (1924–)

James Baldwin eats watermelon, etc.

(University of California at Los Angeles, 1966)

BANANAS

Banana power.

(Men's room, The Dom, New York City—also on a button)

Bananas forever.

(On a wall on St. Mark's Place, New York City)

Chiquita is hooked on bananas.

Come alive, you're in the banana generation.

(Men's room, New York City)

Smoke bananas.

(On a fence in the East Village, New York City)

Smoke more bananas.

Trip on a banana.
[Variation: Trip on a banana peel.]

BARA, THEDA (1890–1955)

Theda Bara is a form of Arab Death.

BARAKA, IMAMU (1934–   )

LeRoi Jones was here.

UNDERNEATH

LeRoi eats white ice cream

(Ladies' room, Le Metro Caffe Espresso, New York City)

BEATLES

This decade would be a *total* loss if not for the Beatles.

(New York University, 1969)

BEATNIKS

Beatnicks are worthless.

UNDERNEATH

Your attitude is worthless.

UNDERNEATH

Beatnicks have been extinct since 1960. Where have you been?

UNDERNEATH

How do you spell beetnick?

(The Forum Coffee House, New York City)

Draft the beat.

To be beat is to be cool.
To be beat-cool is not to be beat.
To be beat-cool and not to be beat is nowhere.

(Café Figaro, New York City, 1966)

BEAUTY

Beauty is only skin deep, but ugly is to the bone.

If you can't make it beautiful—make it sensitive!

May yours be the luck Sabina, to blossom unfading,
Your beauty unwithered. Long a girl may you stay.

UNDERNEATH

Sabina, you suck all in, you don't act prettily.

(Pompeii, 79 A.D.)

BEIDERBECKE, LEON (1903–1931)

(Note: famous jazz cornetist)

Bix lives!

(Men's room, Eddie Condon's, New York City, 1954)

BECKETT, SAMUEL (1906–)

Go! Go! with Godot.

I was here, wait for me

—Godot.

(University of California at Berkeley)

BEETHOVEN, LUDWIG VAN (1770–1827)

Beethoven made overtures.

Beethoven scares little kids.

(Public school wall, New York City)

BELL, ALEXANDER GRAHAM (1847–1922)

Alexander Graham Bell is alive and well in New York, and still waiting for a dial tone.

(Cited by Earl Wilson, columnist, New York Post, *December 13, 1971)*

BEN-GURION, DAVID (1886–1973)

Donald Duck is a Jew.

UNDERNEATH

Ben-Gurion is a duck.

BIBLE

Alcohol is your enemy!

UNDERNEATH

The Bible says: Love thy enemy.

(On a wall, Helsinki, 1970)

All flesh is grass
—Isaiah

UNDERNEATH

Smoke a friend today.

Blessed are the meek for they shall inhibit the earth.

Consult Bishop Sheen for revocation of the 10 Commandments.

(Ladies' room, City College of New York, 1969)

Dow shalt not kill.

(Construction fence, New York City)

Gabriel blows.

(On various walls, also on a button)

God is not dead! He is alive and autographing bibles at Brentano's.

(Subway, New York City)

In the Garden of Eden sat Adam,
Massaging the bust of his madam,
He chuckled with mirth,
For he knew that on earth,
There were only two b——s and he had 'em.

Incest, murder, sodomy, genocide . . . are as close as your nearest Bible.

It wasn't the apple in the tree that drove Adam out of Eden, it was the tomato on the ground.

The meek shall inherit the earth—they are too weak to refuse.

A new Reading about the three Children in the Fiery Furnace. From the Hebrew.

Shadrack, Moshac, and Abednego.
If Shadrac had a Fever and Ague.
Then read in English
Shadrack may shake, and a bed may go. R.F.

(On a window, Merton College, Oxon)

Sodom is a summer festival.

UNDERNEATH

Gomorrah the merrier.

(Kettle of Fish Bar & Restaurant, New York City)

Sodom was a fun city.

Thou shalt not covet thy neighbor's fag.

You think Oedipus had a problem. Adam was Eve's mother.

(Construction wall, Philadelphia, 1969)

BIGOTRY, *see* RACE CONFLICT

BILBO, THEODORE G, (1877–1947)

(Note: An ultra-conservative, Bilbo served as senator from, and governor of, Mississippi)
Bilbo lives on Waverly Place

(Limelight Restaurant, New York City)

BIRTH CONTROL

Ban the bombino.

Birth control pills are habit forming.

Don't litter, stop the population explosion.

(IRT subway, New York City)

Give 11 year old girls the pill.

(Stockholm official graffiti wall (Kotterplank), *1969)*

Have pill—will.

The following were written on prophylactic machines:

Buy me and stop one.

UNDERNEATH

Buy two and be one jump ahead.

(Men's room, pub, Derbyshire, England, 1971)

It takes the worry out of being close.

(Rest room, Shafter, Nevada—takeoff on a Ban deodorant ad)

Practice birth control—people are worse than the bomb.

(Phoenix, 1965)

Head gaskets for hot rods.

(Written on a prophylactic vending machine, men's room, Tex., 1964)

The little old lady who lived in a shoe recommends the pill.

Make love, not babies.

(Ladies' room, John Adams Luncheonette, New York City)

The name for the pill is absorbine junior.

Not too slow, not too fast. Get off at the right time, otherwise you impregnate.

(Men's room, Germany)

Pope Paul *is* a pill!

Oh father, oh father I've come to confess
I've just left a girl in a terrible mess.
Her blouse is all tattered, her tits are bare.
And there's a lump in her belly that shouldn't be there.
Oh son, oh son with you I am vexed
When I was your age I used a Durex.
Oh father, oh father don't be unjust
I used one too, but the bloody thing bust.

(Men's room, London)

Send your pills to the Pope.

(Ladies' room, Limelight Restaurant, New York City, 1968)

Thank God my mother doesn't believe in birth control or I wouldn't be here today.

UNDERNEATH

Who needs you?

This gum tastes just like rubber.
[Scrawl found on a contraceptive vending machine in U.S. Army toilet]

Unilateral withdrawal is the answer to the population problem.

(University of Michigan, 1970)

Use contraceptives: No deposit—No return.

A vasectomy means never having to say you're sorry.

BLOW, JOHN (1648–1708)

(Note: English composer and organist chiefly remembered for his church music; teacher of Henry Purcell)

Do you know the John Blow record?

UNDERNEATH

No, how many times?

BODY, HUMAN, see ANATOMY

BOOKS

Condense soup, not books.

I have two of everything. What shall I do with them?

UNDERNEATH

I should buy some books.

(Men's room, New York City)

The last book on elephant physiology was written in 1936—this was also the first.

(University of Michigan)

Read books—they may be burned tomorrow.

The world is coming to an end! Repent and return those library books!

(Arlington County Public Library, Va.—cited in American Library Association Bulletin, *April, 1969)*

Ye longing Sophs, say it who can,
That Corny's not a learned Man.
He knows well each Edition, Sir,
of Aldus, and of Elzevir;
Of Beza he profoundly reasons,
And talks jocose of Harry Stephens.
Though (says a Wag) all this I grant,
Yet Corny sure must Learning want.
How so?—It's plain, (if that we may
B'lieve what Men of themselves do say,).
For Corny's openly * confess'd,
He's but a Blockhead at the best.

(On window of printer and bookseller's shop, Cambridge, England)

BOONE, DANIEL (1734–1820)

D. BOON
Cilled A. BAR
in ThE
yEAR 1760

(Daniel Boone's carving on a beech tree in Central Tennessee)

BOREDOM

I yawned here.

(Ladies' room, Schrafft's Restaurant, New York City)

Pearl was super-bored today

(Subway, New York City)

People who work get bored when they don't work; people who don't work never get bored.

(Sorbonne, May, 1968)

Philadelphia is not dull—it just seems so because it is next to exciting Camden, New Jersey.

(Construction wall, Philadelphia 1969)

The prospect of tomorrow's joy will never console me for today's boredom.

(Nanterre University, May, 1968)

Same thing day after day—tube work dinner work tube armchair TV sleep tube work—how much more can you take? One in five cracks up, one in ten goes mad.

(Painted in letters 3 ft. high outside a London underground station, 1971)

BOURGEOISIE

Bourgeois elements must go!

The bourgeois state is a tranquilizer with lethal side effects.

(Ladies' room, Goddard College, 1971)

The bourgeoisie has no other pleasure than to degrade everybody.

(Sorbonne, May, 1968)

BRAGGADOCIO

Few hairs but well combed.

(On a truck, Mexico)

The Hawkins Brothers . . . we don't give a rats ass.

(Men's room, Greyhound bus stop, Arkansas)

I am twelve inches long and three inches around.

UNDERNEATH

Great: How big is your penis?

I hold the record on the deepest probe yet.
Twelve inches and it's all in me pants.
Bisexual is my game.
Any girl or guy that will give up the stuff
I'll make the claim.

(Men's room, Los Angeles Valley College, 1970)

I'll drink like Bacchus, and I'll fight like Mars,
The Kind I'll love, the Cross may kiss my A–se.

(In a tavern in Fleet Street, London, mid-18th century)

I'm not a dollar but I can go up.

(On a truck, Mexico)

I've got what every woman wants.

UNDERNEATH

You must be in the fur coat business.

Think you as I do, and think ye true.

(Men's room, faculty lounge, Hunter College, New York City)

When I drop my drawers,
To display my tool,
The majority of girls,
Just sit and drool.

UNDERNEATH

Why? Does it look like a butterscotch sunday?

UNDERNEATH

Shmuck! There's an e instead of y in sundae.

(Men's room, University of Minnesota, 1972)

The yodeling cowboy from Texas I SATISFY Whoopee.

(Tourist Park, Waterloo, Iowa, 1932)

BRAHMS, JOHANNES (1833–1897)

Brahms not bombs.

(On wall in New York City, also on a button)

BRANDT, WILLY (1913–)

Willy Brandt: don't give Nixon or Agnew political asylum in Germany.

(New York City, 1970)

BROWN, H. RAP (1943–)

Rap Brown is alive and underground and fighting.

(Watts, Los Angeles, 1970)

Rap Brown wears blue contacts.

BRUCE, LENNY (1926–1966)

Lenny Bruce died of an overdose of police morphine.

UNDERNEATH

He died of shit.

(Ladies' room, Max's Kansas City Restaurant, New York City)

Lenny Bruce spoke the truth and truth died of a heart attack.

(Ladies' room, Max's Kansas City Restaurant, New York City)

Lenny Bruce was the great one, believe me girls.

(Ladies' room, Max's Kansas City Restaurant, New York City)

BRUTUS, MARCUS JUNIUS (85?–42 B.C.)

Brutus is a hostile ingrate.

(Lion's Head, New York City)

BUDDHA (c. 563–483 B.C.)

Jesus saves; Moses invests; but only Buddha pays dividends.

BUILDINGS

Help save Lincoln Center.

In case of emergency, break glass and pull down lever.

(In chalk on the sidewalk in front of the glass-and-steel Lever building in New York City)

The Prudential Center is a Phallic symbol.

(Boston University)

Save the Pan Am Building.

BUREAUCRACY

An elephant is a mouse drawn to government specifications.

Eliminate Government Waste no matter how much it costs.

The reason the govt. thinks you're just a number is because it's just a machine.

(San Francisco State College, 1970)

When the last of the sociologists has been strangled with the intestines of the last bureaucrat, will we still have problems?

(Sorbonne, May, 1968)

C

CAPITALISM

All the rich are the same exploiters.

(Construction fence near Harvard University, 1972)

Communism: Socialism at its highest potency.
Capitalism: Democracy at its lowest impotence.

(Stockholm official graffiti wall (Kotterplank), *November 7, 1968)*

Down with the merchandising society.

(Paris, May, 1968)

Merchandise is the opium of the people.

(Paris, May, 1968)

Socialism: Forwardness, humanism, "what one is."
Capitalism: Backwardness, egoism, criminality, "what one has."

(Stockholm official graffiti wall (Kotterplank), *November 7, 1968)*

Support the rich.

CAPONE, AL (1899–1947)

Al Capone went to public school.

(On cover of The Critic, *which was a picture of a wall covered with graffiti, December, 1966–January, 1967)*

CAPOTE, TRUMAN (1924–)

Truman Capote stays in bed on Father's Day.

(Cited by Jim Moran, columnist, Chicago Daily News, *May 27, 1967)*

CARS, *see* AUTOMOBILES

CASANOVA (1725–1798)

Casanova was a latent homosexual.

(IRT subway, New York City)

CASTE, *see* SOCIAL CLASSES

CASTRO, FIDEL (1926–)

Castrate Castro.

(Written in a doorway, New York City)

Castro is gay.

(Men's room, bar, San Francisco)

The following was written on a poster that said: "I got my job through The New York Times":
So did Castro.

Lenin won
Fidel won
We will win

(Columbia University, April 30, 1968— the day of the student strike)

CENTRAL INTELLIGENCE AGENCY

All you fuckin' queers are being observed on closed TV by the CIA.

(Men's room, University of Minnesota)

 IA

LBJ and the CIA did away with JFK.

(Subway, New York City)

Tutti-Frutti is supported by the CIA.

U.C.I.A. (University of).

CÉZANNE, PAUL (1839–1906)

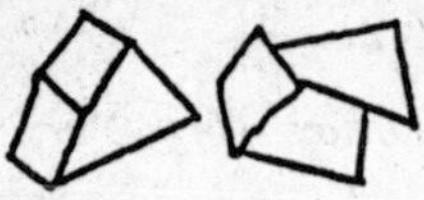

Balls by Cezanne

(Cited in Graffiti *by Richard Freeman)*

CHASTITY

An Epitaph on an Old Maid:
Beneath this Place there lies an ancient Maid,
Whose secret Parts no Man did e'er invade;
Scarce her own Finger she'd permit to touch
That Virgin Part, altho' it itched much.
And in her last expiring dying Groans,
Desir'd no Tomb, if it was built with Stones.

(England, mid-18th century)

Carry me back to old virginity.

(McGraw Tower, Cornell University)

Chaste makes waste.

(On various walls, also on a button)

Chaste makes paste.

(Free Library of Philadelphia, 1968)

Chastity belts are Waist Pollution.

(Men's room, University of Maryland, 1972)

Chastity is its own punishment.

(Paradox Restaurant, New York City, also on a button)

Chastity is the most perverse of all perversions.
(Ladies' room, Greenwich Village pub, 1971)

Cure virginity.

Don't write dirty things (like chastity) on the fucking walls.
(Ladies' room, Le Metro Caffe Espresso, New York City)

Hail charming Maid! hail my enchanting Fair,
Thy Beauty's such, what Mortal can forbear?
Have Pity on a Youth's despairing Cries,
Compassion shew, or else your Lover dies.
O that I but one good Enjoyment had!
Grant it me soon, or else I shall go mad.
Her Answer:
Alas! poor Youth, if you go mad for Love,
Seek your Relief from mighty Jove above.
No cure I have, my Body's chaste and pure;
A wandering Youth I never can endure.
(Rain-Deer, Bishop-Stafford, England)

If Virtue rules the Minds of Women,
They'll never let you touch their Linnen;
But if they are not Virtue Proof,
Then you may kiss them oft enough.
(Bull-and-Mouth-Street, England)

If you want to be close to a man's chest,
then the hymen must be torn.
(Ladies' room, Breslau—cited in Anthropophyteia, *Vol. 5, 1908)*

I'm a virgin but I'm on the verge.

Isn't it great pain to still be a virgin at age 50.
(Men's room, Germany)

Never be led astray into the path of virtue.

Virginity is a social disease, but there is a cure.
(Men's room, Rutgers University)

Virtue can hurt you.

Whatever happened to virginity?

UNDERNEATH

It got fucked.

(Ladies' room, Max's Kansas City Restaurant, New York City)

CHRIST, *see* JESUS CHRIST

CHRISTMAS

Give your child mental blocks for Christmas.

Keep the X in Xmas.

(Taxi garage, New York City, 1970)

Please God, send me a Lamborghine for Christmas.

(Stockholm official graffiti wall (Kotterplank), *1969)*

Roses are reddish
Violets are bluish
If it weren't for Xmas
We'd all be Jewish.

CIRCUMCISION

Circumcision is the unkindest cut of all.

During circumcision, what spices life now falls to the knife, for love's happiness enough is left however.

(Breslau—cited in Anthropophyteia, *Vol. 6, 1909)*

Here is the only place where Jews have shortcomings.

(Men's room, Germany, 1968)

Why is it that graffiti at Harvard is all homosexual and that at B.U. anti-Semitic?

UNDERNEATH

Queers prefer circumcised Jews.

UNDERNEATH

So does Christ.

(Men's room, Harvard University)

CLEAVER, ELDRIDGE (1935–)

Revive Eldridge.

UNDERNEATH

Is he ill?

(Ladies' room, Hunter College, New York City, 1969)

CLERGY

He who wants to lick a virgin's cunt must hide in the confessional booth.

(Men's room, Breslau—cited in Anthropophyteia, *Vol. 6, 1909)*

I'm in love with a priest and he's a virgin.

UNDERNEATH

How did you ever find a rarity like that?

Keep the Pope off the moon.

(The Rivera, New York City)

Never have I fucked so beautifully as with a priest in a convent.

(Men's room, Breslau—cited in Anthropophyteia, *Vol. 6, 1909)*

Pope Paul *is* a pill!

The priest of Kempton starches his shirts in his own semen. In eternity, Amen.

(Men's room, Germany)

The priest wipes himself when he shits and practically drops his prick off.

(Men's room, Prussia-Silesia—cited in Anthropophyteia, *Vol. 7, 1910)*

Said the priest to the girl
I'll stick my pole in your dirty old hole
Now work your ass to save your soul.

(Tourist Park, Kirksville, Mo., 1926)

Stuff and swill, fuck and gape, you will learn best from the priests.

(Men's room, Breslau—cited in Anthropophyteia, *Vol. 6, 1909)*

On a long-winded Preacher at Coventry:
Twelve Minutes, and one tedious Hour
Mills kept me once in Pain,
But if I had it my Power,
He ne'er should preach again.

(On a window, Coventry, England)

Vat 69 is the Pope's telephone number.

When the Devil was sick, the Devil a Monk would be,
When the Devil was well, the Devil a Monk was he.

(In the Vaults at Chelsea, England, and in a hundred other places)

Whoever does not know how to fuck properly should see how the bishop is doing it.

(Men's room, Breslau—cited in Anthropophyteia, *Vol. 6, 1909)*

Whoever goes to the priest as a virgin, soon bemoans her lost innocence.

(Men's room, Breslau—cited in Anthropophyteia, *Vol. 6, 1909)*

Whoever masturbates in church will soon be ordained a priest.

(Men's room, Prussia-Silesia—cited in Anthropophyteia, *Vol. 7, 1910)*

Whose prick will no longer stand up should go with it to the priest.

(Men's room, Breslau—cited in Anthropophyteia, *Vol. 6, 1909)*

CLOTHING and DRESS, see FASHION

COLLEGE, see UNIVERSITIES and COLLEGES

COMIC STRIPS

Batman is a junky.

(Lion's Head, New York City)

Batman loves Robin.

Clark Kent is a transvestite.

Donald Duck is a Jew.

UNDERNEATH

Ben-Gurion is a duck.

Donald Duck is a Jew.

UNDERNEATH

Donald Jew is a duck.

Donald Duck is a Jew.

UNDERNEATH

So what?

UNDERNEATH

So he can't eat Porky Pig.

(Men's latrine, South Vietnam, 1967)

Donald Duck is myopic.

Flash Gordon is low unintentional camp.

Little Orphan Annie puts out, but she's a lousy lay.

Little Orphan Annie wears contacts.

Major Hoople lives!

(University of Florida)

Mandrake lives!

(Limelight Restaurant, New York City)

Mickey Mouse is a homosexual.

(Scholtz's Beer Garden, Austin)

Mickey Mouse is wearing a Spiro Agnew watch.

Mickey Mouse smokes pot.

Minnie Mouse is a slow maze learner.

Minnie Mouse is a whore.

(Scholtz's Beer Garden, Austin)

Porky Pig is a Jew.

Send Batman to Vietnam.

Superman gets into Clark Kent's pants every morning.
(University of Michigan)

Superman wears mini-pants.
(Simple Simon Hamburger Bar, New York City)

Walt Disney turned me against God and made me believe in Mickey Mouse.

COMMUNISM

Be kind to communists, they're misdirected but they mean well.

Better red than black.

The ideal principle
- Christianity: believes it is only for Christians. Not a single Christian in Christianity.
- Communism: Practice for everybody. All Communists are communists.

(Stockholm official graffiti wall [Kotterplank], *November 7, 1968)*

Communism: Socialism at its highest potency.
Capitalism: Democracy at its lowest impotence.
(Stockholm official graffiti wall [Kotterplank], *November 6, 1968)*

It takes the red to get out of the black.
(Paris, May, 1968)

Kill a Commie for Christ.
(Subway station men's room)

Leave the fear of red to animals with horns.
(Paris, May, 1968)

Read the Red book.
(Jefferson Market Public Library, New York City, 1970)

Young women Reds are always more beautiful.
(Paris, May, 1968)

COMPUTERS

Do not bend, fold, staple or mutilate in any way these walls.

(Florida State University)

I am a human being: do not fold, spindle or mutilate.

I am a masochist: please spindle, fold or mutilate.

I am a U.C. student.
Please don't bend, fold, spindle or mutilate me.

(On a big IBM card)

CONCEPTION

Artificial insemination: getting a girl you don't really love pregnant.

(Men's room, Rutgers University, 1969)

Don't worry. The rabbit died of a heart attack.

(Ladies' room, Max's Kansas City Restaurant, New York City)

Hard Stools proceed from costive Claret;
Yet mortal Man cannot forbear it.
So Childbed-Women, full of Pain,
Will grunt and groan, and to't again.

(Boghouse, Hempstead, England)

"T BG Y T DG 1 BB."
Te Bese Y Te je Un Bebe.
I kiss you and leave you a baby."

(On a truck, Mexico)

I no come,
She no come,
Baby come,
How come?

(Men's room, Garment Center, New York City)

Please don't let me be pregnant.

(Ladies' room, Ninth Circle Restaurant, New York City, 1965)

A poor Woman was ill in a dangerous Cafe,
She lay in, and was just as some other Folks was:
By the Lord, cries She then, if my Husband e'er come,
Once again with his Will to tickle my Bum,
I'll storm, and I'll swear, and I'll run staring wild;
And yet the next Night, the Man got her with Child.
S.M. 1708.

(The Star, Coventry, England)

She who indulges, bulges.

Support the Pope—get pregnant.

Why did I have a baby?

UNDERNEATH

It's hereditary.

(Ladies' room, Le Metro Caffe Espresso, New York City)

CONTRACEPTION, see BIRTH CONTROL

COPPOLINO, CARL A. (1932–)

Thanks, Dr. Coppolino, but I've already had my shots.
(Note: A hypodermic injection was the M.O. used for murder by this physician)

COPROPHAGIA

Austin eats snail shit.

(Ladies' room, Limelight Restaurant, New York City)

Be humble, eat shit.

(University of Florida)

Don't flush the toilet. The next man might be hungry.

(Chicago, 1960)

Eat shit. A million flies can't be wrong.

(Googie's Bar, New York City)

He who doesn't like to eat shit finds nothing here to eat.

(Men's room, Breslau—cited in Anthropophyteia, *Vol. 6, 1909)*

Hippies eat shit and brown rice.

(Co-ed toilet, Alvin's Finer Delicatessen, Detroit, 1971)

In the stinking rat holes there blooms pig shit, but believe me even in palaces people feast themselves on pig shit.

(Men's room, Vienna—cited in Anthropophyteia, *Vol. 5, 1908)*

The man who eats shit is a cad, a fine gentleman doesn't eat shit.

(Men's room, Prussia-Silesia—cited in Anthropophyteia, *Vol. 7, 1910)*

Not even a sow eats her own shit.

(Men's room, Berlin, 1910)

People who write on shit house walls
Should roll their shit in little balls,
And those who read these lines of wit
Should have to eat those balls of shit.

Who eats shit is a pig, I don't even lick my own wife's ass.

(Men's room, Riesengebirge—cited in Anthropophyteia, *Vol. 6, 1909)*

You are what you eat and Nixon eats shit.

(University of California at Los Angeles, 1970)

COUGHLIN, CHARLES (1891–)

(Note: The popular, right-wing "radio priest" of the 1930's)

Unleash Father Coughlin.

(On cover of The Critic, *which was a picture of a wall covered with graffiti, December, 1966–January, 1967)*

CRAB LICE

Butterfly has wings of gold,
Moths have wings of flame
Toilet crabs have no wings at all,
But they got here just the same.

Do not throw toothpicks in the bowl.
The crabs here can pole vault.

I have crabs.

(Ladies' room, Le Metro Caffe Espresso, New York City)

It does no good to line the seat
The crabs here jump fifteen feet.

'Taint no use to stand on the seat,
Power house crabs jump 20 feet.

CRATER, JOSEPH F. (1889–1931?)

(Note: After he mysteriously disappeared in 1931 Judge Crater was never heard from again.)

Judge Crater—please call your office.

CRIME

For heaven's sake, catch me before I kill more i cannot control myself.

(Written in bright red lipstick on the bedroom of one of his victims by triple female slayer William Heirens who was caught and given 99 years, 1946)

Let's take crime out of the streets!—and put it back in the homes where it belongs!

(Men's lockers, Sunken Meadow State Park, N.Y.)

My name is George D. I steal.

Now is my latest Guinea chang'd,
And gone where it was used to range:
When that was broke, it broke my Heart;
For now for ever we must part,
Unless I boldly meet it on the Road,
And bid the Porter give it me, by G–d.
And so I'll do;
Tom. Stout.
Will see it out. Feb. 2.

UNDERNEATH

Win it and take it, says Captain Hector. I defy the bold Robber; and I have an hundred Guineas that I shall travel with to-morrow.

Feb. 16.

(On a window, The White Hart, Windsor, England)

CUCKOLDRY, see ADULTERY

CULTURE

Americans haven't read Chaucer—its *Arse.*

(Feenjon Coffee House, New York City)

Culture is an inversion of life.

(Paris, May, 1968)

Culture is in crumbs.

(Paris, May, 1968)

Culture is like jam, the less you have the more you spread it out.

(Paris, May, 1968)

Help—I'm plastic.

Manners Maketh Man.

(Cited in Graffiti *by Richard Freeman)*

The tears of Philistines are the nectar of the gods.

(Paris, May, 1968)

Whenever I hear the word gun I reach for my culture. (Note: This is a reversal of the statement made by Hans Johnst. He was an unsuccessful playwright who was the president of the Third Reich Theater Chamber. On one occasion he publicly stated, "Whenever someone mentions the word 'culture' to me, I want to reach for my revolver.")

CUNNILINGUS

Al (the bartender) sucks badly.

Ladies' room, bar, New York City)

Beautiful young lady seeks young man with tongue movement of approximately 30–40 horsepower.

(Ladies' room, Switzerland—cited in Anthropophyteia, *Vol. 6, 1909)*

Cunnilingus is next to godliness.

Cunnilingus spoken here.

Eat pussy and last and last.

UNDERNEATH

Stop me before I last more.

(Men's room, New York City)

Eat pussy or busts

Girls—let me suck your moist cunt.

(Ladies' room, Hunter College, New York City)

Hairpie is made of excellent meat.

UNDERNEATH

You're putting me on. I ate one and it tasted awful.

UNDERNEATH

Perhaps you forgot to unwrap it?

(Wall, Helsinki, 1969)

I know a girl who was ate before she was seven.

I'd rather fuck the pizza and eat the waitress.

UNDERNEATH

I did. The pizza's better.

(Men's room, San Antonio)

If Miles Standish had shot a cat instead of a turkey we would all be eating pussy for Thanksgiving.

If you can't fuck it—
suck it—
If you can't dick it—
lick it—
If you can't stuff it—
muff it—
signed, The Fuck.

(May's department store, New York City)

O girls let me fervently kiss your slender body, let me savor the fragrance of your cunty's dew, for I am a woman just like you.

(Ladies' room, Breslau—cited in Anthropophyteia, *Vol. 6, 1909)*

Observe National Cunnilingus Week, take a clitoris to lunch.

Phil Attio loves Connie Lingus.

(Restaurant, Phoenix)

Romeo Julie ate.

(Taxi garage, New York City, 1970)

Those Oakies are a funny bunch
What we call pussy they call lunch.

(Le Metro Caffe Espresso, New York City)

Virgula to her Tertius, you're a naughty boy. Who dips his wick [*probably means tongue*] in a fiery bottom will burn it off.

(Pompeii, 79 A.D.)

CUSTER, GEORGE (1839–1876)

General Custer is alive and well and living on a reservation.

We'll bring peace to this land if we have to kill them all. —Custer

(Vietnam, 1971—cited in Playboy, *August, 1971)*

D

DADAISM

Dada saves!

(Lion's Head Bar, New York City)

Everything is dada.

(Paris, May, 1968)

DARWIN, CHARLES (1809–1882)

Jesus lives!—Darwin survives!

DAYAN, MOSHE (1915–)

Moshe Dayan should run our war in Vietnam.

UNDERNEATH

We will even give him 7 days.

(Wall in Boston)

DEATH

Bridey Murphy lives!

Cowards fear to die, but Courage stout,
Rather than live in Snuff, will put it out.

(Written by Sir Walter Raleigh on the snuff of a candle the night before he died)

Death is a yellow curtain, after death there is no pain.

UNDERNEATH

Yeah, all the pain comes before!

(Florida State University)

Death is camp.

Death is Life's answer to the question "why?"
(Men's toilet, Telephone Company, New York City)

Death is nature's way of telling you to slow down.
(On various walls, also on a button)

Death is necessarily counter-revolutionary.
(Paris, May, 1968)

Death is only a state of mind.
UNDERNEATH
Only it doesn't leave you any time to think about anything else.
("55" Bar, New York City)

Death is only a stepping stone to perfecting oneself.
(Los Angeles Valley College, 1970)

Death is the greatest kick of all, that's why they save it for last.

Death is the price of evolution.
(San Francisco State College, 1970)

(Death is like a shadow which always follows the body.)
(Written in Latin, England, Middle Ages)

Clelia's Epitaph, who was flander'd to Death:
Death, to vindicate her Wrongs,
Gives her Fame which never dies;
So the Life that died with Shame,
Lives in Death with Glorious Fame.
R.S. Oct. 17. 1708.
(The Catherine-Wheel, Henley, England)

The doctor more than illness we should fear;
Sickness precedes, and Death attends his coach,
Agues to fevers rise, if he appear,
And fevers grow to plagues at his approach.
(On the chamber window of a lady, who, on a slight indisposition, sent for S.J.S., England, early 18th century)

Everything is still free especially death.

(On fence at site of brownstone that was blown up by three overactive political activists, New York City, 1970)

For those who think life is a joke, just think of the punchline.

(University of Michigan, 1970)

The greatest high is suicide.

(Ladies' room, Hofstra College, N.Y.)

I believe in death . . . I seen it in a movie, once.

(Florida State University)

I wish I could come back as a bug, to bite an ass.

(Le Metro Caffe Espresso, New York City)

If Death doth come as soon as Breath departs;
Then he must often die, who often farts:
And if to die be but to lose one's Breath;
Then Death's a Fart, and so a Fart for Death.

(On a window, Richmond, England)

If I should die in Tennessee,
Who'll say kaddish over me?

The most sincere form of criticism is suicide—do it.

(Men's room, Goose and Gherkin House, New York City, 1969)

My Swan Song

I go to a better world
Now there will be wild goings-on
And full plates eternally
I have always been hungry on earth,
Yonder I will eat and drink
And one thing will be particularly beautiful,
One doesn't have to go to the toilet.

(Vienna, late 19th century—cited in Leben, Mein-ungen und Wirken, *by Wetti Himmlisch, 1906—this suicide note was left by a starving poet in a toilet stall)*

A Young Lady, who hang'd herself, left the following Lines upon the Table:

O Death! thou pleasing End of human Woe!
Thou Cure of Life, thou best of Things below!
May'st thou for ever shun the Coward Slave,
And thy soft Slumbers only ease the Grave!

The following was written on the tomb of a boy by his mother:
Oh relentless Fortune, who delights in cruel death, why is Maximus so early snatched from me?

(Catacombs, Rome)

Our Bodies are like Shoes, which oft we cast,
Physick the Cobler is, and Death the Last.

(On a chamber window in Queen's College, Cambridge, University)

Our layaway plan—die now, pay later.

(On a funeral parlor ad, IRT subway, New York City)

This City is a World that's full of Streets,
And Death's the Market-Place where Mankind meets;

(On a pillar at the Royal Exchange, London)

To Adeodata, a worthy and well-deserving virgin, and she rests here in peace, her Christ commanding her.

(Catacombs, Rome)

To kick the bucket is beyond the pail.

(Ladies' room, Bennington College, Vt.)

To the Divine Manes of Titus Claudius Secundus, who lived 57 years. Here he enjoys everything. Baths, wine and love, ruin our constitution, but—they make life what it is. Farewell, farewell.

(Catacombs, Rome)

The following was written on a poster advertising a funeral parlor that said, "We understand":
How to exploit sadness and death for our profit.

We're slapped on the ass to give us the breath
To start us off on our march toward death.

Within this piere where bricks are laide
There buried lieth a virgin mayde
Ffrauncys Cordall was her name
She lived and died in godly fame
Anno 1597 June vij.

(On one of the pillars of St. Leonard's Church, Flamstead, England)

Yea, though I walk through the valley of death, I fear no evil 'cause I know I'm the coolest MF in the whole valley.

(University of Michigan)

You kill 'em we chill 'em.

(Written on an undertaker's ad)

DEFECATION

Also in this secondary art
there are dilettantes.
Artists shit through the hole,
Hacks on the rim.

(Cited in Anthropophyteia, *Vol. 6, 1909)*

Americans can't appreciate a good shit, they place too much emphasis on a good lay.

(Ladies' room, Max's Kansas City Restaurant, New York City)

Anyone can piss on the floor, be a hero, shit on the ceiling.

Anyone who wants to crap here will
have to hurry for the railroad
graciously grants you only 5 minutes.
—A North German

(Railroad station, Oderberg, Germany, 1880)

Anything over 10 pounds must be lowered with a rope.

Apollinaris, doctor to the Emperor Titus had a crap here.

(Public lavatory, Herculaneum, c. 79 A.D.)

Be the girl as pretty as can be,
She has to go shitting anyhow.

She may carry her nose way up,
Still it does smell.

(Germany, 1906)

The biggest pig on earth is he
who wipes his ass with his fingers.

(Nordhausen—cited in Anthropophyteia, *Vol. 4, 1907)*

Boys we all must use this throne
Please keep it clean and neat
Shit down the hole, God damn your soul
And not upon the seat.

(Camp Maxey, Paris, Tex., 1945)

D–n their Doublets, and confound their Breeches,
There's none besh–t the Wall but Sons of B—ches.
May the French P–x, and the D—vil take 'em all,
That besh–t their Fingers, and wipe them on the Wall.

(Boar's-Head, Smithfield, England)

Dear friend take my advice:
don't steal toilet paper!
you are like a little child
if you take paper home with you.
Therefore listen well and mark my words
For your ass the coarsest sandpaper
is good enough.

(Police station, Germany, 1906)

Dear people be reasonable!
Shit in the hole and not on the rim.

(Kolberg, Germany, 1902)

The dear sun is shining warm and hot
And the little boy is sitting on his pot.

(Men's room, Berlin, 1910)

The following was written on a notice which read: "Don't use the toilet when the train has stopped"):

Your strange notice gave me a laugh and a surprise, and I want to tell this company that the sphincter has no time table.

Dung, when featter'd o'er the Plain,
Causes noble Crops of Grain:
Dung in Gardens too we want,
To cherish ev'ry springing Plant.
Corn and Plants since Dung affords,
We eat as well as gh— our T——ds.

(In the vaults at Tunbridge, England)

As the eye follows a list of obscenities in a stall the last one reads:

You are now shitting at a 45 degree angle.

Good Bread and Meat, strong Beer withal,
  Will make a T—d more lasting;
Therefore I think he is a Fool,
  That goes out in a Morning fasting.
Tom. Rudge.

We suppose he wants to eternize his Memory by eating a Breakfast.

(On a wall at the Plough Ale-House, near Cripplegate, England)

Good shitting can make me very happy, sometimes more so than fucking.

(Men's room, Prussia-Silesia—cited in Anthropophyteia, *Vol. 7, 1910)*

The greatest Monarch, when a fighting,
Looks not so great as I, when sh—ting.

UNDERNEATH

Such places as these,
Were made for the Ease
Of every Fellow in common;
But a Person who writes
On the Wall as he sh—tes,
Has a Pleasure far greater than Woman.
For he's eas'd in his Body, and pleas'd in his Mind,
When he leaves both a T—d and some Verses behind.

UNDERNEATH

You are eas'd in your Body, and pleas'd in your Mind,
That you leave both a T—d and some Verses behind;
But to me, which is worst, I can't tell, on my Word,
The reading your Verses, or smelling your T—d.

(In a Bog-House at the Nag's Head in Bradmere, England)

He who cannot shit correctly should call Martin Luther.

(Men's room, Langenau in Silesia—cited in Anthropophyteia, *Vol. 6, 1909)*

He who craps on the rim may go straight to hell.

(Men's room, Breslau—cited in Anthropophyteia, *Vol. 6, 1909)*

He who wants to see German unity
needn't travel far, for as one sees
it here, one shits on the other.
An Austrian.

(Oderberg, 1880)

Here every ass opens its gate
and sausages are coming forth
and the tail in all its quiet glory
hangs nearby and watches.

(Men's room, Thüringen—cited in Anthropophyteia, *Vol. 7, 1910)*

Here I sit and shit away
meals that cost six bits a day.

(Outside Inn, Parley's Canyon, Salt Lake City, 1928)

Here I sit in silent bliss, listening to a stream of piss. Suddenly another sound is heard, introducing Mr. Turd.

Here I sit in solemn bliss
Listening to the dribble of piss
And now and then a fart is heard
Then followed by a thundering turd.

(Men's room, Camp Maxey, Paris, Tex., 1945)

Here I sit in stinking vapor
Some sonuvabitch stole the paper.

Here in this big hall,
where no bird sings,
Man lets something drop,
which disastrously stinks.

(Würzburg, 1905)

Here is the court of appeals,
Where every ass pronounces his judgment,
Representatives are not accepted,
Who wants to shit must come by himself.

(Thorn, 1906)

Here is a high tribunal,
Lawyers we need not,
Who wants to shit may come by himself
Lawyers are not accepted.

(Men's room, Prussia, 1850)

Here is the place we all must come
To do the work that must be done
Do it quick and do it neat
But please don't do it on the seat.

Here it is just like Heaven
Here all men are equal
1st, 2nd and 3rd class,
Everyone shits into a mass.

(Men's room—cited in Anthropophyteia, *Vol. 5, 1908)*

Here men and women gather gifts of love for agriculture. Therefore squeeze and press with all your might for the benefit of suffering agriculture.

(Thorn, 1897)

Hold your ass at the proper slant
Don't protest and say you can't
Many a man has done things galore
Things he thought he couldn't do before.

(Lakeside, Lake Tahoe, Cal., July 14, 1928)

I do not like this place at all,
The seat is too high and the hole is too small.

UNDERNEATH

You lay yourself open to the obvious retort,
Your bottom's too big and your legs are too short.

(Somerset House, England—cited in Cleanliness and Godliness *by Reginald Reynolds, 1946)*

If no paper, do not linger. Be a sport and use your finger.

I have a calm conscience: this morning I fucked and now I have shit.

(Men's room, Riesengebirge—cited in Anthropophyteia, *Vol. 6, 1909)*

I need no paper to wipe myself, I have a hand for that.

(Men's room, Prussia-Silesia—cited in Anthropophyteia, *Vol. 7, 1910)*

I wish you on your name day,
Well what shall I wish?
Ah! I just had an idea!
There is nothing better I can wish you
Than noble shitting.
Therefore shit for as many years
as there are hairs on your head.
Shit in the ditches of all streets.
Shit them full up, but don't miss.
Shit on shoemakers and tailors,
Shit on your own clothes,
Shit on lawyers and on priests,
Shit into your own mouth,
Shit into your own face,
But don't shit on me.
(Temesvarer Kolonie.)

(Men's room—cited in Anthropophyteia, *Vol. 5, 1908)*

If I only could shit powerfully, then I would fuck neither women nor men.

(Men's room, Prussia-Silesia—cited in Anthropophyteia, *Vol. 7, 1910)*

Si desit stramen, cum digito terge Feramen.

UNDERNEATH

If you cannot get some Grass,
With your Finger wipe your a–se

And under that, by another.

Such wretched Latin, and such wretched Verse,
Are proper Stremina to clean my A–se.

(Boghouse, Ipswich, England)

If you design to sh–te at Ease,
Pray rest your Hands upon your Knees.
And only give a gentle squeeze.

(Temple boghouse, England)

If you want to shit with reason,
take your head in your hand,
and curve your elbows upon your knees,
then you can shit as never before.

(Chemnitz—cited in Anthropophyteia, *Vol. 4, 1906)*

If you want to shit without pain
put your hands under your knees
and stare directly at the door
then the shit will jump out by itself.

(Travnik—cited in Anthropophyteia, *Vol. 5, 1908)*

In days of old, when knights were bold.
And toilet seats were not invented
They would drop their load on the side of the road.
And walk away contented.

(White Whale Coffee House, New York City)

In memory of those who sat in agony trying to take a shit.

(NBC Studios, New York City, 1966)

In this holy moment
I start to think about
how expensive our food is
and how it turns into . . . this.

(Men's room, Mexico)

In this place fucking is done, standing, farting, shitting is done sitting and who doesn't want to join in is thrown out.

(Men's room, Riesenbegirge—cited in Anthropophyteia, *Vol. 6, 1909)*

In this resplendent place
where so many people come
the most cowardly strain
and the bravest shit.

In this sad place
Where so many people shit.
The cowardly squeeze
The valiant shit freely.

(Trujillo, Peru, 1890)

In this sad shit house
I look in vain for paper
With three wide open eyes
I cannot find it.

(Trujillo, Peru, 1890)

I've shit in England
I've shit in France
But before I'd shit here
I'd shit in my pants.

I've shit in the Mississippi
I've shit in Niagara Falls
But this is the only place I ever shit
where the water washed my balls.

(Tourist Park, Waterloo, Iowa, September 9, 1932)

Like Claret-Drinkers Stools, a Blockhead's Brain;
Hardly conceives what it brings forth with Pain.
Such is my Cafe —— who, while I'm thus inditing,
Prove the Analogy 'twixt it and Sh——.

(In the vaults at Tunbridge, England)

Love and diarrhea cause much pain—
Diarrhea in your belly, love in your heart.

(Halle, Prussia, 1903)

May God give you for this activity the courage of a horse, the strength of a bull and the fleetness of a sparrow—from now until eternity.

(University toilet, Halle, Prussia, 1904)

My dear innkeeper I advise you,
do provide toilet paper,
for otherwise man in his distress
will grab at the wall paper.

(Dennheritz, 1906)

The nicest Maid, with the Whitest Rump,
May sit and sh–te, and hear it plump.

(Boghouse over the water at the Spread-Eagle, Bunny, England)

No Hero looks so fierce in Fight
As does the Man who strains to sh–te.

(Temple boghouse, England)

Nothing better than sitting here with the runs and having something to read.

(Ladies' room, New York University, 1971)

Oh! what a pleasure,
Not even paper!
I should have known that before,
I would have shit at home.

(Elberfeld, 1907)

An old woman wanted to go crapping,
the toilet was locked.
Then she saw a ladder there,
and shit through the rungs.

(Germany, 1906)

On September 17th 1945, Colonel Jeff Crowther sat here after eating a fine fish dinner, and deposited a soft, tan, stool.
—Colonel Jeff Crowther

(Men's room, Roth's Restaurant, New York City, 1945)

One masturbates, one pisses and craps until life's thread is cut.

(Men's room, Munich—cited in Anthropophyteia, *Vol. 5, 1908)*

One step from the nose is the water hose.
One step from the neck is the sausage factory.

(Breslau—cited in Anthropophyteia, *Vol. 5, 1908)*

Only the Jew and the Protestant will shit on the rim.

(Breslau—cited in Anthropophyteia, *Vol. 6, 1909)*

The patron saint of him who shits, this role Dr. Martin Luther fits.

(Men's room—cited in Anthropophyteia, *Vol. 6, 1909)*

Patrons are forbidden to leave seat while bowels are in motion.

(Yosemite National Park, Cal., July 11, 1928)

Pisser don't piss on my bones, I pray,
nor defecate, if you'd be yet more kind.
See the thick pile of nettle—turn away.
Here it's not safe to squat with bare behind.

(Pompeii, 79 A.D.)

Please, make in the middle,
not on the edge,
that would be a disgrace.

(Cited in Anthropophyteia, *Vol. 5, 1908)*

Prussian: Where a Bavarian shits, there you get a big pile. It certainly comes from the fact that they eat and drink too much.
Bavarian: He who wrote this is most certainly from Prussia, for where there is nothing to eat there is nothing to shit.

(Munich, 1905)

Sam, Sam, the janitor man
Chief superintendent of the crapping can.
He washes out the bowls and picks up the towels
And listens to the roar of other men's bowels.

Save paper use both sides.

(Midvale Steel Works, Philadelphia, 1918)

Screwing makes squint eyes and very pale cheeks,
If you want to have a red face—you must shit on the cunt.

(Men's room, Berlin, 1910)

Shit here shit clear
Wipe your ass and disapear
—Shakespear

(Auto Camp, Truckee, Cal., 1928)

Shit, that all the walls will burst,
Shit the devil in his jaw,
Shit the world in the face,
only don't shit on the seat.

(Aus Erfurter Abtritten, 1906)

Shit tranquilly
Shit contentedly
But shit inside.

(Spanish toilet)

Shit until the rocks crack,
Shit into the mouth of the dead,
Shit in a peasant's face,
But don't shit on our friendship.

(Men's room, Vienna, 1850)

Six Pennyworth of Whiting,
A Hole to let Light in,
Will make it fit to sh–te in.

UNDERNEATH

By what's above, I welly ween,
The Fool wants Light to sh–t him clean.

Some come here to sit and think
And some come here to wonder
But I come here to shit and stink
And fart away like thunder.

(Banff, Alberta, 1928)

Some come here to shit and think
I come here to shit and stink.

Some come here to smoke and spit.
Some come here to piss and shit.

Some people come here to read and write
But I come here to shite and shite.

(Railroad station, Galatz, Rumania, 1908)

Something to wipe my ass with would now mean more to me than any other scholarly paper.

(Men's room, Breslau—cited in Anthropophyteia, *Vol. 6, 1909)*

Stand on your ass
not on your feet
Shit down the hole
not on the seat.

(Men's room, Lakeside, Lake Tahoe, Cal., July, 1928)

There is nothing so overrated as a bad fuck and nothing so underrated as a good shit.

(Ladies' room, San Francisco State College, December, 1968)

Supposed to be wrote by one who had a great Antipathy to Tobacco:
This is a Place that's very fitting,
To p–ss, and f–rt, to smoke, and sh–t in.

(Boghouse, Lambeth-Wells, England)

This is Martha's bedroom, for she always shits in her bed.

(Slave's latrine, Pompeii, 79 A.D.)

This little home is not your own
So keep it nice and neat
Bear in mind and be so kind
To not shit on the seat.

(Co-ed toilet, Woodstock, N.Y., 1970)

This little place we call our own
And try to keep it neat
So please be kind with your behind
And don't —— on the seat

UNDERNEATH

And damn your soul
Shit down the hole
And not upon the seat

(Tejon Camp, near Tejon Pass, Cal., July, 1932)

Tom, Tom the lavatory man
He's overseer of the company can
Oh, he picks up the papers
And he rolls up the towels
And he listens to the music
Of the discontented bowels.

Upon this board I have put my sheetings,
Whoever sits here has my greetings.

(Men's room, Prussia-Silesia—cited in Anthropophyteia, *Vol. 7, 1910)*

Use both sides, you only paid a dime.

(Men's pay toilet, bus station in Fargo, N.D., 1972)

What similarity is there between a toilet and a bank business?
In the toilet you get a crash and then the papers fall; in the bank it is the other way around.

(Cited in Anthropophyteia, *Vol. 4, 1907)*

What the baker bakes,
What the butcher chops,
is here quite exactly
crapped out again.

(Halle, 1903)

When adam was a
small lad before
paper was invented
he wiped his ass on
a tuft of grass & went
away contented.

(Banff, Alberta, August 2, 1928)

When you want to shit in ease
place your elbows on your knees
in your mouth with both your thumbs
give a grunt and out it comes.

(Bryce Canyon National Monument, Utah, 1928)

When you want to shit in ease
place your elbows on your knees
Put your hands against your chin
Let a fart and then begin.

(Bryce Canyon National Monument, Utah, 1928)

Whether Social Democrat or German National,
Here is not the place to indicate this,
For here only the ass may speak,
And the mouth must be quiet.

(Vienna, late 19th century—cited in Leben, Meinungen und Wirken, *by Wetti Himmlisch, 1906)*

Whether south or north, whether
Austrian-German you Germans
just have to brawl. Therefore as
an object for your strife I shit
you a big pile to be divided.
—A Hungarian

(Railroad station, Oderberg, 1880)

Who wipes his ass with his hand, doesn't the son-of-a-bitch deserve to be beaten up?

(Men's room, Nordhausen—cited in Anthropophyteia, *Vol. 4, 1907)*

Who can shit six times a day is truly a strong man.

(Men's room, Breslau—cited in Anthropophyteia, *Vol. 6, 1909)*

Whoever shits on the seat
will get his ass chopped off.

(Aus Erfurter Abtritten, 1906)

Whoever would disturb me while I am crapping, to that one I would swear revenge.

(Men's room, Riesengebirge—cited in Anthropophyteia, *Vol. 6, 1909)*

Why do [*sic*] everybody think about their sexual functions while they're excreting?

(Ladies' room, Manhattan College, New York City, 1972)

Why go West young man, when you can make your own pile here?

(Men's room, Princeton University, 1970)

Why wipe your ass with three papers while one will do the job.

(Men's room, City Park, Lansing, Iowa, August, 1932)

Ye Cantabs mind when ye are sh–t—ng,
How nearly 'tis allied to Writing.
—To Writing, say you?—pray how so?
An uncouth Simile, I trow.
—Hold, pray—Condemn it not untry'd,
Hear only how it is apply'd.

As learned Johnian wracks his Brain—
Thinks,—hems—looks wise,—then thinks again;—
When all this Preparation's done,
The mighty Product is—a Pun.
So some with direful strange Grimaces,
Within this Dome distort their Faces;
Strain,—squeeze,—yet loth for to depart,
Again they strain—for what? a Fart.

Hence Cantabs take this moral Trite,
'Gainst Nature, if ye think or sh–te;
Use all the Labour, all the Art,
'Twill ne'er exceed a Pun, or Fart.

(Boghouse, Trinity College, Dublin)

You have 5 minutes to shit,
who shits longer is thrown out.

(Men's room—cited in Anthropophyteia, *Vol. 4, 1907)*

You who instead of Fodder, Fingers use,
Pray lick 'em clean, and don't this Wall abuse.
Under which is written;

These House-of-Office Poets, by the L—d,
Instead of Laurel, should be crown'd with T—d.
(Boghouse, Trinity College, Dublin)

DE GAULLE, CHARLES (1890–1970)

France has her De Gaulle,
And we have our Neanderthal.

Long live de Gaulle. (A French masochist)
(France, May, 1968)

DEMOCRACY

Communism: Socialism at its highest potency.
Capitalism: Democracy at its lowest impotence.
(Stockholm official graffiti wall [Kotterplank], *November 7, 1968)*

Democracy is letting the other fellow have your way.
(University of Michigan)

Forced democracy is hypocrisy.
(Ladies' room, Queens College, New York City)

DESCARTES, RENÉ (1596–1650)

Coito ergo sum.
(Greenwich Village, New York)

I care, therefore I am.

I peed, therefore I am.
(Ladies' room, "55" Bar, New York City, 1971)

I think I exist; therefore I exist, I think.
UNDERNEATH
I think I think; therefore I think.
(Cornell University)

I think, I think, therefore I think I might be.

I'm sure I'm something, I think.
(Goddard College, Plainfield, 1971)

DESPAIR

Despair—the only way.

(On a doorway, East Village, New York City, 1972)

I began crying the moment I was born, and each following day teaches me the reason why.

(Free Store Theatre, New York City)

O God help me I am suffering—

UNDERNEATH

Sweetheart so am I.

UNDERNEATH

From what? Everything?

UNDERNEATH

Who cares.

UNDERNEATH

We care at A. & P.

(Ladies' room, Lion's Head, New York City)

Somewhere a man is catching glimpses of himself and crying.

(University of New Hampshire)

DEWEY, MELVIL (1851–1931)

(Note: Mr. Dewey, who invented the Dewey decimal system, spelled his name Melvil. He believed in phonetic spelling)

Melville Dewey died for our sins.

(Free Library of Philadelphia, 1968)

Melvil Dewey played the numbers and lost.

(Library staff lounge, after library had converted to the Library of Congress classification system—cited in American Library Association Bulletin, *January, 1969)*

DICKINSON, EMILY (1830–1886)

Emily Dickinson doesn't have a date for the senior prom.

(Cited by Jim Moran, columnist, Chicago Daily News, *May 27, 1967)*

DILLINGER, JOHN (1902–1934)

Stranger, stop and wish me well,
Just say a prayer for my soul in Hell.
I was a good fellow, most people said,
Betrayed by a woman all dressed in red.

(Written on brick wall a day after John Dillinger was shot by the FBI on July 22, 1934)

DIRKSEN, EVERETT (1896–1969)

Senator Dirksen is a leprechaun.

DISCONTENT

Don't hate yourself in the morning—sleep till noon.

I am envious (green)
UNDERNEATH
I am furious (yellow)

(Men's room, Princeton University, 1970)

I want to leave this hostile environment.
UNDERNEATH
And yet I can't get away.

(Antioch College, Ohio)

I wish, I wish, I wish in vain
That I could be a child again.

(Ladies' room, The Old Spaghetti Factory, San Francisco)

It's me and you against the world—when do we attack?

(Graffiti Restaurant, New York City)

Stop the world, I want to get off.

(Appeared on several toilet walls long before Anthony Newley used it as the title of his musical)

This mirror is a liar.

(In red crayon on a mirror)

DISENCHANTMENT

The fucking you get is not worth the fucking you take.

A hippo sat at the sandy shore
and wiped its ass with desert sand.
Oh! would your heart be as clean
as the asshole of the hippo.

(Halle, Prussia, c. 1903)

Isabel.

UNDERNEATH

You mean Jezebel.

It's not the face you fuck, it's the fuck you face.

*(Ladies' room, Limelight Restaurant,
New York City, 1965)*

A man hanging for Love, drawn when Painting was in its Cradle, with his Dog barking at him, viva voce.

(The Three Pigeons, Brentford, England)

The Occasion of this dangling Story, was from
a Lady who hated him, and set him about it.
Go hang thyself, quoth cruel She,
Go hang thyself I say.
The Man obey'd her presently,
And made himself away. Mary Worthless.
The Criticks do not make out whether he walk'd off, or went off; neither does the Figure determine which.
Hang me, if I will hang for any Woman,
For most of them alike are very common;
I'd sooner trudge as I have done before,
Than hang upon a d——d confounded Whore.

Men once they possess, they either throw them away or use them until they are no good to anyone.

*(Ladies' room, Ninth Circle Restaurant,
New York City)*

Roses are red
Violets are blue
Sugar is sweet
But you're not!!

Tell me where is Fancy bred?
In the Heart, or in the Head?
How begot, how nourished?

UNDERNEATH

Had not Celia come this Way,
My Heart would be my own this Day,
Fancy's engender'd in the Eyes,
With gazing fed; and Fancy dies
In the same Cradle where it lies;
For she's a Wh–re, and I despise.
—R.L. 1710.

(Star-Inn, Coventry, England)

Thank you for being what you almost were.

(Coffee house toilet, New Orleans)

When Mr. H— was chosen Mayor,
We thought our Peace stood very fair,
And hollow'd when he took the Chair.
But see how Mortals may prove civil,
They change their State from Good to Evil:
Set a Begger on Horseback, he'll ride to the Devil.
And so it prov'd.

(On a window, York, England)

DISNEY, WALT (1901–1966)

Jonas Mekas loves Walt Disney.

Walt Disney turned me against God and made me believe in Mickey Mouse.

DOCTORS, *see* PHYSICIANS

DODD, THOMAS J. (1907–1971)

Dodd is dead.

(Men's room, U.S. Senate)

DONNE, JOHN (1572–1631)

Shakespeare eats Bacon.

UNDERNEATH

It can't be Donne.

(Lion's Head, New York City)

DRACULA, COUNT (*d.* 1462)

Count Dracula, your Bloody Mary is ready.

Dracula sucks.

(On various walls, also on a button)

Dracula wears dentures.

I never drink wine.
—Dracula.

DRAMA, *see* THEATER

DRUG ADDICTION, *see also* HEROIN, MARIJUANA

Amy needs tranquilizers.

(Cited in The New Yorker, *1959)*

Blow your mind . . . smoke gunpowder.

Don't be a bring-down.

(Sidewalk in Tomkins Park, New York City, also on a button)

Dope kills.

(East Harlem, New York City, 1970)

Frodo has been busted.

(Men's room. Back Fence Bar, New York City)

Give me librium or give me meth.

(Scrawled in chalk on a piece of sculpture, New York City)

God is not dead—he's been busted.

Have you taken your soma?

(Swansea University, Wales, 1971)

Help feed my hobbit.

(Café Figaro, New York City, also on a button)

I fly/Hashish.

(Nanterre, May, 1968)

Jesus takes it in the palm.

Joe exists to get high.
Bill gets high to exist.

("A" train, IND subway, New York City)

Keep me high and I'll ball you forever.

(Ladies' room, Café Figaro, New York City, also on a button)

Legalize narcotics for addicts.

(On various walls, also on a button)

Little Boy Blue, come blow your mind!

(Arlington County Public Library,—cited in American Library Association Bulletin, *April, 1969)*

Mary Poppins is a junkie.

(Various IRT subway toilets, New York City, 1965, also on a button)

My mental condition is highly illegal.

(Ladies' room, Café Figaro, New York City, and on a button)

Nirvana needed.

The only dope worth shooting is Nixon.

(Men's room, bus stop, Seattle, 1972)

One good turn-on deserves another.

Speed kills.

(On various walls, also on a button)

Speed kills—don't meth around.

(Siena College, Loudonville, N. Y., 1972)

Support your local habit.

The Exit Coffee House, New York City)

Up is a nice place to be.

(Ladies' room, Village Gate, New York City, and on a button)

Tea is a groove
and AMT is really boss,
LSD is a trip,
Hash is too much, but
being high on love is the most precious because you don't buy it or con it or substitute.

(Ladies' room, Limelight Restaurant, New York City)

There's a methedrine to my madness.

The up must be higher than the down's down.

(Paradox Restaurant, New York City)

With booze you lose, with dope you hope.

(Men's room, Holly Tavern, Bellingham, Wash., 1970)

DRYDEN, JOHN (1631–1700)

Glass with a Diamond does our Wit betray;
Who can write fure on that smooth slippery Way?
Pleas'd with our scribling we cut swiftly on,
And see the Nonsense, which we cannot shun.

(White-Hart, Watford, England—a parody of four lines by Dryden)

DUNN, MICHAEL (1935–1973)

(Note: Mr. Dunn is a highly talented actor who is quite short)

Michael Dunn was here.

(High on a wall in the Fedora Restaurant, New York City)

E

ECOLOGY, *see also* AIR POLLUTION

Ecology, the last fad.

(Fence in San Francisco, 1970)

Forest fires prevent bears.

The forest precedes man, the desert follows him.

(Sorbonne, May, 1968)

Green plants are friendly.

(Bottom of the Barrel Café, Atlanta)

Is the balance of nature hanging in the balance?

Keep America beautiful. Swallow your beer cans.

Keep New York green, throw your trash in New Jersey.

Lake Erie died for your sins.

(University of Michigan, 1970)

Mankind has an incestuous relationship with mother earth.

(University of Michigan, 1970)

Never mind about ecology, what about the human waste?

People are uneatable, they contain too much DDT.

(Exeter College, Oxford University, 1971)

Piss on the environment; everyone else does.

(University of Michigan, 1970)

Pollution's cost proves grime doesn't pay.

Power to the earth.

(San Francisco State College, 1970)

Preserve wild life—throw a party.

A real part of the national debt is a logged-out redwood forest.

(San Francisco State College, 1970)

The following was written on a poster that said, "Smokey the Bear says, 'Help preserve our virgin forests' ":
Vote 'yes' on chastity belts for trees.

There's too much water in our chlorine supply.

The following was written on a fence near a lone tree:
This tree is spared, but its sex life is ruined forever.

We should be the symbiants of the earth, not the parasites.

(San Francisco State College, 1972)

ECONOMICS, *see also* CAPITALISM

The cost of a thing is the amount of life required to be expended for it.

UNDERNEATH

For those who live life rather than expend it everything is free.

(Men's toilet, Telephone Company,
New York City, 1969)

Damn the Joke
Of all the Folk:
I've lost my Estate;
And all Men I hate:
I shall look through a Grate,
For I see 'tis my Fate.
The Devil take the Bubbles,
I'm in a Pack of Troubles,
—X.B. 1721.

UNDERNEATH

Happy's the Man
That well could scan,
Which way his Fortune led him:
I have got what he lost,
I am gay while he's cross'd,
So adieu to good Mr. B—n.
Ha! ha! ha! 1722.

(In one of the summer houses at the Swan, at Chelsea, supposed to be written by one who lost his estate in the South-Sea year)

The economy is wounded, I hope it croaks.

(Paris, May, 1968)

How're gonna keep 'em down on the farm after they've seen parity?

If Life were Merchandize, that Men could buy,
The Rich would only live, the Poor must die.

John Maynard Keynes is a spendthrift.

(John Adams Luncheonette, New York City, 1968)

Up the Crown!! There will always be an England.

UNDERNEATH

As long as there's a Fort Knox.

(Limelight Restaurant, New York City, 1970)

What this country needs is a good 5 cent anything!

EDUCATION, *see also* UNIVERSITIES AND COLLEGES

Cemetery.

(On University wall, Nanterre, May, 1968)

Coarse syllabus—take one.

(Written on wall with arrow pointing to toilet paper, men's room, Princeton University)

The following was written on a poster that said, "Don't be a high-school dropout":

No, stay in school and learn to read and riot.

Don't write on our walls
We don't shit in your notebooks.
—The Regents

UNDERNEATH

What's found in our notebooks is shit anyway.
—The Students

Examination = servility, social promotion and hierarchical society.

(Paris, May, 1968)

Fail now and avoid the June rush.

Feces on theses.

Fuck the faculty.

(Hunter College, New York City, 1970)

Help retard children, support public schools.

High school causes brain damage.

The following was written on a poster that said, "I quit school when I were 16":
And now I are a millionaire.

UNDERNEATH

Became a rock and roll star.

If SDS closes down the school you won't be able to get your diploma and graduate.

UNDERNEATH

Too Bad! No diploma to Plasticland.

(San Francisco State College, 1968)

Life is elsewhere.

(Sorbonne, May, 1968)

Marie Montessori taut me to rite at age too.

(On cover of The Critic, *which was a picture of a wall covered with graffiti, December, 1966–January, 1967)*

May he who gives me the fee for teaching get what he seeks from those aloft.

(On a school wall, Pompeii, 79 A.D.)

Mr. Kirschenbaum is a good teacher.

(IRT subway, New York City, 1957)

Open the school to the people.

(University of California at Los Angeles, 1970)

The pen is mightier than the switchblade.

Long Island Courthouse, Mineola, N. Y., 1970)

Rape your Alma Mater.

(Nanterre University, May, 1968)

Something to wipe my ass with would now mean more to me than any other scholarly paper.

(Men's room, Breslau—
Cited in Anthropophyteia, *Vol. 6, 1909)*

Such futility in learning facts—to what end? . . .
One does not learn wisdom one grows into wisdom.
. . . I have found the supreme bean.

(Antioch College)

Teachers have two things in common: low mental capacity and high sucking power.

(Men's room, University of Maryland, 1972)

There will be no irrelevant Greek courses with pacing professors.

(New York University, 1969)

This desk is dedicated to those who died waiting for the bell to ring.

(Traditional desk graffito found in countless schools)

Write larger.

(Found on many desk chairs in public schools—
circumstantial evidence of attempted cheating)

Yellow walls of timeless folly,
Frozen scar of melancholy
Id and ego synthesized.
Testaments before my eyes.
Deck the halls with boughs of holly,
Ivy creeping up your thighs.

(Men's room, Princeton University, 1970)

You don't need a professor if you can read a book.

(Hunter College, New York City, 1970)

EGOTISM

An egotist thinks he's in the groove when he's in a rut.

Fat Mark loves himself.

(New York City)

Me loves I.

(IRT subway, New York City)

EISENHOWER, DWIGHT D. (1890–1969)

Another load of golf balls for Ike.

(Scrawled on a huge trailer truck during Eisenhower administration)

FDR, Ike and Rutherford B. Hayes all ate H.O. oatmeal.

I miss Ike.

UNDERNEATH

Hell, I miss Harry.

(Cited by Norton Mockridge, columnist, Boston Herald, *December 2, 1966)*

Nixon is the first president to have an ass-hole for a vice president.

UNDERNEATH

No, Eisenhower was.

(University of Michigan, 1970)

ELECTIONS

All thieves vote for Cassius Marcellus.

(Wall, Ancient Rome)

Anyone who removes my election announcement shall have an apoplectic seizure.

(Wall, Ancient Rome)

18! Thank you Supreme Court.

(Subway, New York City, 1971)

If anyone refused to vote for Quintius, let him be carried through this town on a donkey.

(Pompeii, 79 A.D.)

It's their election.

(Columbia University, October, 1968—Commentary by students on their inability to affect the upcoming presidential election results)

Referendum = voting for one's ball and chain.

(Paris, May, 1968)

The united fruitman with Helvius Vestalis urge you to make Marcus Holconius Priscum duumvir with judiciary powers.

(Pompeii, 79 A.D.)

Vote Buddhist.

You fight and die but can't vote at 18.

ELIOT, T. S. (1888–1965)

May is crueler than April.

(New York City, c. 1957)

T.S. Elliot loves D.H. Lawrence.

UNDERNEATH

Eliot is spelled with one l, you ass.

(Washington, D.C.)

EMPLOYEE MORALE

The boss is vacationing at the annual conference.

(Library staff lounge—Cited in American Library Association Bulletin, *January, 1969)*

The difference between this firm and a cactus plant is that the plant has the pricks on the outside.

It's a pain to put up with one's bosses; it's even more stupid to choose them.

It's not the work that gets me down, it's the coffee breaks.

Women my delirium
Pedestrians my martyrdom.

(On a truck, Mexico)

ENCOURAGEMENT

Illegitemi no carborundum.
[*Don't let the bastards grind you down.*]

(Harvard University)

In any case no remorse.

(Paris, May, 1968)

Keep on Truckin'

(On various walls, also on a T shirt, 1972)

Let the sun shine.

(Watts, Los Angeles, 1970)

Right on!

(University of Michigan, 1970)

ENGINEERS

Engineers blow.

UNDERNEATH

No, we just build the horns.

*(Men's room, engineering building,
University of Maryland, 1972)*

Mother Grumman is a whore.

UNDERNEATH

No, Mother Grumman is the madam, the engineers are the whores.

*(Men's room, Grumman Aerospace Corp.,
Bethpage, N. Y., 1972)*

Student—gets his prick up in a moment
Engineer—takes an hour to get his prick up.

*(Men's room, Polytechnic Institute, Petrograd, 1917
—comment on the long and tedious road
leading to an engineering degree)*

10% of all engineers have hemmeroids [*sic*]—the rest are all perfect ass-holes.

(Men's room, Princeton University, 1972)

ERUCTATION

A belch is a wind from the stomach
That could not find its way to the ass.

(Men's room, Berlin, c. 1907)

Belch when you're happily drunk and dare to assert the bottom's rude delights. Blurt and still blurt.

(Pompeii, 79 A.D.)

If you belch and don't fart,
Then your ass thinks it has been cheated.

(Men's room, Berlin, c. 1907)

ETHICS

Be vertuous and assure thyselfe thou canst not then but thrive in only vertu is it sayfe that men themselves survive.

(Well Tower in Tower of London, 16th century)

Dishonor before death.

Do unto others—and then cut out.

Do unto others before they undo you.

(Men's room, ferry terminal, New York City, 1972)

Don't fuck yourself anymore! Fuck the others!

(Nanterre University, May, 1968)

Down with the categorical imperative.

(University of California at Los Angeles, 1972)

Everything not forbidden is compulsory.

Evil works.

The greatest evil becomes a trifle if you scorn it.

(Pompeii, 79 A.D.)

Hire the morally handicapped.

I can resist anything but temptation.

If at first you don't succeed . . . Cheat!!!

It is all right to copy but not to envy.

(Pompeii, 79 A.D.)

Think Rotten!

ETHNIC PRIDE

white
All power to the ∧ people.

Be ethnic.

~~Black is beautiful.~~

~~White ain't so bad.~~

Black is still beautiful.

(Northwestern University)

Black peoples must fight back!

(Watts, Los Angeles, 1970)

Black power

(On various walls, also on buttons)

Dare to struggle, dare to win.

(Watts, Los Angeles, 1970)

Dig yourself.

(Watts, Los Angeles, 1970)

Don't fuck with me.

Don't rip off your brothers and sisters.

(Wall near People's Park, Berkeley, Calif., 1970)

Get off your knees praying to be white.

(Watts, Los Angeles, 1970)

Irish power.

Italian power.

Jewish power.

Know your heritage.

(Watts, Los Angeles, 1970)

Say it loud, I'm yellow and I'm mellow.

(IND subway, New York City)

The Songs of Watts must be heard.

(The Forum Coffee House, New York City)

Think Ethnic.

(Blimpie's, New York City)

Viva la Raza.

(Mexican-American barrio, Los Angeles, 1970)

Wasp power.

We don't need a gun, we've already won.

(Los Angeles, 1970)

We got to do things. Blacks must act.

(Watts, Los Angeles, 1970)

Venceremos!
[*We shall conquer*]

(East Harlem, New York City, 1970)

White power.

(On various walls, also on a button)

EUCLID (*fl.* c. 300 B.C.)

Euclid was square.

EVOLUTION

I just cannot picture you as the end result of millions of years of evolution.

Modern man is the missing link between apes and human beings.

(University of Michigan)

We are all god in the process of evolution.

(Ladies' room, Goddard College, 1971)

You are now part of the cosmic plot to evolve the human race into the next dimension.

UNDERNEATH

With the other reptiles.

(Coed toilet, East Village Other, *1970)*

You could be extinct too! Think about that!

(New York University, 1969)

EXISTENTIALISM

The act creates conscience.

(Nanterre, May, 1968)

If you can keep your head when those about you are losing theirs, perhaps you've misunderstood the situation.

You are who you fuck.

EXPLOITATION

All the rich are the same exploiters.

(Construction fence, Harvard University, 1972)

Bone and Skin,
Two Millers thin,
Would grind this Town and Places near it.
But be it known
To Skin and Bone,
That Flesh and Blood won't bear it.

(On the pillory in a certain market town in Shropshire, England—on two millers, named Bone and Skin, who exacted extravagant toll)

Down with variable annuities.

(Metropolitan Life Insurance Building, New York City)

If I had a wish I would wish that people would stop eating each other's brains out.

(Ladies' room, Limelight Restaurant, New York City, 1965)

The public is a patient beast—beat it gently.

(Arlington County Public Library,—cited in American Library Association Bulletin, *April, 1969)*

Publicity is manipulating you.

Society is a carnivorous flower.

(Paris, May, 1968)

Those you walk on are always kinder than those who command you.

(Paris, May, 1968)

The following was written on a poster advertising a funeral parlor that said, "We understand":

How to exploit sadness and death for our profit.

F

FASHION

Brown shoes don't make it.

(Construction fence, Harvard University, 1972)

Down with pants!
Up with penises!

(Engagé Coffee House, New York City)

Dress British, think Yiddish.

(Men's room, Madison Avenue building, New York City, also on a button)

A Fox was drawn in for Cakes and Ale,
And by a fly Stratagem lost his Tail.
'Tis no Matter, says Reynard, by Dint of Persuasion,
I'll make all my Brethren believe 'tis the Fashion,
Though at the same Time, he was in a d——d Passion.

UNDERNEATH

—Although they all come in,
There's none can laugh, but those that win.
New Fashions are Gins that I mortally hate,
I'll keep my old Fashion, and keep my Estate.
No coaxing, no wheedling, good Mr. Fox.
Recruiting Officer
Getting is a Chance; but keeping is a Virtue.

(On a window, Chester, England, 1726)

God damn all those dirty minded naked dames.

(IRT subway, New York City, 1969—probably written by a gentleman who couldn't cope with the erotic excitement of modern fashion)

Midis went too far out on a limb.

Up with minis.

FATALISM

I shit on society, but she gives it back to me with ease.

(Paris, May, 1968)

If fate promised you to pass by here you will.

*(Ellis Island, N.Y., 1953—
written in Greek on a wall in the main building)*

FECES, *see also* DEFECATION

All, all are gone, the old familiar faeces.

The caretaker wept and well he might to see these walls covered with shit.

(Peel, Isle of Man, England, 1929)

Free lunch.

*(Written over toilet bowl in men's room,
University of North Carolina, 1959)*

From costive Stools, and hide-bound Wit,
From Bawdy Rhymes, and Hole besh–t.
From Walls besmear'd with stinking Ordure.
By Swine who ne'er provide Bumfodder
(Libera Nos—

(Boghouse at the George Inn, Whitchurch, England)

Gefilte feces.

(Steinberg's Dairy Restaurant, New York City)

The greatest masterworks of the kitchen
Give off here the most awful smells.
The more the cooks show their skills,
The worse do smell the flavor of the excrement
What use is esthetics and devotion?
Here you are a simple son of the earth.

(Vienna, late 19th century—cited in Leben, Meinlungen und Wirken, *by Himmlisch, 1906)*

Here in this soft butter
There lies buried Dr. M. . . . Lu . . . .

UNDERNEATH

Yet when you grasp into it a little more deeply: there lies P . . . . the fat pig.

(Zwickau, 1905—possibly referring to Martin Luther)

I cannot fathom what this pig has
eaten and that thing that stinks
so out of the behind.

(Men's room, Weissenfels, Prussia—cited in Anthropophyteia, *Vol. 4, 1907)*

If shit could be sold by the pound, assholes would be rationed.

(Men's room, Santa Cruz University)

In the stinking rat holes there blooms pig shit, but believe me even in palaces people feast themselves on pig shit.

*(Men's room, Vienna—*cited in Anthropophyteia, *Vol. 5, 1908)*

In this hotel there are hot
sausages without the skin.

(Rügen, Prussia—cited in Anthropophyteia, *Vol. 4, 1907)*

McManus was a man who was quite thin,
One day while he was on the john he fell in.
Along came another man who flushed it,
he was not meek,
Now McManus is really up shit creek.

Oh! that I were a turd, a turd,
Hid in this secret place,
That I might see my Betsy's ass,
Though she shit me in my face.

UNDERNEATH [*in a woman's hand*]

'Tis pity but you had your wish.

(Boghouse, Hampton Court, England, 1703 —cited in The Merry Thought, *1731)*

Poor little cook, your art goes through this hole.

(Men's room, coffee house, Vienna, 1910)

Shit stinks.

UNDERNEATH

Only if you smell it.

(Men's room, University of Maryland, 1972)

The South will rise again because shit floats.

(Men's room, New York University, 1969)

This plumbing eats shit.

(Antioch College, Ohio)

What Difference between Kings T——ds and mine?
One may be costive, one be full of Slime;
Yet equally will any Hog that feeds,
Produce good Pork by feeding on our Needs.

UNDERNEATH

You nasty Dog, you may eat your Pork yourself.

(Wall, Hoxton, England)

What lies under here no one steals.

(Men's room—cited in Anthropophyteia, *Vol. 6, 1909)*

Whoever is a prude should look away
and not enjoy every piece of shit.

(Men's room, Germany)

FEDERAL BUREAU OF INVESTIGATION

Defend anal freedom, support your FBI.

(On a button)

I was a pseudo Bohemian for the FBI.

(Café Figaro, New York City)

FELLATIO

Auto-fellatio is its own reward.

Blow job?

UNDERNEATH

Try Jesus.

UNDERNEATH

Why? Is he well hung?

(Archie Café, Abilene, Tex.)

Blow my fuse.

(Men's room, University of Maryland, 1972)

Cocksuckers of the world unite—bite Birchers.

Don't start sucking cocks, it's a bad habit to break.

UNDERNEATH

Now he tells us.

(West Side Y.M.C.A., New York City)

Eat at the "Y."

(On a button)

Fellatio is not a felony, fellas, it is a misdemeanor.

Fucking in the mouth is best.

(Toilet, Vienna, 1910)

Get the dick out of the White House and into your mouth.

(Men's room, Montclair State College, N. J., 1971)

Have gums, will travel.
—The Prairie Fairy.

Here's to the * * * the human vine
who blooms every month and bears
every nine the only thing this side
of hell that can take the juice from
a nut without cracking the shell.

(Yosemite National Park, California, 1928)

I am the night cleaning man. I'm looking for a chick who wants to have a little fun. I love to suck dik [*sic*] and eat womand's [*sic*] asshole.

UNDERNEATH

You're sick, cleaning man.

(Ladies' room, City College of New York, 1971)

I can lick any man.

(Men's room, bus station, Boston)

I play the flute and swallow the music

(Men's room, Chinese Real Food Restaurant, New York City)

I want to be fucked in the mouth by a young student.

(Men's room, Vienna—cited in Anthropophyteia, *Vol. 7, 1910)*

If you want to suck a prick—break your back and suck your own.

(Cedar River Park, Waterloo, Iowa, 1932)

I'm a beautiful, tall girl but the lower part of my body doesn't feel well, however, I would enjoy being fucked in the mouth every hour on the hour.

(Ladies' room, Breslau—cited in Anthropophyteia, *Vol. 6, 1909)*

Larry I want your head because you are a good cocksucker so you should be a good asssucker [*sic*].

(Men's room, Hunter College, New York City, 1972)

Let 'em eat cock.

(Men's room, University of California at Berkeley, 1971—response to Women's Liberation Movement)

Little Jack Horner eats it.

Male cocksuckers suck best. I tried it.

(Men's room, IRT subway, New York City)

My daughter 4½ sucks me off every Saturday morning.

UNDERNEATH

Wishful thinking.

(Toilet, London)

Notice: I will suck off all boys' (over 16) cocks next Sunday—July 25th at 12 p.m. All wishing to be sucked off get a bone on and wait. I will choose the best looking pricks. My friend will jerk off the rest.

(Chief Ranger Martindale Geyser Baths Swimming Pool, Old Faithful Camp, Yellowstone National Bank, 1928)

Old fags unite!

UNDERNEATH

Don't bite.

(Co-ed toilet, Alternate U., New York City)

Old fairies never die, they merely blow away.

Out of love, I'd let myself be buggered and fucked in the mouth by a dashing young student with a big prick. Let me know when I can meet such a person. I am here every day from 10:00 to 10:30.

(Men's room, Philosophy Faculty, University of Vienna, 1910)

Peter, Peter, pumpkin eater.
Pumpkin, pumpkin, Peter eater.

Phil Attio loves Connie Lingus.

(Restaurant, Phoenix)

Sex has no calories.

UNDERNEATH

Wrong Fatso, you're getting 8 in every load you swallow.

Sucking a cock every day keeps the doctor away.

(Men's toilet, Fortune Theatre, New York City)

Think about him, talk about him, but don't go down for him.

(Ladies' room, Ninth Circle Restaurant, New York City)

Uncut cock tastes better.

(Men's room, Fortune Theatre, New York City)

Which pretty young man
will let himself for 1 mark be
sucked off and fucked in the ass.

(Halle, Prussia, 1905)

A white whore sucked my black dick all night last night and loved it and this morning I fucked her in the ass—her pussy stinks to [*sic*] bad.

(Men's room, Greyhound Bus Terminal, Chicago, 1970)

Will you suck this cock of mine?
You will find it really fine
I think it is unusually great
But if you're scared just masturbate.

FIELDS, W. C. (1880–1846)

W. C. Fields is alive and drunk in Philadelphia.

(Top of the Gate, New York City)

FILLMORE, MILLARD (1800–1874)

Millard Fillmore was the last Pres. born in the 19th century.

UNDERNEATH

Actually he was the first, being born in January 1800.

UNDERNEATH

Who was Millard Fillmore?

UNDERNEATH

Millard Fillmore is an Aggie.

UNDERNEATH

Millard Fillmore was a dirty commie rat.

UNDERNEATH

Millard Fillmore is secretly alive and awaiting the call of his country.

(Scholtz's Beer Garden, Austin)

Don't knock President Fillmore. He kept us out of Vietnam.

FLATTERY

When great ELIZA saw at Redgrave-Hall,
The Apartment few, and those indeed but small,
Thus to its Lord, bespoke the gracious QUEEN;
Methinks for you, this Mansion is too mean.
For me, my Liege, quoth he, of old 'twas meet
But you have made me for my House—too great.

(Over the Gate of Redgrave Hall—on a visit made by Queen Elizabeth to Sir Nicholas Bacon, then Lord Keeper)

When the emperor lets one go
Geoffray would say he smells a rose,
and the Senate aspires
to the honor to prove it.

(Vienna, late 19th century—cited in Leben, Meinungen und Wirken, *by Wetti Himmlisch, 1906)*

Who speaks to please in ev'ry Way,
And not himself offend,
He may begin to work to Day,
But Heaven knows when he'll end.

(In the summer house on Gray's Inn Terras, England)

FLATULENCE

As on the throne of the gods
you sit yourself on this gadget
and let the storm, the thunder
crash loudly under you.

(Men's room—cited in Anthropophyteia, *Vol. 4, 1907)*

Blow me a Kiss, says a Nymph to her Swain,
And when I have got it, I'll give it again,
The Swain had been working, as sometimes Men do,
Till he'd hardly got Breath for to buckle his Shoe;
But turning around, he let a great F—t,
And blow'd her a Kiss according to Art.
B.R. 1715

(On a window, Beaconsfield, England)

A belch is a wind from the stomach
That could not find its way to the ass.

(Men's room, Berlin c. 1907)

Belch when you're happily drunk and dare to assert the bottom's rude delights. Blurt and still blurt.

(Pompeii, 79 A.D.)

Do not fart too loud because the walls are weak.

(Banff, Alberta, 1928)

Farting pressure over 200 pounds.

(Iowa State Teachers College Library, 1928)

Hail to thee Helvetia, hail!
A fart is no arrow
otherwise the old comrades of the oath
(Helvetians) would have shot their
wives in bed.

Here I sit all brokenhearted,
Paid a dime and only farted.

UNDERNEATH

Don't cry brother
You had a chance
I didn't have a dime
And shit in my pants

Here I sit broken hearted
Tried to shit and only farted
But think of the man who took a chance
Tried to fart and shit his pants.

An Encomium on a Fart:

I sing the Praises of a Fart.
That I may do't by Rules of Art;
I will invoke no Deity,
But Butter'd-Peace and Furmity;

And think their Help sufficient
To sit and furnish my Intent:
For sure I must not use high Strains,
For fear it bluster out in Grains.
When Virgil's Gnat, and Ovid's Flea
And Homer's Frogs strive for the Day;
There is no Reason in my Mind,
That a brave Fart should come behind;
Since that you may it parallel,
With any Thing that doth excel.
Musick is but a Fart that's sent
From the Guts of an Instrument:
The Scholar farts; but when he gains
Learning with cracking of his Brains;
And having spent much Pain and Oil,
Thomas and Dun to reconcile,
For to learn the abstracting Art,
What does he get by't? Not a Fart.
The Soldier makes his Foes to run
With but the Farting of a Gun;

That's if he make the Bullet Whistle,
Else 'tis no better than a Fizzle:
And if withal the Winds to stir-up
Rain, 'tis but a Fart in Syrrup.
They are but Farts, the Words we say,
Words are but Wind, and so are they.
Applause is but a Fart, the crude
Blast of the fickle Multitude.
The Boats that lie the Thames about,
Be but Farts several Docks let out.
Some of our Projects were, I think,
But politick Farts, Foh! how they stink!
As soon as born, they by-and-by,
Fart-like, but only breathe, and die.
Farts are as good as Land, for both
We hold in Tail, and let them both:
Only the Difference here is, that
Farts are let at a lower Rate.
I'll say no more, for this is right,
That for my Guts I cannot write;
Though I should study all my Days,
Rhimes that are worth the Thing I praise:
What I have said, take in good Part,
If not, I do not care a Fart.

The Italian Gout:

If a Man lets a Fart in fair Italy,
From Lovers he never is after free;
For why —— amongst those Dons, 'tis said.
'Tis a certain Sign of a Male Maidenhead.
If a Man should breathe backwards, and happens to stink,
You may say, if you will, it is natural instinct.

UNDERNEATH

You may quibble upon the Word Instinct, if you will, but I think 'tis better out than in considering the Case.
—I.M. of Oxon.

(Boghouse, Uxbridge, England)

If Death doth come as soon as Breath departs;
Then he must often die, who often farts:
And if to die be but to lose one's Breath;
Then Death's a Fart, and so a Fart for Death.

(On a window, Richmond, England)

If you belch and don't fart,
Then your ass thinks it has been cheated.

(Men's room, Berlin, c. 1907)

My fart is short.

(Men's room, Stuttgart)

Silence is golden some people say,
But I don't care, I fart anyway.

(Men's room, University of Maryland, 1972)

Solomon the Wise says: Loud farts do not smell but the soft ones, the delicate ones are an odorous flower bed.

(Toilet, Austrian inn, 1904)

To preserve our good Health,
Let us let a good F—t;
It is better than Wealth,
It will comfort your Heart;
And when you have done,
With the Crack of your B–m,
Bend your Knees,
And then squeeze,
And something will come,
You'll be better, tho' it's not so big as your Thumb.
—G.S. 1716.

(Boghouse, Richmond, England)

Reader,
Within this Place two Ways I've been delighted;
For here I've f——, and likewise here have sh——d.
They both are healthful, Nature's Ease require 'em,
And though you grin; I fancy you desire 'em.

UNDERNEATH

What Beast alive, could bear to f——
  In such a filthy Hole as this is;
The nauseous Stink, might, one would think,
  Disturb his Taste for amorous Kisses.

UNDERNEATH

This was wrote by some Beau, the Fop you may know,
His squeamish Exception would make one believe it;
Though the Smell where we sh——t, is not grateful a Bit,
Yet I ne'er knew a C——y that favour'd of Civet.

(Boghouse, Carlisle, England, 1718)

A Scrap of a Lady's Life:

When first she wakes, a Sigh or two she fetches,
Then rubs her Eyes,—and Arms and Legs she stretches!
Oh! for a Husband, out she gently cries,
If he were here,—he would not let me rise;
But I must up, for Fear my Love should stay,
And we should be too late at the new Play.
Here, Jenny, reach my Slippers, bring the Pot;
Then out she jumps, and down she gives a Squat,
I think I need not tell you what to do,
And then she lets a merry Crack or two.
W. Overb—ry.

(On a window, Kidderminster, England)

Who first smells it is the culprit.

(Found in Germany, written in French)

FLYING SAUCERS

The truth is within the saucers.

(Engagé Coffee House, New York City)

UFO's are for real; the Air Force doesn't exist.

(University of Michigan)

FLYNN, ERROL (1909–1959)

Erroll Flynn holds the record.

FOOD

An apple a day keeps the doctor away, but an onion a day keeps everyone away.

Apple pie is fluoridated.

Apple pie makes you sterile.

Bagel power!

A cauliflower is just a cabbage with a college education.

(Ladies' room, University of California at Berkeley)

The following was written under a stenciled sign over a coffee urn that read, "Coffee 10 cents. please pay, Ali Baba had less trouble with his 40 thieves":
Yes, but Ali Baba had good coffee.

(U.S. Naval Air Station, New York, 1970)

Down with macrobiotics!

(Coed toilet, Paradox Restaurant, New York City)

The following was written on a poster that said, "Drink Milk It's Good for You":
Contains Strontium 90.
Contains Cholesterol for good hard arteries.

Fuck home cooking.

(Four Seasons Restaurant, New York City)

He who hints
For a blintz
Gets his wish
With a knish.
A pox on your lox;
I'll inveigle
A bagel.

He who makes soup from sanitary napkins will never get a job as a cook.

(Men's room, Germany)

Honolulu is as American as apple poi.

I'd rather fuck the pizza and eat the waitress.

UNDERNEATH

I did. The pizza's better.

If you have cheese on your stollen.
you can fuck like a bull.

(Men's room, Germany)

Kohlrabi is coming.

(Laundry room, Princeton University, 1971)

Life is Kreplach.

The Puddings are so good in Sandy-Lane,
That if I chance to go that Way again,
I'll not be satisfy'd unless I've twain,
The one stuck thick with Plumbs, the other plain.

*(Wall at the George in Sandy-Lane—
a place famous for puddings)*

Yone Shimmel put Kennel Rations in his kashe knishes.

*(Wall in lower Manhattan East Side
near Katz's Delicatessen)*

FRANCO, FRANCISCO (1892–   )

Viva Franco.

UNDERNEATH

American spaghetti.

(Yale University)

FREEDOM, see LIBERTY

FREUD, SIGMUND (1856–1939)

Before Freud sex was a pleasure, now it's a necessity.

FRIENDSHIP

Earn cash in your spare time—blackmail your friends.

I know that I can never see
Completely through your mind
For you have strangers in your life
And I have friends in mine.

(Paradox Restaurant, New York City)

Identify your friends by their enemies.

(Co-ed toilet, Alternate U., New York City)

I'll blow your mind if you suck my soul.

Pyrrhus to his pal Chius: I'm sorry to hear that you are dead.

(Pompeii, 79 A.D.)

True Friendship multiplies our Joys;
It mends our Griefs, and makes them light as Toys.

(On a window at Christ-Church, Oxford University, 18th century)

When you share a joy it becomes two joys; when you share a grief it becomes half a grief.

(California Rehabilitation Center for female drug addicts, Norco, 1970)

Whene'er a Man has gain'd his Ends,
He is encompass'd by his Friends;
But when that Man has lost his All,
And wants his Friends, he'as none at all.

In gay Prosperity we see,
That ev'ry one will bend the Knee,
And treat you with their Flattery;
But in a contrary State,
When Gaiety's destroy'd by Fate,
The Man they lov'd before
——They hate.

(Devil-Tavern, England, 1721)

FRODO

Frodo has been busted.

(Men's room, Back Fence Bar, New York City)

Frodo is God.

Frodo lives.

(On various walls, also on a button)

FROMMER, ARTHUR (1929-)

(Note: Frommer publishes the *$5-A-Day* travel guides)

Arthur Frommer spends $10 a day.

(Ladies' room, National Gallery, London, 1970)

FRONDIZI, ARTURO (1908-)

Frondizi will return.

UNDERNEATH

To make peace.

(Toilet, Buenos Aires)

FULLER, R. BUCKMINSTER (1895-)

Bucky Fuller for President.

UNDERNEATH

Of the world.

(Iowa State University, 1972)

G

GALLANTRY

Her lips were as pink as a rooster's dink
Her eyes were a hen turd brown
Her tits were as loose as the balls of a moose
But she came from a damned good town.

(Men's room, train station, Minneapolis)

A little old but very obliging.

(On a truck, Mexico)

Mrs. or Miss, if you need what I'm carrying, tell me now, tomorrow is too late.

(On a truck, delivering eggs, Mexico)

GALLO GANG

Bring back the Gallo gang, the gang with a soul.

GAMBLING

The following were written on the seats of buses that go to Yonkers Raceway:

Fixed races nightly at Yonkers.

Fools go to vacume [*sic*] cleaners Yonkers.

The human race is fixed.

I won at Niceria, dicing, 855 sesteras, no cheating.

(Baths at Pompeii, 79 A.D.)

Keep grandma off the streets—legalize bingo.

Outlaw church gambling.

(On various walls, also on a button)

GANDHI, MAHATMA (1869–1948)

Reporter: Mr. Gandi [*sic*] what do you think of Western Civilization?

Mr. Gandi: I think it would be a good idea!

(Co-ed toilet, Alternate U., New York City)

GANGS

The Assassins.

UNDERNEATH

The Royal Bishops.

UNDERNEATH

The Non-Violent Stompers.

(Painted on wall; names denoting violence and power are frequently taken by gangs)

From the smiling daughter mongers, and kill, fight,
Drink and sing many happy songs on cold Knights.

(Chalk on pavement around fountain in Washington Square Park, New York City, December, 1966)

Hello to the 119th Street Savage Knight Purple Killer Warrior Demon Saint Bishop Mystic Unknown Mother-Hater Carrot Mutilators Sons of the Smiling Butcher Fathers.

(Chalk on pavement around fountain in Washington Square Park, New York City, December, 1966)

Hell's Angels wear training wheels.

(Ladies' room, Chumley's Restaurant, New York City)

Stamp out Rockers.

(Cited in Graffiti *by Richard Freeman, London)*

GENETICS

Do the gaullists have one chromosome too much?

(Medical School, Paris, May, 1968)

I was born this way, what's your excuse?

Save your seeds!

(Engagé Coffee House, New York City)

GENITALIA

Are you nervous, tense? Try my 8-inch relaxer.

(NBC Studios, New York City, 1966—inspired by commercials)

At the Foot of a Bed where a Woman lay dying,
A Parcel of Gossips in Council were sat;
And instead of good Prayers, condoling and crying;
A Thing was the Subject of all the Debate.
One wish'd for a thick one, and swore 'twas the best;
Altho' 'twere as short to the full as her Snout;
But a finall One procur'd the Applause of the rest,
Provided in Length the Defect were made out.
Hold, quoth the sick Sister, you are all in the Wrong;
So I'll in a Case of this Weight to decide,
Heav'n send me at once both the Thick and the Long;
So closing her pious Petition, she dy'd.

(The Silver Lion, Calais)

Big girl, big cunt. Small girl, all cunt.

(Men's room, Wolfie's, Brooklyn)

Callahan tunnel is a large vagina.

(Boston University)

An Acrostick upon something or other:

Commodious for a Haven made,
Under a rising Bank,
Nature has fix'd a Place of Trade,
To men of any Rank.

UNDERNEATH

Riddle my ree, &c.
And read the four first Letters, and you'll see.
—R.M.

Cunt plays no gramaphone,
neither does she sing songs;
she is only a resort for stiff members.

(Men's room, Germany)

A cunt with long hair,
is good in the winter
because it protects
the prick from freezing.

(Men's room, Thüringen—cited in Anthropophyteia, *Vol. 7, 1910)*

Do you have split ends? Then you're in the wrong bathroom.

(Men's room, University of California at San Diego, 1971)

Eunuchs of America unite!
You have nothing to lose.

Every man has one too small
And every woman has one too big.
If a man sticks it in well
Then it has to be a virgin who can
be trusted to give pleasure.

(Ladies' room, College in Berlin, 1910)

The future of America is in your hands.

Genitals prefer blondes.

(Cyrano Restaurant, New York City)

God the Father
Why did he create the prop?
That man will use it
To continue the race
And also to let out his water.
A maiden of fine sensibilities
Must be ashamed if she sees
That the instrument of high love
Becomes the most vulgar gutter.
What man uses for his pissing
With that he creates his equals.
(Heinrich Heine)

He who wears trousers of cunt,
will have an erection all year.

(Men's room, Konsantz am Rhein—cited in Anthropophyteia, *Vol. 5, 1908)*

The heat of the meat is inversely
proportional to angle of the dangle.

UNDERNEATH

and directly proportional to the mass of the ass.

I am six foot two, have blond wavy hair and a ten-inch prick. I am looking for a girl five foot three and likes to shake her box. I am not prejudiced.

UNDERNEATH

You must look like a fag if you got in here. What the hell do you do, anyway, sew it on?

(Ladies' room, City College of New York, 1971)

I believe in capital punishment, but I don't think women should be hung like men.

If looking down embarrasses you don't look.

It's better to fuck a hairy cunt than a smooth one.

(Pompeii, 79 A.D.)

It was the day of the King's castration and the royals balls were coming off.

KOTEX: Not the best thing on earth, but next to the best.

(Yosemite National Park, Cal., 1928)

The man with the golden rod is suffering from allergies.

(University of Michigan)

$Me^2 = 144$

(Men's room, Broadway Bar, San Francisco—the length of the writer's penis squared; the conclusion is that his organ is 12 inches long)

Meet me in front of the pawnshop and I'll kiss you under the balls!

The men of Essen have long hard steel flutes made by Krupp.

(Men's room, Essen)

My girl has a lovely pussy.

UNDERNEATH

Mozel tov.

O cunt, o cunt you have it easy:
In winter you don't need a hat
And when everybody perspires in the summer,
You can sit in the shade of the ass.

(Men's room, Germany)

On this site will be a block long erection.

(On a construction fence, Madison, Wis.)

The penis is mightier than the sword.

Perfume doesn't help nor does make-up, the hole must stink like a hole.

(Men's room, Germany)

Peter Piper picked a peck of pickled peckers.

Remember the alum, Moe.

(The White Whale, New York City.)

So let me state in this woeful dirge
That life played a horrible trick
On the man possessed by a giant's urge
And cursed with a pygmy's stick.

(Public toilet, San Francisco, 1948)

There was a man from Boston
Who traded his Ford for an Austin.
He had room for his ass
And a gallon of gas
But his balls hung out the window
And he lost them.

(Men's room, Standard Oil station, Salmon, Id.)

Third cock wanted for a party.

UNDERNEATH

You're lucky and a freak if you've got two!

(Toilet, London)

This is the little English cock
Look at him sit without letting on,
erase its beak and feet
and stick it in your ass.

(Men's room, Mexico)

To find out if a girl is ticklish, give her a couple of test tickles.

Vagina envy.

(On sidewalk in front of Brooklyn College, November, 1969)

What help is crying, man has only one.

(Men's room, coffee house, Vienna, 1910)

What would you do if you had a 2″ cock?

UNDERNEATH

Join the Jewish army.
Act real big, bad, militant.
Marry a girl with a 2″ pussy.
Use my head.
Attend Hunter College.
Fuck you in the left nostril.
Become a priest.

UNDERNEATH

How about a 14″ cock?

UNDERNEATH

Fold it.
Make 2 7″s.
Display it in the Smithsonian.
Buy a bigger jock.

(Men's room, Hunter College, New York City, 1972)

When one reflects on how it hangs
Between his legs, one could cry!

UNDERNEATH

You have fucked too much.

(Men's room, coffee house, Vienna, 1910)

ON THE CEILING

Why are you looking up here, are you ashamed of it?

UNDERNEATH

No, but neither am I obsessed with it.

You are now shaking your best friend
And he stood up for you on your wedding night.

(Camp Maxey, Paris, Tex., 1945)

GINSBERG, ALLEN (1926–)

Ginsberg for Pope.

(The Old Quarter, Houston)

Ginsberg revises.
[*Refutation of the idea that Allen Ginsberg writes without revisions*]

Vote Row A: Allen Ginsberg for Messiah.

GOD

Allah
~~God~~ is dead.

And we said "go home, God" and he did . . . but he still comes to eat chicken at our house on Thursdays.

(Florida State University)

Art is Love is God.

(Engagé Coffee House, New York City)

Contrary to popular belief "Damn It" is not God's last name.

(Construction wall, Philadelphia, 1969)

Curb your God
i.e. curb Allah
i.e. curb caballah

UNDERNEATH

i.e. curb Cat Ballou

(The Forum Coffee House, New York City)

The death of God is yesterday's story.

(Ladies' room, Ninth Circle Restaurant, New York City)

God is dead.
—Voltaire

UNDERNEATH

Voltaire is dead.
—God

(Odeon Metro station, Paris)

Do not fear tomorrow for God is already there, let him fear tomorrow.

(New York College of Music, New York City)

Does God have a navel?

(Florida State University)

Feare fortuns flateri, fraile of felicitie,
dispayre not in danger, God is defender.

(Salt Tower, Tower of London, 16th century)

Find God within yourself.

UNDERNEATH

God's a lower intestinal tract.

(Men's room, Rutgers University, 1971)

God ain't dead, he's just playing possum.

God come home—all is forgiven.

God did not create the world in 7 days; he screwed around for 6 days and then pulled an all-nighter.

(University of Michigan)

God don't pay his debts in money.

(Airport lounge, London)

God eats the dead.

(Men's room, Minetta Tavern, New York City, 1965)

God for rent—Apply Sundays.

(On brick wall, Church of God, Long Beach, Cal.)

God fucks those who fuck themselves.

(Taxi garage, New York City, 1970)

God grows good grass.

(University of Michigan)

God has an authoritarian personality.
(Men's room, Brooklyn College, 1969)

God hips those who hip themselves.
(Men's room, Harlem, New York City)

God in the form of a white dove came before the Americans and said kill, kill, kill all unfree, undemocratic people in my name.

God, inventor of the unique principle.
(Paradox Restaurant, New York City)

God is a concept by which man judges his potentialities.
(Men's room, University of California at San Diego, 1971)

God is a prisoner in the Sandoz factory.
[*Sandoz factory is where LSD is made.*]

God is a 6000-foot tall, red jellybean.
(Piazza Haven, Berkeley, Cal.)

God is a voyeur.

God is a whore and what's more she's black.
(Men's room, Slug's, New York City)

God is alive and away for the season in Miami.
(On various walls, also on a button)

God is alive and living in a sugar cube.
(Wall near Tomkins Square Park, New York City, also on a button)

God is alive and living in Argentina.

God is alive and well in Mexico City.
(On various walls, also on a button)

God is alive—everyone else is dead.

God is alive he just doesn't want to get involved.
(On various walls, also on a button)

God is alive in Burbank, Calif., if in doubt call (214) 9687.
(Ladies' room, Ninth Circle Restaurant, New York City)

God is an April Fool's joke.

(Boston College)

God is an atheist.

God is an undefined term.

(On various walls, also on a button)

God is coming to St. Louis, tickets on sale now.

God is dead.

UNDERNEATH

Did he ever live?

(Men's toilet, Newport Jazz Festival, 1967)

God is dead.

UNDERNEATH

Would you believe seriously ill?

(Ladies' room, Eighth St. Ice Cream Parlor, New York City)

GOD IS DEAD, and indexed—H.W. Wilson.

(Arlington County Public Library, Va.—cited in American Library Association Bulletin, *April, 1969, also cited in* Library Journal, *January 1, 1968, with slight variation, the indexer was Bowker)*

God is dead, but don't worry the Virgin Mary is pregnant again.

("Private" men's room, Central Cleveland Police Station, 1968)

God is dead.
—Nietzche [*sic*]
Nietzche is dead.
—God

God is dead.
—Nietzche [*sic*]
Nietzche is dead.
—God
They're both dead.
—Odin

God is dead.
—Nietzche [*sic*]
Nietzche is dead.
—God

UNDERNEATH

Who cares?
—Moses
Me—God

God is dead.
—Time
Time is dead.
—God
God is not dead.
—Billy Graham
Who is Billy Graham?
—God

(Limelight Restaurant, New York City)

God is gay and living on E. 59th St.

(Ladies' room, Ninth Circle Restaurant, New York City)

God is good.

UNDERNEATH

Cheeses is also delicious.

(Fence, New York City, 1972)

God is love.
Love is blind.

(Ladies' room, Ninth Circle Restaurant, New York City)

God is not dead! He is alive and autographing bibles today at Brentano's.

(Subway, New York City)

God is not dead, he is just very, very sick.

God is not dead, he just moved to a better neighborhood.

God is not dead; he lives with me.

(Ladies' room, Tin Angel, New York City)

God is not dead—he's been busted.

God is not dead—he's hiding because he's ashamed.

God is not dead, he's just trying to avoid the draft.

(Subway, Boston)

God is not dead, just currently unemployed.

(California State College, California, Pa.)

God is not on our side.

God isn't dead he's just taking a "trip."

God is omnivorous; chitlins, bagels, pizza, even enchiladas.

UNDERNEATH

Napalm too?

(IRT subway, New York City)

God is polytheist.

(Bleecker Street Restaurant, New York City, 1970)

God is regressive and hostile.

God is silly putty, can do anything!

UNDERNEATH

I believe in silly putty.

God is the answer.

UNDERNEATH

What is the question?

(IRT subway, New York City)

God is 300% American.

God is watching so give him a good show.

God isn't dead he just couldn't find a parking place.

(Ladies' room, Queens College, New York)

God isn't dead—he just doesn't want to get involved.

(Lamont Library, Harvard University)

God isn't dead . . . he's just in a state of shock.

God marks on the curve.

(Cornell University)

God nibbles.

UNDERNEATH

One does what he can.

(New York University)

God sometimes allows us to take credit for his work.

UNDERNEATH

Yea; disease, famine, war, pain, suffering, death, etc., etc.

(University of Michigan)

God speaks Sanskrit.

God twinkles and shines.

God was here.

UNDERNEATH

I sure was.
—God

(Limelight Restaurant, New York City)

I am god
thou art god
god is in each of us
So why do you brag?

(Ladies' room, Le Metro Caffe Espresso, New York City)

I found God in Gimbels.

I suspect you, God, of being a left-wing intellectual.

(Paris, May, 1968)

If God is dead what do you say when somebody sneezes?

If God is omnipresent, does that explain wet dreams?

(Men's room, Rutgers University, 1971)

If God is perfect, why did he create discontinuous functions?

UNDERNEATH

He didn't, man did.

UNDERNEATH

Since God is perfect, the theory of discontinuous functions must be wrong.

(University of Michigan)

Impeach God and his bright ideas.

(Ladies' room, Max's Kansas City Restaurant, New York City)

Is God dead? No, but his children are all sick.

Lovemaking is God's will!
For that reason he made the penis.
Girls, why do you still want to resist?
Why did he create for you the cunt?

(Kolberg, 1904)

The following was written on a religious poster:
MAN created god in his image.

My God is alive sorry about yours.

(University of Michigan)

Neither master, nor God. God is I.

(Paris, May, 1968)

A noble God is the highest work of man.

To serve God, to endure penance, to obey the fates, is to reign.

(Written by Arthur Poole in Latin on Beauchamp Tower, Tower of London, 1564)

Tomorrow is called off.
—God

Walt Disney turned me against God and made me believe in Mickey Mouse.

Walter Lippman—God is not dead. He is alive and appearing twice a week in the Washington Post.

(Cited by Art Buchwald, columnist, Washington Post*)*

We are all god in the process of evolution.

(Ladies' room, Goddard College, 1971)

We don't even trust God.

Weary, weary is the Lord of hosts. So weary is he in fact that I hear he is dead of it.

What is the difference between God and Santa Claus?
Answer. There is a Santa Claus.

GODARD, JEAN-LUC (1930-)

Art is dead. Godard can't do a thing about it.

(Sorbonne, May, 1968)

GODIVA, LADY (*fl. c.* 1040–1080)

Lady Godiva wore a fall.

Lady Godiva had short hair.

GOGOL, NIKOLAI (1809–1952)

Russian Lit. à Gogol!

(Library staff lounge, Fort Belvoir, Va.—cited in American Library Association Bulletin, *April, 1969)*

GODZILLA

Vote for Godzilla.

(The Forum Coffee House, New York City)

GOLDWATER, BARRY (1909-)

Goldwater in '64. Hot water in '65. Bread and water in '66.

(In various subway stations, New York City, 1964)

Hari-Kari with Barry.

(On various walls, also on a button)

In your guts you know he's nuts.
In your heart you know he is far right.

(Variants on Goldwater slogan "In your heart you know he is right")

When I look down I see Goldwater.

(Men's room, City College of San Francisco, 1964)

GOLEM

Beware the wrath of the Golem.

(Free Store Theatre, New York City)

The Golem will eat your false Gods.

(Free Store Theatre, New York City)

GOSSIP, *see also* SLANDER

Abramowitz is a neo-classicist.

UNDERNEATH

Bullshit: He's a fairy.

(P. J. Clarke's Bar, New York City)

Adele will do anything in the name of love.

(Railroad station, Freeport, N.Y.)

All of the Bear Garden's waitresses fuck.

UNDERNEATH

If it was true they wouldn't have to work here.

(Bear Garden Restaurant & Coffee Shop, New York City, 1966)

Baby Jane is nearly ripe!

Beth is hostile and regressive.

Big Red takes bubble baths.

(IRT subway, New York City, 1969)

Charlie Chan started the Hong Kong flu.

Daddy Colepius Kisses the Ladies where he shouldn't.

(Pompeii, 79 A.D.)

Dave Bromberg is more fun than a National Park.

(Ladies' room, Café Figaro, New York City)

David W—— wears a corrective jockstrap.

UNDERNEATH

David W—— wears a training jockstrap.

UNDERNEATH

David W—— is a corrective jockstrap.

(Co-ed toilet, East Village Other, *1970)*

The dear beautiful Miss Stark
shows her ass for a mark.
But, if you pay her a dollar
She will show much more.

(Men's room, Leipzig—cited in Anthropophyteia, *Vol. 5, 1908)*

Dorothy wears blue panties.

(Wall, New York City)

Enrico Banducci is happening

UNDERNEATH

in his pants.

Garry Wills is a secret liberal.

(On cover of The Critic, *which was a picture of a wall covered with graffiti, December 1966–January, 1967)*

George Schleppington washed here.

It's really true what they say about Tom Clancy.

(Ladies' room, New York City)

J.C. puked on this spot 11/29/68.

(Wall, New York City)

Jack the bartender is a great lay.

(Ladies' room, Greenwich Village, New York City; it was later discovered that Jack had written the message himself as self-advertisement)

Jimmy fucked Nancy (almost).

(Junior H.S., Brooklyn)

Lamont Cranston is afraid of his shadow.

Little Jack Horner's problem is more serious than he thinks.

Lum Fong was here.

UNDERNEATH

Ah! So!

Mickey R. mainlines paprika.

(Ladies' room, Max's Kansas City Restaurant, New York City)

Millie, the best kid in town.

(Cited in The New Yorker, *February 10, 1934)*

Morris Feinberg is psychopathic.

(Fence, Brooklyn, 1938)

Mrs. Moynahan eats watercress.

(On public school wall)

Oscar eats meat.

(Oscar's Salt of the Sea Seafood Restaurant, New York City)

Quinn is in—when in Minneapolis he can be found at the Triangle.

(Lion's Head, New York City)

Sally is a Humpty Dumpty with hair.

(Little Red School House, New York City)

Serena hates Isadore.

(Pompeii, 79 A.D.)

Sir John at this Place
Kiss'd her Grace,
Which he proved Face to Face.
—C.W. April 14. 1710.

UNDERNEATH

While this was a-doing.
Her Maid I was wooing:
She did like her Lady,
But made me a Daddy.
—J.W. April 12. 1711.

(On a window, Spinham-Land, England)

Sister Carita is a tomato.

(On cover of The Critic, *which was a picture of a wall covered with graffiti, December, 1966–January, 1967)*

Steve is a bum teeny-bopper

(IND subway, New York City)

Successus the weaver loves the innkeeper's maid servant, Iris by name. She, however, does not return his love. But he begs her to take pity on him. Written by his rival. Goodbye.

UNDERNEATH

You who burst with jealousy you take care though I don't want to prove what's true who's handsomer, most worthy and fine chap of us two.

(Pompeii, 79 A.D.)

Sue Itman is an anal-neurotic.

(Over urinal in the Dallas Art Museum)

This week I'm going with Bill but I like Jim.
—Alice

UNDERNEATH

This week I'm going with Jim but I like Bill.
—Alice

UNDERNEATH

This week we are not going with Alice.
—Bill and Jim

Tom Siegal is no longer a virgin.

(Engagé Coffee House, New York City)

Vicki Jones is
f - - - - - - this week.

UNDERNEATH

Who is Vicki Smith?

UNDERNEATH

Who is this week?

(Antioch College)

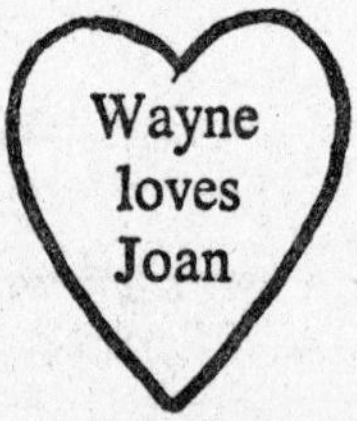
Wayne
loves
Joan

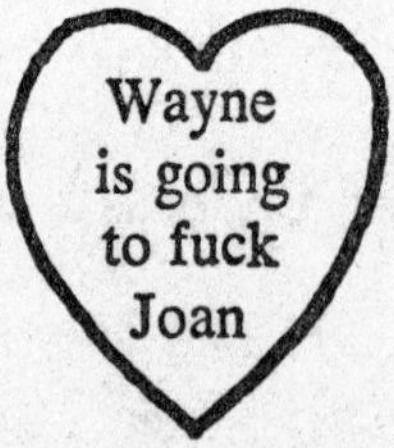
Wayne
is going
to fuck
Joan

Where the tacos make you puke and your chick falls in love with Duke.

*(Tortilla Flats Restaurant, New York City—
Duke is the owner of the restaurant)*

Wong is a very naughty boy.

(Chinatown, New York City, 1966)

Zorro is a homo.

(Men's room, The Alibi Bar, Bloomington, Ind.)

GOVERNMENT

All previous revolutions have strengthened the power of the state over people.

(Wall near People's Park, Berkeley, Cal., 1970)

Any government that's strong enough to give all the people what they want is a government that's strong enough to take it away.

Down with the State.

("55" Bar, New York City)

The mark of primitive religion (or big Gov't) is sacrifice.

The state is a disease.

These days, govt. is a four-letter word.

(San Francisco State College, 1970)

GRAFFITI, *see also* WALL WRITERS

Cut out the shit on the goddam walls.
—Mother Superior

(Co-ed toilet, Alternate U., New York City)

Do not bend, fold, staple or mutilate in any way these walls.

(Florida State University)

Down with graffiti.

UNDERNEATH

Yeah, down with all Italians.

(Chumley's Restaurant, New York City)

Down with protests.
Up with graffiti.

(Ladies' room, Graffiti Restaurant, New York City)

Everything has its place, even the stupid writings in this cold john, may they never see the daylight. Amen.

(Ladies' room, Ninth Circle Restaurant, New York City)

For total involvement see Stall 3.

(Men's room, Rutgers University)

Graffiti is now respectable.
See New York Times et al.

(Ladies' room, Lion's Head, New York City)

Graffiti has changed de face of de nation.

The graffiti in here is all fucked up.

(Ladies' room, Lion's Head, New York City)

The graffiti in the men's room is better.

(Ladies' room, Lion's Head, New York City)

Graffiti is dead.

(Kettle of Fish Bar & Restaurant, New York City)

Graffiti is the Express to the solution of life.

(Ladies' room, Brooklyn College, 1969)

Graffiti sucks!

(Wall on Bleecker Street, New York City)

Graffiti was Mussolini's Secretary of Defense.

The handwriting is on the wall.

(Chumley's Restaurant, New York City)

Happiness is a white wall and a magic marker.

Hello to all my readers.

Hereafter, submit all graffiti in four copies.

(Vietnam, 1971)

How strange: ♂ and ♀ graffiti.

(Co-ed toilet, Paradox Restaurant, New York City)

I am an enemy of Graffiti—they killed my mother.

I claim this wall for Queen Elizabeth.

(Wall, Yale University)

I who read am a sucker, he's a sucker who reads this.

(Pompeii, 79 A.D.)

If you're going more often and enjoying it less—try the men's room.

(Ladies' room, office building, New York City)

Is the noticeable lack of graffiti on the wall the result of
a) irregular use
b) overcleaning
c) all of the above
d) none of the above
e) both c and d.

(Ladies' room, University of Maryland, 1972)

Keep on doin it!!!

(Subway, New York City, 1972—defiant statement of young spray can scrawlers in answer to stepped-up campaign against them)

My graffiti will fail,
Because my lipstick's so pale.

(Ladies' room, Lion's Head, New York City)

No truth is allowed here anymore.

(Ladies' room, Limelight Restaurant, New York City)

The only difference between graffiti and philosophy is the word fuck.

(Men's room, Limelight Restaurant, New York City)

Paint can't stop progress.

(Toilet, The Cave, New York City—written after walls were painted)

Phone 411-000—Graffiti made up to take out.

(Goodale's Restaurant, New York City, 1969—in the men's room they have a three-foot ruler attached to the wall and men note their measurements)

Preserve graffiti.

Remember graffiti doesn't grow on walls.

Santini is a book burner.

(Chumley's Restaurant, New York City; this was written after owner Ray Santini had his restaurant's bathroom walls painted)

Slob, you could at least wash your wall.

(Paris, May, 1968)

Take one toilet, one poet, plant in a warm area, water frequently and up sprouts graffiti.

(Men's room, Princeton University, 1970)

Take sex, religion and politics out of the john.

(Engagé Coffee House, New York City)

These are the most interesting, dirtiest walls in town. No shit.

(Ladies' room, Lion's Head, New York City)

This wall has bad rap.

(University of Michigan)

This wall shall be the Rosetta Stone of the next civilization, consider your words well.

(Men's room, Telephone Company, New York City, 1969)

This wall soon to appear in paperback.

(On a wall covered with obscenities)

Today's graffiti is tomorrow's headline.

Wall bathing infinitely in its own glory.

(Nanterre University, May, 1968)

Walls are for writing on.

UNDERNEATH

No, tearing down.

(Ladies' room, Brooklyn College, 1969)

Were this Place to be view'd by a Herald of Note,
He would find a new Charge for the new-bought Coat,
Which Guillim ne'er thought of, nor one of the Herd,
Viz. a Wall erect Argent, Gutte de T—d,
And as a Reward for improving the Art,
He should bear on a Fess (if he paints it) a F—t.

UNDERNEATH

A Pox on your Writing, I thought you were sh———g,
My great Gut has giv'n me such Twitches:
Had you scribled much more, I'm a Son of a Whore,
If I should not have don't in my Breeches.

(Boghouse, White Hart, Petersfield, England)

What happened to all the high class graffiti?

UNDERNEATH

It got read.

UNDERNEATH

Better read than ded.

(Lion's Head, New York City—written after the walls were painted)

Who reads this, may he never read anything else.

(Pompeii, 79 A.D.)

Why do gnomes always wash stuff off the walls?

(Men's room, Bates College, Lewiston, Me.; "gnomes" is affectionate name for custodians)

Why do you wash these walls? Graffiti is a learning experience.

UNDERNEATH

So is washing walls.

(Men's room, University of Michigan)

Why no graffiti on this wall?

REPLY

Because the people here have done it all.

(Ladies' room, Bleecker Street Restaurant, New York City)

Write your graffiti soon, this wall to be demolished by urban renewal.

(Wall, San Francisco, 1972)

You can't whitewash everything.

(Max's Kansas City Restaurant, New York City)

GRANT, ULYSSES S. (1822–1885)

Lee:
Make it.
—Grant

GREAT SOCIETY

(Note: Lyndon B. Johnson and his administration popularized this term denoting what America could be, with the aid of his proposed reforms)

Conspicuous only in its absence—The Great Society.

(Construction wall, Philadelphia, 1969)

Great Society: a new leech on life.

Great Society, abominable snow job.

Great Society: bombs, bullets, bullshit.

Great Society, the big snow job.

GUEVARA, CHE (1928–1967)

All the way with Che.

(Men's room, Brooklyn College, 1969)

Che lives like a pit in the throat of all capitalists and fascists.

(Mr. Waffles Ice Cream Parlor, New York City)

El Exigente killed Che Guevara.

(IRT subway, New York City)

I am the light of the world.
—~~Jesus~~ Che

(Wall near People's Park, Berkeley, Cal., 1970)

To sell some Guevara, to slip in some
Trotsky, is to be a traitor two times.

Viva Ché

(University of Michigan)

H

HALLUCINOGENS, *see also* LSD

Alter reality through politics not psychedelics.

(Men's room, Green Hornet, New York City, also on a button)

Bird seed is psychedelic.

UNDERNEATH

Sassparailla is psychedelic.

DMT [*a hallucinogen*]

(On various wall, also on a button)

End psychedelic unemployment—send me a dollar.

Enter the psychedelic world of the lost.

The following were written on a poster for a Broadway Presbyterian Church:
Psychedelic psalms for psoriasis.
Preparation LSD shrinks hemmeroids [*sic*]

Psychedelize suburbia.

(On various walls, also on a button)

Scientology is the next step after psychedelics.

HAMILTON, GEORGE (1939–)

Ad Hoc Committee to draft George Hamilton.

UNDERNEATH

Would you really feel secure with George Hamilton in uniform?

(On various walls, also on a button—George Hamilton was deferred on the grounds that he was the sole support of his mother)

HAPPINESS

Happiness is all the rotten kids going back to school.

Happiness is:
Having your tent not blow away.
Catching two lemmings in one trap.
A dry sleeping bag.

(Men's room, Arctic Institute's Devon Island Research Station, Lat. 75°40′ North, 1972)

Happiness is not a goal. It is a by product.

(San Francisco, 1971)

I decree the state of permanent happiness.

(Paris, May, 1968)

I dream of being a happy idiot.

(Nanterre, May, 1968)

Oh how happy a man feels as long as he can piss, masturbate and shit; fucking can be added to this and this soul can have peace.

(Riesengebirge—cited in Anthropophyteia, *Vol. 6, 1909)*

Shit on happiness. Live.

(Sorbonne, May, 1968)

HAUPTMAN, BRUNO (1899–1936)

(Note: Hauptman was electrocuted after he was convicted as the kidnaper and murderer of the infant son of Charles A. Lindbergh)

Bruno Hauptman is innocent—I am the Lindbergh baby.

(Wine Cellar Restaurant, New York City, 1970)

HAWTHORNE, NATHANIEL (1804–1864)

Hester Pryne was a nymphomaniac.

HEALTH

Belly to belly, mouth on mouth,
makes your heart healthy at all times.

A healthy asshole that doesn't shit.
Healthy teeth that do not bite.
Healthy cock that doesn't stand up.
And you, idiot, ask how I am?

(Men's room, Germany)

HEDONISM

Do it! There's always bail.

Live now—pay later.

(Los Angeles Valley College, 1970)

The Novelty this Crowd invites,
'Tis strange, and therefore it delights;
For Folks Things eagerly pursue,
Not that they're good, but that they're new.
Pleasure must vary, or must cease,
We tire of Bliss, grow sick of Ease.
And if the Year we're doom'd to Play,
To Work would be a Holiday.

(On the window of a fine assembly room on a vast appearance at its opening, England)

While I lived, I lived well. My play is now ended, soon yours will be. Farewell and applaud me.

(Catacombs, Rome)

HEFNER, HUGH (1926–)

Hugh Hefner is a virgin.

HEGEL, GEORG (1770–1831)

For Hegel contradiction was a moment in totality. For Marx totality was a moment in contradiction.

(Men's room, New York University, 1969)

HELL

Beneath this Stone there lies a cursed Sinner,
Doom'd to be roasted for the Devil's Dinner.

(An Epitaph on a wicked man's tomb written by Doctor Wild the famous nonconformist minister, England, early 18th century)

Hell is a blast.

(Men's room, The Flick Restaurant, New York City, 1968)

Hell is empty, for the devils are all here.

(Bates College, Lewiston, Me.)

HELLER, JOSEPH (1923–)

Yossarian lives.

HEMINGWAY, ERNEST (1891–1961)

Lucky is he for whom the belle toils.

UNDERNEATH

Lucky is she for whom the balls toil.

HENDRIX, JIMI (1942–1970)

Jimi was here but now he's gone,
But left his mind to carry on.
—Jimi

(Men's room, Princeton University, 1970)

HENRY VIII (1491–1547)

Henry VIII was a chauvinist pig.

UNDERNEATH

And he had bad table manners.

HENTOFF, NAT (1925–)

Nat Hentoff is a Protestant.

(Half Note, New York City)

HEREDITY, *see* GENETICS

HEROIN, *see also* DRUG ADDICTION

Fuck Black Power, let's hear it for the greatest force on this earth that which has subjugated even the so-called black force—I speak of King Heroin, White Powder!!!

(Men's room, Rutgers University, 1971)

Legalize pot!
legalize heroin!
legalize outlaws!
legalize me!
and legalization.

(Ladies' room, Limelight Restaurant, New York City)

Living in the land of Nod
coke is king and scag is God.

Pay your taxes, it goes to welfare, to pay for heroin.

(Wall, South Bronx, New York City)

HERSHEY, LEWIS B. (1893–)

Bar Hershey.

HETEROSEXUAL INTERCOURSE

Arescusa [*sic—probably Arethusa*], like a sensible girl took a firm hold of his best part for her own good.

(Pompeii, 79 A.D.)

As dear N—y B—k look'd into the Street,
  From this Window where now I am musing,
I poop'd her behind, but no Body see't,
  And she prov'd ne'er the worse for my using.
—T.B.

UNDERNEATH

Ungrateful Wretch, thou'rt scarcely fit to live,
Much less such Favours worthy to receive.
A greater Curse than leading Apes in Hell,
The Fool deserves, that dares to kiss and tell.

UNDERNEATH

Dear Madam, pray dont let your Anger abound,
  For Faith what you've wrote has no Charm in't;
You often have try'd me, and know I am found,
  Then prithee now where was the Harm in't?
You did me a Favour, I did you one too,
  And, if I'm not mistaken, a greater;
I'll swear I can't love the Sport better than you,
  So pray say no more of the Matter.

(On a window, Carlisle, England)

Beautiful girls make the flesh stiff,
Stiff flesh makes the girls pregnant.

(Men's room, coffee house, Vienna, 1910)

Behind the apron, the girl has a nest, I have been there quite often.

(Men's room, Riesengebirge—cited in Anthropophyteia, *Vol. 6, 1909)*

C. Valerius Venustus soldier of the first Praetorian Cohort Company of Rufus, I had a most satisfying night of embraces in this bed.

(Pompeii, 79 A.D.)

Copulate for coexistence.

Floronius, seconded on special duties, soldier of Legion VII, was here and the women didn't recognize him, all but a few, that is, and they succumbed on the spot.

(Pompeii, 79 A.D.)

For what did Venus love Adonis,
But for the Gristle, where no Bone is?

(Boghouse, Spread-Eagle, Bunny, England)

Fortunatus made it with Anthusam.

(Pompeii, 79 A.D.)

Fresh water
Pure wine
Tight cunt
Hard prick.

(Toilet, Little Italy, New York City)

Fuck me daft.

(Sterling, Scotland)

Fucking, fucking, oh my life,
to it I want to give myself completely.

(Thüringen, 1910)

Fucking, fucking what a lust,
under the arms, between the breasts,
from behind, from the front, it doesn't matter
if it only stays hard each time.

(Men's room—cited in Anthropophyteia, *Vol. 4, 1907)*

Fucking is a gass [*sic*].

Fucking, it is beautiful, for that reason I am immediately going fucking.

(Ostern, 1905)

George K is the best—in this bar.

UNDERNEATH

Obviously you haven't fucked much.

(Ladies' room, New York City—cited in article by Lindsay Van Gelder in New York Post, *March 28, 1972)*

Have you not in a Chimney seen
A sullen Faggot, wet and green,
How coyly it receives the Heat,
And at both Ends doth fume and sweat:
So fares it with the harmless Maid
When first upon her Back she's laid.
But the kind experienc'd Dame.
Cracks and rejoices in the Flame.

(On a window, Woodstock, England)

Here fucking goes well,
I must grant you that:
The old one had a fat cunt
and a fat stomach.

(Rügen, 1903)

Here I have found many girls who make love.

(Pompeii, 79 A.D.)

Here Festus made it with Sodalibus.

(Pompeii, 79 A.D.)

Here I recall I had a girl of late
The intimate details I shall not relate.

(Pompeii, 79 A.D.)

Hickory is the best of wood,
Fuckin' does a maiden good,
—opens her eyes
—strengthens her thighs,
And gives her ass some exercise.

How much cunt is enough?

(The Village Gate, New York City)

I am happy and like to fuck,
I fuck girls from near and far.
I love the big ones and the little ones,
the ugly and the fine ones.
For fucking they are good enough,
as for getting children—well,
I don't pay for them!

(Rügen, 1903—written in a very childish hand)

I let myself be ridden front and back
and permit myself to be taken from both sides.

(Slavonia, 1908)

I like a girl with a proper mat, not depilated and shorn.
Then you can snug in from the cold, as an overcoat she's worn.

(Pompeil, 79 A.D.)

I screwed my girl in this toilet.

UNDERNEATH

Your girl friend has class.

I want to seduce my history teacher.

UNDERNEATH

I did and got an F.

(Ladies' room, Hunter College, New York City)

I was fucked here.

(Ladies' room, Graffiti Restaurant, New York City)

I was here—I left to fuck,
You are here—good luck.

(Ladies' room, Limelight Restaurant, New York City)

I will believe anything if you can answer this question; why are there people.

UNDERNEATH

Sex.

(Ladies' room, Ninth Circle Restaurant, New York City)

If I am sleeping and you want to wake me, don't shake, take me.

(Ladies' room, Café Figaro, New York City)

If kisses were the only joys in bed,
Then women would with one another wed.

(On a window, Mainwaring's Coffee House, London, c. 1720)

I'm so horney the crack of dawn better watch out.

(Men's room, Salem State College, Mass.)

Jenny demure, with prudish Looks,
Turns up her Eyes, and rails at naughty Folks;
But in a private Room, turns up her lech'rous Tail,
and kisses till she's in for Cakes and Ale.
—L.M. July 17. 1727.

(On a summer house window, at the Swan, Chelsea, England)

Jim fucked Margie Cambel & Jane Slapfer at the Depot.

(Iowa City, 1928)

Long live all girls,
who lift their skirt on their own
and lead the prick with their hand
into the promised land.

(Würzburg, c. 1903)

The Maiden's Prayer:
Lay me down gently, and turn up my frock,
Pull off my drawers, and get out your cock,
Spread my legs wide, and insert your knob,
Then frig it about until I start to throb.

(Gentleman's Lavatory, Victoria Station, England, 1950)

May I always and everywhere be as potent in dealing with women as I was here!

(Pompeii, 79 A.D.)

O, God, Yes!

Peggy came in with a smiling Face,
And every Feature had its Grace:
Her Cheeks were blooming, as I'd wish to see;
Her something else above her Knee,
Fill'd all my Mind with Extasy;
And so we went to't.
—L.T.

(The Devices, Wiltshire, England)

Says Sir John to my Lady, as together they sat,
Shall we first go to Supper, or do you know what?
Dear Sir John, (with a Smile,) return'd the good Lady,
Let us do you know what, for Supper's not ready.

(The Great Room, The Red-Lion, Brentwood, England)

Scordopordonicus here made love well with whomever he wished.

(Pompeii, 79 A.D.)

Screwing a woman is better than screwing her.

She that thinks upon her honour,
Heeds no other guard upon her.
UNDERNEATH

She that has a man upon her,
Never thinks upon her honour.

(Red Lyon, Egham, England, early 18th century)

Sollemnis was here, an accomplished performer.

UNDERNEATH

Sollemnis you're a perfect lover.

(Brothel, Pompeii, 79 A.D.)

Some girls have watches of gold,
Some girls have watches of brass,
My girl hasn't any watches at all,
The movement is in her ass.

There was a young couple named Kelly,
Who went around belly-to-belly,
Because in their haste
They used library paste
Instead of petroleum jelly.

(University of California at Berkeley)

The time that one is married one must use for fucking.

(Ostern, 1905—written in a childish hand)

To go together is blessed, to come together divine.

A toast to a German virgin—Goesintight!!!

Twinkle twinkle little twat,
How I wonder where you squat,
High above the dick somewhere,
How I wish I could be there.

(Ladies' room, Ninth Circle Restaurant, New York City)

Up with dresses
Down with pants.

(The Exit Coffee House, New York City)

Victor von Stein
who does it right fine
and puts him quite sweetly in mine.

(Ladies' toilet, Klause St. Lukas, 1903)

We are all under cuntrol.

(Men's room, Under The Stairs Bar & Restaurant, New York City)

The Wedding-Night past, says Sir John to his Mate,
Faith Madam I'm bit (tho' I find it too late)
By your d—n'd little Mouth, or else I'm a Whore's Son,
For the Cross underneath's quite out of Proportion.
Good Sir John, says my Lady, then under the Rose,
I'm as bad bit as you, by your plaguy long Nose:
You have not by half so much as I wanted,
I've more than you want, yet y'are not contented.

(On a window, Dolphin Inn, Southampton, England)

By Desire not to insert the Place.
What care I for Mistress May'ress;
She's little as the Queen of Fairies:
Her little Body like my Thumb,
Is thicker far than other some;
Her conscience yet would stretch so wide;
Either on this, or t'other Side,
That none would tell when they did ride.

UNDERNEATH

Swim for thy Life, dear Boy, for I can feel
neither Bottom nor Sides.

What Lacing,
What Dressing,
What Moulding,
What Scolding,
What Painting,
What Fainting,
What Loving,
What Shoving,
What Cooing,
What Wooing,
What Crosses,
What Tosses,
What Actions,
What Fractions,
Before the Day was done.

(Star, Coventry, England)

When I lay with my bouncing Nell,
I gave her an Inch, and she took an Ell:
But I think in this Case it was damnable hard,
When I gave her an Inch, she'd want more than a Yard.

When my brisk Lass
Upon the Grass,
Will sport, and Give her Love;
She'll wink and pink,
Till she can't think;
That's Happiness, by Jove!
Per Jovem Juro.
—J.M.

(On a window, Epsom, England)

Who rides so late on mother's belly?
It is father with his hose.
He is grabbing mother's tits,
so he can ride better

(Men's room, Germany)

Willie S— is a transcendental fuck.

(Ladies' room, Ninth Circle Restaurant, New York City)

With such violent rage,
Sir John did engage
With the damsel which he laid his leg on,
That his squire, who stood near,
Swore it look'd like the spear
Of St. George in the mouth of the dragon.

(Boghouse, Oxon, England—cited in The Merry-Thought*)*

Yesterday my wife was completely crazy, I fucked myself almost dead.

(Men's room, Prussia-Silesia—cited in Anthropophyteia, *Vol. 7, 1910)*

HILLBILLIES

Attention hillbillies—the rock candy in the urinals is not for you.

(Greenwich Village Coffee House, 1962)

Do mountain men keep mountin' women?

A hill billy farmer named Hollis,
Used possums and snakes for his solace.
The children had scales and prehensile tails,
and voted for Governor Wallace.

(Men's room, Princeton University, 1970)

If billies had brains as big as their balls,
They wouldn't write on shithouse walls.

(Men's room, Hillbilly Tavern, Chicago)

HIPPIES

All those long haired pinko fags out to get fucked.

UNDERNEATH

We're ready!

UNDERNEATH

Hey, that looks like a girls handwriting!

(University of Michigan)

Boy hippy: A guy who looks like a Jill and smells like a John.

Cops eat flowers.

(San Diego State College, 1970)

Flower children of the world unite.

UNDERNEATH

Your mothers were all laid by pansies.

The flower generation has a tin ear.

Flower power.

Hippies eat shit and brown rice.

(Co-ed toilet, Alvin's Finer Delicatessen, Detroit, 1971)

Hippy power.

(On various walls, also on a button)

I came to San Francisco with flowers in my hair—and I starved.

(Rex Hotel, San Francisco)

Merry Christmas and a Hippy New Year.

Old Hippies never die, they just trip away.

St. Marks Pl., the place to die physically and spiritually.

(The Dom, New York City, 1969—
St. Marks Place is an area heavily populated by hippies)

This is hipness: Dig going, before staying, means not becoming.

Thoreau was a hippie.

UNDERNEATH

But at least she [*sic*] could read and write.

(Fedora Restaurant, New York City)

HITLER, ADOLF (1889–1945)

Back Mac.

UNDERNEATH

If you liked Hitler—you'll love McNamara.

(New York City—refers to Robert McNamara,
Secretary of Defense 1961–1967)

Hitler is alive in the White House.

(BMT subway, New York City, also on a button)

I shot Hitler.

UNDERNEATH

You missed me, schweinhunt.

(Men's toilet, Decanter Bar, Detroit, 1971)

HO CHI MINH (1880–1969)

Foreign aid to Ho Chi Minh.
North Vietnam Care Package.

(Messages painted on bombs in Vietnam, 1967)

Ho lives!

You don't have to be Chinese to love Ho Chi Minh.

UNDERNEATH

He's not Chinese either.

(Lion's Head, New York City)

HOMESPUN ADVICE

On A Drinking-Glass:
Guard well your Credit, for 'tis quickly gone:
'Tis gain'd by many Actions, lost by one.

If at first you don't succeed try reading the directions
(Graffiti Restaurant, New York City)

HOMOSEXUALITY

The Devil says: legalize abortion, pot, homosexuality.
(IRT subway, New York City)

Equality for homosexuals.

Fight heterosexual supremacy
(Co-ed toilet, Alternate U., New York City, 1969)

Gay power! *(Scrawled on various fences and sometimes accompanied by the following symbols:*

Go gay and live.
(The Riviera, New York City)

Help! I'm a lonely heterosexual.

Heterosexual love is a convention not found in the animal world.
(Men's room, University of Maryland, 1972)

Lavender.

My husband really wants a man.
(Limelight Restaurant, New York City)

My mother made me a homosexual.
UNDERNEATH
If I sent her some wool would she make me one?

An Address to our present Petit-Maitres:
No more let each fond foppling court a Brother,
And quit the Girls to dress for one another;
Old maids, in Vengeance to their slighted Beauty,
Shall one Day make you wish you'd done your Duty;

Thro' H–ll they drag ye on most aukward Shapes,
Yoak'd in their Apron-Strings, and led for Apes.

(On a tavern window, Fleet Street, London)

Nobody loves you when you're young and gay.
[*Also seen as "Nobody loves you when you're old and gay." This is a parody of the song "There'll be some changes made," in which the line is "Nobody loves you when you're old and gray."*]

Nothing frustrates me like a rectal exam.

(Men's room, University of Maryland, 1972)

Old fags unite!

UNDERNEATH

Don't bite.

(Co-ed toilet, Alternate U., New York City)

Old fairies never die they merely blow away.

Only his hairdresser knows for sure.

Let your fingers do the cruising.

(Variant on New York Yellow Pages slogan: "Let your fingers do the walking.")

Let's face it we're all queer.

More deviation, less population.

Now being organized the Greenwich Village Heterosexual Club (underground).

(Howard Johnson's, New York City, 1965)

HOMOSEXUALITY (FEMALE)

Draft Lesbians.

UNDERNEATH

What—another beer!

Ex-les says, "Fucking is better than sucking."

(Ladies' room, New York City)

Girls are better than boys—you can't get pregnant from a girl.

(Ladies' room, Hunter College, New York City, 1970)

Girls—let me suck your moist cunt.

(Ladies' room, Hunter College, New York City)

Hey boy, get your finger out of that dike.

(Free Store Theatre, New York City)

I like girls—is there anything wrong with me?

UNDERNEATH

Not if you're a girl.

I'm bisexual.

UNDERNEATH

Hey me too—Let's get in touch really.

UNDERNEATH

There's no such thing, you're kidding yourselves.

UNDERNEATH

Leave her alone—let the kid live.

(Ladies' room, Hunter College, New York City, 1970)

I'm so horny, I'm joining a convent.

UNDERNEATH

Watch out for the lesbians there.

(Ladies' room, Bernard Baruch College, New York City, 1970)

Joan of Arc was a dyke.

The lesberated woman refuses to betray her body.

(Ladies' room, Gay Liberation Front, New York City, 1970)

Lesbians read John Updike.

Lesbians unite!

UNDERNEATH

Against whom?

UNDERNEATH

For each other.

Minnie Mouse is a giant spade bull-dyke.

(Co-ed toilet, The Forum Coffee House, New York City)

O girls let me fervently kiss your slender body, let me savor the fragrance of your cunty's dew, for I am a woman just like you.

(Ladies' room, Breslau cited in Anthropophyteia, *Vol. 6, 1909)*

Support our girls in Lesbos.

When I'm reincarnated, I hope I'm Queer. At least the problems and frustrations will be different.

(Ladies' room, Lion's Head, New York City)

HOMOSEXUALITY (MALE)

All boys who go to Harvard are fags.

UNDERNEATH

Except one and he's a lesbian.

(The Casablanca, Harvard Square, Cambridge, Mass.)

All you fuckin' queers are being observed on closed TV by the CIA.

(Men's toilet, University of Minnesota)

Am in the next booth—tap foot for plow.

Better latent than never.

(Men's room, Boston University)

Blow my fuse.

(Men's room, Engineering Building, University of Maryland, 1972)

Call beautiful blonde at 444—if a man answers, it's me.

Call 265-6791 for info re The Mattachine Society—if you're inquisitive sweetie, I'll tell you everything!

(Lion's Head—the Mattachine Society is an organization devoted to explaining the viewpoints and rights in society of homosexuals)

Castrate all queers.

(Men's room, IRT subway, New York City, 1972)

Do fairies fuck?

UNDERNEATH

Yes, if you believe in them.

(West End Café, New York City)

Dr. Strangelove or how I learned to love the bum.

(Toilet, London)

Don't start sucking cocks, it's a bad habit to break.

UNDERNEATH

Now he tells us.

Eat at the "y."

Faggots are maggots.

Faggots to the fray!

Fags are fun.

Fags fornicate.

Fellatio is not a felony, fellas, it is a misdemeanor.

Gay is good.

UNDERNEATH

Bi is better.

(Men's room, Goddard College, 1971)

Get your finger out of my ass and stop your fooling.
That ain't my finger, and I ain't fooling!

(Frontier Bowling Lanes, Scottsdale, Ariz.)

God is gay and living on E. 59th St.

(Ladies' room, Ninth Circle Restaurant, New York City)

God save the Queens!

Have gums, will travel.
—The Prairie Fairy

Here I stand alone and confused
Tried to hustle but was only cruised.

(Wall, 54th Street and Lexington Ave., New York City)

Here in this beautiful place
Hans met his sweetheart.

*(Men's room, Thüringen—
cited in* Anthropophyteia, *Vol. 7, 1910)*

Homosexuality is a pain in the ass.

(Wall, New York City)

I am cured, I'm not a queer anymore.

I have just become the father of a lovely baby boy.

UNDERNEATH

How butch!

(Men's room, Dorset, England, 1971)

I love men with thick pebble lensed glasses.

(Men's room, London)

I once met a bar girl named Noy,
Who wasn't unfriendly or coy
Yet in my hotel, I let out a yell
When I found Noy was really a boy.

(Men's room, Vietnam, 1972)

I play the flute and swallow the music.

(Real Chinese Food Restaurant, New York City)

I screwed my old father in the ass because my black tom cat had run away.

(Men's room, Prussia-Silesia, 1910)

I take it 2 ways for a $1.

(Men's room, Greyhound bus station, New York City, 1940)

I'm for boy love.

(Men's room, Mama's Chicken 'n' Rib, New York City, also on a button)

In this place fucking is done standing, farting and shitting is done sitting and who doesn't want to join in is thrown out.

(Men's room, Riesengebirge—cited in Anthropophyteia, *Vol. 6, 1909)*

A Jewish fag = a ju ju fruit.

(Ladies' room, Lion's Head, New York City)

John Smith is a queer!

UNDERNEATH

Listen darling . . . I resent this!

(Men's room, bar, Charlottesville)

Kilroy was queer.

(Spokane, Wash.)

Lenny is a stupid faget.

UNDERNEATH

I may be stupid but at least I can spell fagget [*sic*].

(IRT subway, New York City)

Make boys! Avoid the draft!

(Wall, New York City, also on a button)

Male cocksuckers suck best. I tried it.

(Men's room, IRT subway, New York City)

Male lesbians united.

Men that I can't get are men that I ain't met.

UNDERNEATH

Listen sweetie, you're in the wrong bathroom.

(Men's room, Hunter College, New York City, 1972)

Mickey Mouse is a homosexual.

(Scholtz's Beer Garden, Austin, Tex.)

My father is a very stern man; he doesn't let me approach him, even from behind.

(Men's room, Prussia-Silesia—cited in Anthropophyteia, *Vol. 7, 1910)*

On poster entitled "Super Summerall," with balloon coming out of character's mouth stating, "I was a black belt in karate, judo, jung-fu, aikido, champ in boxing," was the following:

Now I'm gay and unafraid.

One man's meat is another man's perversion.

Pederasty is with it.

Peter is a fag, he plays potsy, he is 42 years old.

(On a sidewalk on Jane Street, Greenwich Village, New York City)

Le Petit Prince is a fairy.

(University of Florida)

Practice makes pervert.

(Men's room, homosexual bar, Greenwich Village, New York City)

Queen power.

(Chalk on building on Gay Street, Greenwich Village, New York City, also on a button)

Rob the queer.

(Subway, Boston)

60 days I leave all the queers up here. Thanks a lot for all the cock.

(Men's room, Fort Richardson Army Base, Anchorage, 1965)

Steve is a group gay.

Stop the homosexual revolution, wear baggy pants.

Suck me for a penny.

(Men's room, Lyric Theatre, New York City, 1940)

When two each other kiss,
And then go out for pisses,
And don't come back—
You've got your sissies.

(Men's room—cited in Anthropophyteia, *Vol. 7, 1910)*

Where are all the beautiful buns?

UNDERNEATH

In the bakery you dizzy bitch.

(Men's room, Hippodrome Garage, New York City, 1970)

Where are all the gay boys?

UNDERNEATH

In my phone book and in your pants.

(Men's room, Bernard Baruch College, New York City, 1970)

Where is a good Turkish bath to have some fun?

(Men's room, subway, New York City, 1940)

W(h)ines and lickers.

(Men's room, Idle Hour Bar, New York City, 1940)

White gentleman 48 years old needs colored boy with big ass. Leave no.

(IRT subway, New York City)

Whoever likes to fuck assholes and considers that his goal in life, he is, and know that for a fact, a picture of horror for every woman.

(Men's room, Vienna coffee house, 1910)

Why are straight boys afraid of gay boys?

(Men's room, Hunter College, New York City, 1972)

Why are there so many queers in this place?

UNDERNEATH

Maybe because you're sexy.

(Men's room, Hunter College, New York City, 1972)

Why is it that graffiti at Harvard is all homosexual and that at B.U. anti-semitic?

UNDERNEATH

Queers prefer circumcised Jews.

UNDERNEATH

So does Christ.

(Men's room, Harvard University)

Wiggle your toes for sex.

(Men's room, railroad station, Stamford, Conn., 1960)

Wipe out male prostitution—adopt a hustler today. Get murdered tonight.

(Free Store Theatre, New York City)

You really should call Larry 888— p.m.

(Mama's Chicken 'n' Rib, New York City)

Young man, well hung, with beautiful body is willing to do anything. P.S. If you see this Bill don't bother to call, it's only me, Tony.

(Howard Johnson's, New York City)

HOOVER, J. EDGAR (1895–1972)

All persons involved in the conspiracy report to stockyards 4:30 p.m. for head bashing.
—J. Edgar Tumor

(Co-ed toilet, East Village Other, *1970)*

J. Edgar Hoover sleeps with a night light.

(Horn & Hardart Automat, New York City, also on a button)

HOPE

As long as I breathe I hope

(Ellis Island, N.Y.—written in Greek on a wall in the main building, Oct. 21, 1953)

They who sow in tears shall reap in joy.

(Beauchamp Tower, Tower of London—written in Latin by Edmund Poole in 1562)

HOPE, BOB (1903–)

Bob Hope was so funny I missed my period.

(Men's room, Vietnam, 1972)

Vietnam
Is a
Bob Hope
Joke

(Vietnam, 1970)

HOSPITALITY

The Cook, confound her, boil'd no Roots;
The Hostler never clean'd my Boots;
The Tapster too, would hardly stir;
The Drawer was a lazy Cur;
The Chamberlain had made no Bed;
The Host had Maggots in his Head:
But Millicent, who kept the Bar,
Was worse than all the rest by far;
She was as many others are.
I kiss'd her till she had her Fill,
I thought it Love, and with her Will.
But then——
She made a da–n'd confounded Bill.
Captain R.T. 1718.

UNDERNEATH

See the Bill Gentlemen.
Thrice was I reckon'd for my Meat
Thrice was I reckon'd for Miss Milly's treat;
Thrice was I reckon'd for my dirty Boots;
Thrice was I reckon'd for not having Roots;
Thrice was I reckon'd by the lazy Fellows;
And thrice I swore, I wish'd them at the Gallows;
And if I come here any more,
Then call me a Son of a Whore.
R.T. 1718.

(On a window, inn on the West Country Road, England)

The Drawer, Tom, had scarce forgot,
Since I was here last Easter;
I broke his Head with the Pewter Pot,
And gave him not a Teaster.
But why, d'ye think, I serv'd him so?
What Flesh alive could bear it?
I'd call'd a dozen Times, I trow,
Yet the Dog would bring no Claret.
This Discipline was not in vain,
For h'as his Manners mended;
I've been here twenty Times since then,
And always well attended.

(Red-Lion, Shrewsbury, England)

If you shit here, eat here—
We don't just want the tail end of your business.

(Legend put in some diners' rest rooms by the management)

They are all Bears at the Angel,
And all Angels at the Bear.
N.B. There are very pretty girls at the Bear.

(The Bear at Oxford, London, 1710—by a gentleman who had been affronted at The Angel)

HUBBARD, L. RON (1911-   )

(Note: Founder and head of Scientology organization, a pseudoscientific cult)

L. Ron Hubbard is not making himself clear.
Lobotomize L. Ron Hubbard.

(Ladies' room, New York University)

HUMOR, see WIT and HUMOR

HUMPHREY, HUBERT H. (1911-   )

H. H. H. for President.
This was change to:
H.a H.a H.a.
Hubert Humphrey, what a schmuck you turned out to be.

(Various walls, also on a button)

Hump with Humphrey.

(Ladies' room, Putney School)

Humphrey for vice.

Humphrey is a product of our times—a waste product.

(Men's room, Bates College, Lewiston)

Johnson gets his Humphrey.

Keep America Hump-free.

Richard Nixon the evil of two lessers.

(On a billboard in subway during the 1968 Humphrey-Nixon campaign)

HUNTER COLLEGE

Hunter belongs in Hanoi.

(Wall, Hunter College, New York City, 1970)

HYGIENE, *see* PERSONAL HYGIENE

I

IDEATION

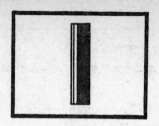

A thought which stagnates is a thought which rots.

(Sorbonne, May, 1968)

To exaggerate is to begin to invent.

(Paris, May, 1968)

To lack imagination means not to imagine the lack of it.

(Nanterre, May, 1968)

Unbutton your brains as often as you unbutton your fly.

(Paris, May, 1968)

Xerox never comes up with anything original.

(Time *magazine's graffiti contest open only to ad men, May, 1967)*

IMPOTENCE

After a tedious Journey, and my Supper,
And d——d neasy with my Crupper,
Jenney came up to warm my Bed,
A pretty Girl; but I was dead,
Or else I'd had her Maidenhead.
R.T.

(The Crown, Uxbridge, England, 18th century)

Drunk at Comb-Abbey, horrid drunk;
Hither I came, and met my fav'rite punk.
But she as well might have embrac'd a log,
All night I snor'd and grunted like a hog,
Then was not I a sad confounded dog?

(On a window, Star of Coventry, England)

I'll never get drunk again,
For my head's full of pain,
And it grieves me to think,
that by dint of good drink,
I should lie with my Phillis in vain.

(On a window, Star of Coventry, England, 1712)

Impotence, where is thy sting?

IMPRISONMENT

Arrived on the ninth of March, 1944. Don Quixote.

*(Prison, Dijon, 1944—
during German occupation of France)*

Avenge Attica!

(Various walls, New York City, 1972)

Bi-torture — strange — my — troulh — was — tryed — yet — of — my — libertie — denied — there — for — reason — hath — me — persuaded — that — paysans — must — be — ymbraced — though — hard — fortune — chassyth — me — with — smart — yet — paysans — shall — prevayl.

(Bell Tower, Tower of London, written by the Irish prisoner Thomas Mehoe [Mick O'More], 1581)

The cell will give you a greater appreciation of wine, tobacco, life, women and liberty.

*(Prison, Dijoin, 1944)
during German occupation of France)*

Faith, courage, hope. But where are the snows of yesteryear. May God have pity on me.

(Prison Rue d'Auxonne, Dijon, during German occupation of France, 1943)

Help us—we don't want to see our children in prison any more.

(Paris, May, 1968)

I feel like weeping, that my fortune flies and my hope goes to the wind, and my last days are always a source of sadness and discontent to me.

(Cited in Graffiti *by Richard Freeman, London, Hutchinson, 1966)*

I'm innocent, the warden done it.

(Popular prison graffito)

Is is the poynt of a wyse man to try and then triste, for happy is he who findeth one that is just. T.C.

I live in hope and I give credit to my friends in time did stande me moste in hande; so would I never do againe excepte I had him in bonde and to all men wish I so, unless ye sustaine the like love as I do. Unhappie is the man who actes doth procure the miseri of this hous in prison to endure. Thomas Clarke. 1586.

(Beauchamp Tower, Tower of London)

Keep your tears; it is strength which flows out.

(Prison, Dijon, 1944—during German occupation of France)

Since fortune has chosen that my hope should go to the wind to complain, I wish that time were destroyed and unpropitious.

(Beauchamp Tower, Tower of London, 16th century—written by Sir William Tyrell, Knight of Malta)

They enter here as lambs and exit as lions.

(Prison, Dijon, 1944—during German occupation of France)

Thomas Rose, within this tower strong, kept close by those to whome hee did noe wrong.

(Beauchamp Tower, Tower of London, 16th century)

We deserve to go to Heaven,
Because we've spent our time in hell.

(Burlington County Jail, N. J.—the 160-year-old-jail which resembles a medieval dungeon is now a museum)

What do we want? Freedom!
What do we get? Bologna sandwiches.

(Jail, Washington, D.C., c. 1966)

When my bird is through
And the governor asks me to recall
the best screw of 'em all
Well then I'll tell him I remember youoooo

*(Prison wall, England—
"I Remember You" was a popular song)*

While robed in the sacred vestments and administering the sacred mysteries, I was taken and held in this narrow cell.

*(White Tower, Tower of London, 1612—
written by Father Robert Fisher with a nail)*

INCEST

Call it incest—but I want my mommy.

Electra loves daddy.

(Ladies' room, Ninth Circle Restaurant, New York City)

Incest—a game the whole family can play.

Incest is relative.

(Button)

Incest, murder, sodomy, genocide . . . are as close as your nearest bible.

Oedipus was a mater violater.

*(Ladies' room, Limelight Restaurant,
New York City, 1966)*

Oedipus was the first man to plug the generation gap.

(Men's room, Princeton University, 1970)

Only yesterday I fucked my aunt who only knew of such a thing from hearsay.

*(Men's room, Riesengebirge—
cited in* Anthropophyteia, *Vol. 6, 1909)*

Public Notice: Oedipus come home, all is forgiven. Mother loves you.

(Ladies' room, Under The Stairs Restaurant, New York City)

Vice is nice, but incest is best.

(Ladies' room, Limelight Restaurant, New York City)

INDIVIDUALISM

Hire a freak today.

I am a non-conformist and I wear a suit.

(The Dom, East Village, New York City, 1966)

The world is good!

UNDERNEATH

And so?
And so be thankful.
What, are you crazy?
Sure, I'm a conformist too.
No, just a fool.
Nonconformity is a myth perpetuated by fools.

(Antioch College, Yellow Springs, Ohio)

INDUSTRIAL MILITARY COMPLEX

Draft the industrial complex.

(Wall near People's Park, Berkeley, Cal.)

The Industrial Military Complex Fucks.

Men's room, Hunter College, New York City, 1969)

INFERIORITY COMPLEX

I am a fetal failure.

(University of Florida)

I am a mistake—legalize abortion.

I came, I saw, I fucked up.

(Men's room, Princeton University, 1970)

I feel like a factory reject of the Dodge rebellion.

(Engagé Coffee House, New York City—variation on a current advertising slogan)

I go for you whoever you may be.

I hate myself.

(Free Church, Berkeley, Cal., 1971)

I'm sure I'm something, I think.

(Goddard College, Plainfield, 1971)

My thoughts aren't worth a penny.

(Men's room, Princeton University, 1970)

Nature never gives up.

UNDERNEATH

It did on me.
Out of order.

(On a mirror in a saloon toilet)

Imago in Speculo loquitur ad T—p—n.

Thou pretty little fluttering Thing,
That mak'st this gaudy Shew,
Thou senseless Mimick of a Man,
Thou Being, call'd a Beau.
Like me thou art an empty Form,
Like me alone, thou'rt made;
Like me delusive seem'st a Man,
But only art a Shade.

(On the looking glass of Mr. T—p—n, Fellow-Commoner of Trinity College, Cambridge)

INSULT, *see also* SLANDER

The Alternate U is run by a Polish Gusano [*worm*].

(Co-ed toilet, Alternate U., New York City)

Christ! I never saw so many phonies in one place in all my life.

(Co-ed toilet, Paradox Restaurant, New York City)

He that loves a Glass without a G,
Leave out L, and that is he.

(In a window of the Rene-Deer-Inn,
Bishop's Strafford, England)

Hide yourself, thing.

(Richelieu Hall, Sorbonne, Paris, May 1968)

Hullo, hullo Mago fare you well, you're obviously castrated.

(Pompeii, 79 A.D.*)*

If I had a face like yours I'd be ashamed to go to the toilet.

(Cited in Anthropophyteia, *Vol. 9, 1912)*

The Mistress by her Window's represented,
For why, 'tis brittle Ware, and painted.

(Written on the window of a coffee house;
underneath: coffee, tea, &c.)

This Glass, my Fair's the Emblem of your Mind,
Which brittle, slipp'ry, pois'nous oft we find.

UNDERNEATH

I must confess, kind Sir, that though this Glass,
Can't prove me brittle, it proves you an Ass.

(Written in a window at a private house by a
despondent lover in the presence of his mistress)

Two D——s, and a Doctor, 'tis said, wrote this Piece,
Who were modest as Whores, and witty as Geese.
They penn'd it, it seems, to shew their great Parts,
Their Skill in Burlesque, and their Knowledge in Arts.
But what say the Town—that't has fully desected,
That Fools they are all—which had long been suspected.

(Written in the first leaf of Arbor Vitae*)*

You are a poet among poets
like an ass among faces.

(Men's room, cited in Anthropophyteia,
Vol. 4, 1907)

You are empty.

(Nanterre, May 1968)

INTELLECT

Eggheads of the world unite! You have nothing to lose but your yokes.

(Yale University)

In every family tree there's some sap.

Is there any intelligent life on Earth?

UNDERNEATH

Yes, but I'm only visiting.

(Wall, Cambridge University, 1969)

Machines can never replace human stupidity.

Most minds are not fit for human habitation.

(IRT subway, 1970)

The following is often written under one of those many office signs that say "THINK":

or

THWIM.

Those who think they know it all upset those of us who do.

(University of Michigan)

INTERNATIONAL RELATIONS, *see also* NATIONALISM

Continentalism is treason.

(Found all over the Canadian North)

Cuba is Soviet Union's Albania.

(Wall, Helsinki, 1971)

Free Ireland's head—its ass will follow.

(Loeb Student Center, New York City, 1972)

Free Jerusalem from the anti-Christ.

Frontiers = repression.

(Paris, May, 1968)

Golda—get out of Arab Land.

Listen to your ears, ears have walls.

(Czechoslovakia, September, 1968—during Russian occupation)

Resist British bully boys!

(Bogside in Londonderry, Northern Ireland, 1972)

Russian circus in town. Don't feed the animals.

(Wall, Czechoslovakia, 1968—during Russian occupation)

They're here. Take off your watches and hide your wives.

(Painted on the side of a Russian tank by a Czechoslovakian who took a big chance, 1968)

INTRIGUE

All Russian spies leave info. here.
—a comrade
(info is a code word for information)

(Loeb Student Center, New York University, 1972)

IHS 1571 Die, 10 April. Wise men ought circumspectly to see what they do—to examine before they speake—to prove before they take in hand—to beware whose company they use, and above all things, to whom they truste.
—Charles Bailly

(Beauchamp Tower, Tower of London, 1571)

INVOLVEMENT

Be enraged!

(Nanterre, May, 1968)

Be salty, not sugar-coated.

(Paris, May, 1968)

Come alive you're in the spontaneous generation.

(Bus stop, Brattleboro, Vt.)

Come on in!

(Wall, Berkeley, Cal., 1970)

Death to the tepid.

(Paris, May, 1968)

Die for

(This graffiti was left unfinished. Watts, Los Angeles, 1970)

Don't write your will before dying for an ideal.

(Sorbonne, May, 1968)

For Brotherhood Week—take your brother hood to lunch.

Fuck complacency.

(The Village Gate, New York City)

God isn't dead—he just doesn't want to get involved.

(Lamont Library, Harvard University)

I came, I saw, I believed.

(Sorbonne, May, 1968)

I came, I seen I SAW

(Timpanoos Cave, Utah, 1928)

If you don't like it, change it.

(Berkeley, Cal., 1970)

If you're not part of the solution, you're part of the problem.

(University of California at Los Angeles, 1970)

Open the windows of your heart.

(Paris, May, 1968)

The Silent Majority has nothing to say about it.

(University of Michigan, 1970)

The Silent Majority is a nice way to speak to a nation of sheep.

(Ann Arbor, Mich., 1970)

Vote with your feet.

UNDERNEATH

Do you have prehensile toes?

(Columbia University)

IRVING, CLIFFORD (1930–)

McGraw-Hill banks at Irving Trust.

McGraw-Hill found the Clifford Irving book Hughesless.

IVES, CHARLES (1874–1954)

(Note: American composer who has been receiving more interest in recent years)

Ives Lives 1874—eternity.

(Men's toilet, Judson Memorial Church, New York City, 1969)

J

JAMES, HENRY (1843–1916)

Henry James must have fucked somebody.

(Ladies' room, Lion's Head, New York City)

JESUS CHRIST

The following was written on a sign that said "Call on Jesus now":

If no one answers, leave a message at the candy store.

Christ comes on cat's paws.

Christ died for our sins, lets not disappoint him.

(Construction wall, Philadelphia, 1969)

Christ died for your sins. What have you done for him lately?

UNDERNEATH

What does he deserve?

UNDERNEATH

He died for you. Won't you even try to see why?

(Los Angeles Valley College, 1970)

Dear Jesus, I would like to remind you that you are due.

(Toilet, Free Church, Berkeley, Cal., 1971)

God is good.

UNDERNEATH

Cheeses is also delicious.

(Fence, New York City, 1972)

I love Jesus, but oh you kid!

(Men's room, Goddard College, Plainfield, Vt., 1971)

If Christ had been hanged, would priests wear a miniature gallows around their necks?

UNDERNEATH

Only a noose.

If Heaven was so cool, why did Christ leave it?

(Men's room, The Steppenwolf Tavern, Berkeley, Cal.)

Jesus Christ.

UNDERNEATH

Say! that's a better name than Gunther.

Jesus Christ was a Temple drop-out.

(Men's room, Princeton University, 1970)

Jesus Christ was a Yid.

Jesus had an Oedipus complex.

(Men's toilet, Telephone Company, New York City)

a slum
Jesus is∧Lord.

(Construction fence, Harvard University, 1972)

Jesus isn't going to save nobodies [*sic*] ass.

Jesus lives!—Darwin survives!

Jesus lives, over the river and down the road.

The following was written on a poster put out by The New York Bible Society that read, "Jesus said, Whoever drinks of the water that I shall give him will never thirst":

He should be appointed water commissioner.

Jesus Saves.

UNDERNEATH

He couldn't do it on my salary!

Jesus saves at the Bowery.

Jesus saves, but Moses invests.

(Popular wall inscription and often quoted)

Jesus saves but the Mongol hordes.

Jesus saves; Moses invests; but only Buddha pays dividends.

Jesus saves S & H Green Stamps.

Jesus saves tin foil.

(Found during World War II)

The following was written on a Gillette billboard ad:
Jesus Shaves!

Jesus takes it on the palm.

Jesus was a dropout.

Jesus was raised in a kosher home.

(BMT subway, New York City; also on a button)

Jesus will return!

UNDERNEATH

We got him before and we'll get him again.

Jesus wore long hair.

John not Jesus.

(Pub, London—refers to a remark by John Lennon that the Beatles were more popular than Jesus)

News note!!!—No Easter, they found the body.

(IRT subway, New York City)

Take a trip with Jesus.

(Wall near the Fillmore East, New York City, also on a button)

Would Christ carry a draft card?

JEWS, see *also* ANTI-SEMITISM

Black girls are better. They're not hung up like Jewish princess virgins.

(Men's room, Brooklyn College, 1970)

Dress British, think Yiddish.

(Men's room, Madison Avenue building, also on a button)

Here is the only place where Jews have shortcomings.

(Men's room, Germany, 1968)

The Renaissance was a Zionist conspiracy.

The following comments were added to poster that read, "You don't have to be Jewish to love Levy's real Jewish Rye":

To be offended by this ad.
To be called one.
To oppose the war in Vietnam.
To go to Columbia University, but it helps.
To wear levis.
To be circumcized.
To be a lousy lover.

JOAN OF ARC (1412–1431)

Joan of Arc was a dyke.

JOHN THE BAPTIST (*d.* 29 A.D.)

John the Baptist was a head.

JOHN BIRCH SOCIETY

Cocksuckers of the world unite—bite Birchers.

Defrock John Birch cops.

JOHNSON, HOWARD (1897–1972)

Howard Johnson eats at home.

(Men's room, Howard Johnson's, New York City, 1970)

Howard Johnson lives!

(IRT subway, New York City)

JOHNSON, LYNDON B. (1908–1973)

All the way with L.B.J.

UNDERNEATH

Barbecue Lyndon.

All the way with LIB. J.

(Arlington County Public Library, Va.—cited in American Library Association Bulletin, *April, 1969)*

Commit LBJ, not the USA.

France has her DeGaulle,
And we have our Neanderthal.

(Wall, Queens College, New York City, 1967)

Give LBJ an enema.

UNDERNEATH

Then he'll disappear forever.

Gypsy Johnson—Napalmistry.

Half the way with L.B.J.

Hey, hey L.B.J. how many kids did you kill today?

(A popular chant around 1966, found on many walls)

Impeach Johnson.

UNDERNEATH

We already tried it stupid, in the late 19th century.

(On February 24, 1868, the House passed a resolution of impeachment against President Andrew Johnson; by a narrow margin, the Senate failed to convict)

Jettison Johnson in '68.

Johnson and Jenkins in '69.

(Lion's Head, New York City)

Johnson gets his Humphrey.

Johnson pull out (like your father should have).

(Men's room, Library, Colby College, Waterville, Me.)

LBJ and the CIA did away with JFK.

(Subway, New York City)

L.B.J. either way.

(Lion's Head, New York City)

L.B.J. for ex-President.

LBJ is the Boston strangler.

(Kettle of Fish Bar & Restaurant, New York City)

LBJ takes trips.

(Ladies' room, Le Metro Caffe Espresso, New York City)

LBJ will go down in history.

Lethal-Bird Johnson beware.

(The Forum Coffee House, New York City)

Lynd not Lyndon.

Lyndon Johnson is suffering under the misconception that his mother was a virgin.

(Men's room, Colby College, Waterville, Me.)

President Johnson is a latent human being.

(BMT subway, New York City)

Turn on LBJ.

Write below the dirtiest expression you can think of.

UNDERNEATH

L.B.J.

JONSON, BEN (1572–1637)

When Hope and Prudence kept this House,
The Angel kept the Door;
  Now Hope is dead,
  And the Angel fled,
And Prudence turn'd a Whore.

(The Crown at Basingstoke, England—tradition informs us that Ben Jonson was acquainted with the house when it was The Angel and was operated by Mrs. Hope and her daughter Prudence; when he found strange people there, and the sign changed, he wrote these lines)

JOPLIN, JANIS (1943–1970)

I want to dig up Janis and fuck her.

(Goddard College, Plainfield, Vt., 1971)

JUDAS

Come home Judas—all is forgiven.

(Men's toilet, Telephone Company, New York City)

Judas needed the money for a sick friend.

JUSTICE, *see also* LAW

Amnesty is an act by which rulers must often pardon the injustices they have committed.

(Sorbonne, May, 1968)

Dick, on two Words, thought to maintain him ever:
The first was Stand, and next to Stand, Deliver.
But Dick's in Newgate, and he fears shall never,
Be blest again with that sweet Word Deliver.

(Traced with smoke of a candle in Newgate, England)

I hope in the end to deserve that I would have men.

(Beauchamp Tower, Tower of London, 16th century—written by a prison keeper, Hugh Longworths, who was killed by one of his charges, Peter Bourchet)

K

KAFKA, FRANZ (1883–1924)

Franz Kafka is a kvetch.

Gregor Samsa—live like him.

(Samsa becomes a cockroach in Kafka's Metamorphosis*)*

KANT, IMMANUEL (1724–1804)

Concentrate on Rousseau instead of your trousseau. Sorry I Kant.

(Library staff lounge, Fort Belvoir, Va.—Cited in American Library Association Bulletin, *April, 1969)*

Immanuel Kant but Kubla Khan.

KEANE, WALTER STANLEY (1920–)

(Note: Keane is painter of large-eyed children)

Walter Keane eats burnt umber.

(Pier 23, Bar, San Francisco)

KEATING, JOHN B. (1900–)

Stop Keating.

UNDERNEATH

But I never keated.

KELLY, EMMETT (1898–)

Emmett Kelly is a Negro in whiteface.

(Ladies' room, Le Metro Caffe Espresso, New York City)

KENNEDY, JOHN F. (1917–1963)

Ask not what your country has done to you.
Rather ask what you can do to your country.
[*This is a variation on the famous line in JFK's inaugural address: "Ask not what your country can do for you, but rather what you can do for your country."*]

The following was written on an ad for Walter B. Cooke funeral home:
John F. Kennedy was a great man who endeavor [*sic*] to bring peace to eradicate all vestige of racial hatred.

UNDERNEATH

Outasight.

LBJ and the CIA did away with JFK.

(Subway, New York City)

President Johnson was behind the asignation [*sic*] of Kennedy.

(Max's Kansas City Restaurant, New York City)

KENNEDY, ROBERT (1925–1968)

Bob Kennedy wears a toupee.

(Subway, New York City)

Bob Kennedy is sex, but Eugene McCarthy is love.

Cardinal Spellman you should be ashamed and ask God's forgiveness.

UNDERNEATH

You're forgiven.
—Bobby

I actively unsupport Bobby Kennedy.

(Engagé Coffee House, New York City)

KEYNES, JOHN MAYNARD (1883–1946)

John Maynard Keynes is a spendthrift.

(John Adams Luncheonette, New York City, 1968)

KILROY

(Note: "Kilroy was here" was a ubiquitous phrase popular during World War II. There was a Canadian counterpart known as Clem. These names were all over to voice popular army gripes. On one army post all the men were called out by the commanding officer and were told that if the name Clem was written again the inscriber would be severely punished. When he returned to his desk to his amazement he saw a scrawl on his wall which read: "What, no Clem?")

Kilroy wouldn't dare come in here.

(University of North Carolina, January 20, 1959)

No grass atoll, no trees atoll, no water atoll, no women atoll, no liquor atoll, no fun atoll, and no Kilroy atoll.

UNDERNEATH

I just didn't pause atoll.
—Kilroy.

(Kwajalein Atoll, Marshall Islands, 1944)

I leap and jump and dance with joy
For I was here before Kilroy.

UNDERNEATH

I hate to spoil your fun,
I hate to spoil your joke,
For I was here long, long ago, but my pencil point was broke.
—Kilroy

(Men's room, Rancheria camp ground, Alaska Highway, Yukon Territory, 1963)

Killjoy was here.

(Arlington County Public Library, Va.—cited in American Library Association Bulletin, *April, 1969)*

Kilroy was queer.

(Spokane, Wash.)

KING, MARTIN LUTHER (1929–1968)

King leaves, riots follow.

(IND subway, New York City—written a week after the King assassination, which occurred April 4, 1968)

KING KONG

King Kong—he died for our sins.

(The Forum Coffee House, New York City)

King Kong taught me to love.

(On various walls, also on a button)

KISSINGER, HENRY (1923–)

Do you realize that if Kissinger was shot today Nixon would become President.

(Library, New York University, 1972)

KNOWLEDGE

Be a knowbody!

Forget all you have learned. Begin by dreaming.

(Sorbonne, May, 1968)

Knowledge, thou Darling of the Soul,
Be thou my Help-Mate o'er a flowing Bowl;
Then will my Time slide easily along,
And ev'ry gen'rous Mortal grace our Song.

UNDERNEATH

D—n your Knowledge, says Captain Blunt;
swear, drink, and smoke, and you're an honest Fellow.
Feb. 13. 1720.

(On a window, Oxon, England)

You can't win except thru ignorance.

KRAFFT-EBING, RICHARD VON (1840–1902)

Krafft-Ebing taught here.

(Wall near Columbia University, also on a button)

KUBLA KHAN (1216–1294)

Immanuel Kant but Kubla Khan.

KY, NGUYEN CAO (1930–)

Kill none, not even Ky.

(Mother Hubbard Restaurant, New York City)

Lock up McNamara and throw away the Ky.

Vote Premier Ky or else!

(Lion's Head, New York City)

L

LSD

Acid—better living through chemistry.

(Wall on St. Mark's Place, New York City, 1968—variation on Dow Chemical Company's slogan: "Better living through chemistry")

Acid heads! Call me anytime and I'll tell you where life is really at. 684-55—Lucy.

(The Forum Coffee House, New York City)

Acid indigestion can be fun.

(Toilet, Washington Square Park, New York City, 1968)

Acid indigestion? Check your source.

(Men's room, Back Fence Bar, New York City, also on a button)

Acid—takes the worry out of being.

(Men's room, St. Adrian Company Restaurant & Bar, New York City)

Alcohol kills. Take L.S.D.

(Nanterre University, May, 1968)

Be placid with acid.

(Men's room, Stanley's Bar, New York City)

Chiquita Banana is an acid head.

Come alive, you're in the LSD generation.

Develop in acid for beautiful pictures.

(Men's room, Germain School of Photography, New York City, 1970)

Fragile—don't drop the acid.

(Yale University)

God is alive and living in a sugar cube.

(Wall near Tompkins Square Park, New York City, also on a button)

God isn't dead he's just taking a "trip."

LBJ takes trips.

(Ladies' room, Le Metro Caffe Espresso, New York City)

LSD is fattening.

LSD is the best. Pot and Hatch are the second best.

UNDERNEATH

I think you mean "hash."

(Ladies' room, Max's Kansas City Restaurant, New York City)

LSD is there only if you care.

(Lexington Avenue subway, New York City)

LSD = Love—Sex—Dreams.

LSD saves!

(The Forum Coffee House, New York City)

LSD support your local travel agent.

LSD the groovy movie.

(On various walls, also on a button)

*L*egalize *S*piritual *D*iscovery.

*L*et the *S*tate *D*isintegrate.

(Engagé Coffee House, New York City, also on a button)

L(ibrary) S(ervices) D(ivision)

(Library staff lounge, Fort Belvoir, Va.—cited in American Library Association Bulletin, *April, 1969)*

Melts in your mind not in your hand.

Old Hippies never die, they just trip away.

Promise her anything but give her LSD.

The following were written on a poster for a Broadway Presbyterian Church:
Psychedelic psalms for psoriasis.
Preparation LSD shrinks hemmeroids [*sic*]

Take a longer trip. Take LSD with platformate.
(Men's room, Rutgers University, 1970)

Take a trip with Jesus.
(Wall, Judson Memorial Church, Greenwich Village, New York City, also on a button)

Take LSD and see.

Take the trip every day of your life.
(Nanterre University, May, 1968—written in English)

Turn on, tune in, drop dead.

Turn on, tune in, drop out.
(The LSD motto found in bathrooms and on buttons all over the East Village and other urban Bohemias)

LABOR

I fight poverty: I work.

Lives there a man with soul so dead
Who never to himself hath said,
"Fuck this shit, I'm going to bed!"
(Laundry room, Princeton University, 1971)

Look at your labor. Oblivion and torture have a part of it.
(Sorbonne, May, 1968)

The people who work are bored when they have no work. The people who do not work are never bored.
(Sorbonne, May, 1968)

They all moved to the country and took jobs as barns.
(Tavern, Seattle)

Wives are unpaid labor.

Workers of the world unite, or we shoot you!
(Wall, Helsinki, 1970)

LAGUARDIA, FIORELLO (1882–1947)

LaGuardia ruined N.Y.C.

(Club Lunch Restaurant, New York City, 1967)

LANDLORD AND TENANT

Death to the slumlords.

(Building on Lower East Side, 1969)

If you lived here you'd be home now.

(Harvard University—takeoff on urban housing ad)

If you want to be happy, hang your landlord.

(Paris, May, 1968)

Landlords, the roaches around here are getting entirely too cocky.

May you be cheated yourself and then repine.

Landlord, you sell us water, while drinking wine.

(Pompeii, 79 A.D.)

Save our slums.

LAVAL, PIERRE (1883–1945)

(Note: A pro-Nazi leader of the French Vichy government during World War II)

Pétain, you have no shame. You, Laval, old rascal, old stinking coyote, we'll get you.

LAW, *see also* JUSTICE

Down with ordinances.

(Sorbonne, May, 1968)

It costs more money to plead not guilty than guilty. This proves that a man can't afford to be innocent these days.

(Wall, Hall of Justice, San Francisco, 1971)

Let's legalize vandalism.

No liberty without law.

(Stockholm official graffiti wall [Kotterplank], *November 7, 1968)*

Obey good laws, break bad ones.

To go to Law
I have no Maw,
Altho's my Suit be sure,
For I may lack
Cloaths to my Back,
E'er I that Suit procure.

(In pencil on a panel in one of the Courts of Justice in Guild-Hall, England)

When law is tyranny, revolution is order.

(University of California at Los Angeles, 1970)

LAWRENCE, D. H. (1885–1930)

T. S. Elliot loves D. H. Lawrence.

UNDERNEATH

Eliot is spelled with one l, you ass.

(Old O.P.A. Building, Washington, D.C.)

LAWYERS

Come hither, Barristers of Dress,
That once your Lips may meet Success;
From Rufus' filthy Hall withdraw;
Here only ye can live by Law.

(On a window in the Inner Temple-Hall, England)

Here is the court of appeals,
Where every ass pronounces his judgment,
Attorneys are not welcome.
Who wants to shit must come by himself.

(Men's room, Thorn, 1906)

In vain poor fable Son of Woe,
  Thou seek'st a tender Ear;
In vain thy Tears with Anguish flow,
  For Mercy dwells not here:
From Cannibals thou fly'st in vain,
  Lawyers less Quarter give;
The first won't eat you till you're slain,
  The last will do't alive.

(Wall of Clements-Inn, when the dial was put up which is supported by a black slave in a kneeling posture, England)

LEARY, TIMOTHY (1920–)

Hands off Tim Leary.

(On various walls, also on a button)

I'm leery of Leary.

Tim Leary is an alcoholic.

Unleash Tim Leary.

(Lion's Head, New York City)

Weary Leary isn't really eerie dearie.

(The Exit Coffee House, New York City)

LEE, PINKY (*n.d.*)

Pinky Lee is secretly alive in Argentina.

(Ladies' room, Café Figaro, New York City)

LEE, ROBERT E. (1807–1870)

Lee:
  Make it.
    Grant.

LEIBNITZ, GOTTFRIED VON (1646–1716)

Leibnitz has the answers, baby.

(Men's room, New School for Social Research, New York City)

LEIF ERICSON (*fl.* 1000)

Greenland: love it or Leif it.

(Men's room, Princeton University, 1970)

Leif Ericson is a fink.

(Boston)

LE MAY, CURTIS (1906–)

Le May's wet dream—Vietnam.

(Boston University)

LENIN, NIKOLAI (1870–1924)

B loves Lenin.

(Municipal Building, New York City, August 26, 1939—written inside hammer and sickle emblem instead of heart and arrow, cited in The New Yorker*)*

Lenin won
Fidel won
We will win.

(Columbia University, April 30, 1968—the day of the student strike)

LENNON, JOHN

(Note: Ex-Beatle who once made the controversial remark that the Beatles were more popular than Jesus)

I am 33 years old, I love John Lennon. I wish I had eyebrows like Paul McCartney.

(Ladies' room, Ninth Circle Restaurant, New York City, 1965)

John has a bigger member than Jesus.

UNDERNEATH

But Jesus has been screwing us for 2000 years.

John Lennon is Jesus in drag.

John Lennon is the once and future king.

(Ladies' room, Bennington College, Vt.)

John Lennon writes his own bibles.

(IRT subway, New York City)

John is not Jesus.

(Pub, London)

LESBIANISM, *see* HOMOSEXUALITY (FEMALE)

LIBERTY

The cost of Liberty is less than the price of oppression.

(Wall near People's Park, Berkeley, Cal., 1970)

Czechoslovakia has gun control.

(IRT subway, New York City, October, 1968)

Don't liberate me, I'll take care of it myself.

(Nanterre University, May, 1968)

Down with repression.

The dreams of those who will not act; the reality of those who are not afraid to be free.

UNDERNEATH

What about the fuck-offs who are still afraid to *fight* to be free.

(New York University, 1969)

Emancipation of man will be either total or not at all.

(Paris, May, 1968)

End all political repression.

(University of California at Los Angeles, 1970)

Free Bobby Seale.

UNDERNEATH

Free the people.

UNDERNEATH

Free me.

(Watts, Los Angeles, 1970)

Freedom is in the milk of those who love liberty.
(Construction fence, New York City, 1973)

How can you free me, when you can't free yourself.
(Free Church, Berkeley, Cal., 1971)

I am my freedom.

Liberty is not a right that we possess. It is a right that we have been prevented from acquiring with the help of laws, rules, prejudice, ignorance, etc. . . .
(Nanterre, May, 1968)

Liberty is the crime which includes all other crimes. It is our absolute weapon.
(Sorbonne, May, 1968)

Liberty is the right to silence.
(Paris, May, 1968)

I will never consent, in order to live, to give up the very reason for living.
(Prison, Dijon, 1944—during German occupation of France)

Loud speaker = programmed environment = repression.

A man is not stupid or intelligent, he is free or he's not.
(Medical School, Paris, May, 1968)

Neither robot nor slave.
(Paris, May, 1968)

No liberty without law.
(Stockholm official graffiti wall [Kotterplank], *November 7, 1968)*

No slave should die a natural death.
(Watts, Los Angeles, 1970)

Prohibiting is prohibited, May 10, 1968.
(Paris, May, 1968)

Total equality.

We must silence those who oppress freedom of speech!

LIBRARY SCIENCE

All the way with LIB. J.

(Arlington County Public Library, Va.—cited in American Library Association Bulletin, *April, 1969)*

Be all you can be . . . WEED!

(Library staff lounge, Fort Belvoir, Va.—cited in American Library Association Bulletin, *April, 1969)*

GOD IS DEAD, and indexed—H. W. Wilson.

(Arlington County Public Library, Va.—cited in American Library Association Bulletin, *April, 1969; also cited in* Library Journal, *January 1, 1968, with slight variation, the indexer was Bowker)*

File now; pray later.

(Library staff lounge, Fort Belvoir, Va.—cited in American Library Association Bulletin, *April, 1969)*

I'm a different kind of librarian. I'm a young adulteress.

(Library staff lounge—cited in American Library Association Bulletin, *January, 1969)*

L(ibrary) S(ervices) D(ivision)

(Library staff lounge, Fort Belvoir, Va.—cited in American Library Association Bulletin, *April, 1969)*

Library statistics are reliable if you don't count on them.

(Library staff lounge—cited in American Library Association Bulletin, *January, 1969)*

Make luv, not catalog cards.

(Arlington County Public Library, Va.—cited in American Library Association Bulletin, *April, 1969; cited also in* Library Journal, *January 1, 1969)*

Melvil Dewey played the numbers and lost.

(Library staff lounge, after converting to the Library of Congress classification—cited in American Library Association Bulletin, *January, 1969)*

Take a reference librarian to a catalogers' luncheon.

(Arlington County Public Library, Va.—cited in American Library Association Bulletin, *April, 1969)*

What is social responsibility to you is an acquisition problem to me.

(Library staff lounges; in one version on the West Coast the words "social responsibility" were crossed out and "Berkeley Barb" written in—cited in American Library Association Bulletin, *January, 1969)*

LIFE

Life is a bowl of shit with the handle in the inside.

(Men's room, Rutgers University, 1971)

Life is a constant *now*.

(Free Store Theater, New York City)

Life is a hereditary disease.

Life is a sandwich & it's always lunchtime.

(Cornell University)

Life is a yo-yo and mankind ties knots in the string.

Life is Kreplach.

Life is like a diaper—short and loaded.

(Men's room, Bates College, Lewiston, Me.)

Life is like a fan—turn it one way and it blows, turn it the other way and it sucks.

(Men's room, Hunter College, New York City, 1972)

Life is like a penis—when its hard you get fucked, when its soft you can't beat it.

(Men's room, Princeton University, 1970)

Life to me is merely sorrow.
Here today, gone tomorrow.

Nobody gets out of life alive.

Syllogism:
1. Life is a four lettered word.
2. Shit is a four lettered word.
   Life is shit. q.e.d.

UNDERNEATH

One premise is missing

3. All four-lettered words are equivalent in meaning.

UNDERNEATH

Not needed—all necessary is that both be four lettered words (In ecto in profondi es establi.)

UNDERNEATH

I agree, an empirical contrapositive might go:

1. Shit is a four lettered word.
2. Life is a four lettered word.

Shit is life as any expert in bio-physiology (or agricultural fertilizers) will tell you, q.e.d. and finis.

(Men's room, Princeton University, 1970)

To live means trouble.
To die means no trouble.
It's better to have something than nothing.

(Loeb Student Center, New York University, 1972)

LINDSAY, JOHN V. (1921–)

(Note: Mayor of New York City, 1965–1973)

Dump Mayor Linseed.

(IRT subway, December 5, 1968)

John Lindsay for President in 1972.

UNDERNEATH

He ruined New York City he can do the same for the country.

(Construction fence, New York City, 1971)

Lindsay couldn't clean up the snow in N.Y., how do you expect him to clean up the shit?

(Men's toilet, New York University, October 1969)

Lindsay has sold his soul to the blacks.

(Men's room, Hunter College, New York City, 1969)

Lindsay is a man?
Who thinks he's all afire.
but all he really is,
is N.Y.'s biggest liar.

(IND subway, 1970—one of the many irate wall messages because of the subway fare hike to 30 cents)

Mayor Lindsay is on welfare.

Lindsay is fresh when everyone is polite.

(Variant on his campaign slogan: "He is fresh when everyone is tired")

Tow Lindsay away.

UNDERNEATH

Lindsay's Garage Inc.

(Property Clerk Storage Pier 96, New York City, April, 1969—place where they impound cars)

Who is the Mayor of New York City?

UNDERNEATH

My name is John Lindsay and I've got a secret.

(Men's room, New York University, 1972)

Why not make N.Y. State a welfare state? Reelect Lindsay.

UNDERNEATH

How about making it Racket State for the Whops [*sic*]?

(IRT subway, October, 1969)

LIPPMANN, WALTER (1889-)

Walter Lippmann—God is not dead. He is alive and appearing twice a week in the Washington Post.

(Cited by Art Buchwald, columnist, Washington Post*)*

LITTER

Keep Lewiston clean—eat a pigeon today.

(Bates College, Lewiston, Me.)

Make love, not litter.

(San Francisco State College, 1970)

The following was written on a garbage truck:
Satisfaction guaranteed or double your garbage back.

(Princeton, N.J., 1972)

LOGIC

Arra, now what signifies the making the two great Lights?
The Sun to light the Day, and the Moons to light the Nights:
For the Sun in the Day-Time there is no Occasion;
Because I can see very well after my Persuasion:
But for the Moons, they are very good in a dark Night,
Because when we cannot see they give us a Light.

(Hollyhead, England)

Dear Johnny if you don't see my message on this wall then you know I wasn't here.

Hurrah, hurrah it's Spring,
The boid is on the wing
How utterly absoid,
The wing is on the boid!

(Laundry room, Princeton University, 1971)

I am here and you isn't
Now you is here and I isn't.

(Ladies' room, Limelight Restaurant, New York City)

It is better to be rich and healthy
Than to be poor and sick.

Things are more like they used to be than they are now.

(The Alibi Bar, Bloomington, Ind.)

LONELINESS, *see also* SOCIAL ISOLATION

Alienation can be fun.

Alienation ends where yours begins.

(Nanterre, May, 1968)

Girls, I just wish I could fuck with anybody.

(Ladies' room, Limelight Restaurant, New York City)

I am anonymous, help me.

I'm so lonesome in my saddle since my horse died.

(University of California at San Diego, 1971)

In vain are they called happy whom nobody can bear.

(Pompeii, 79 A.D.)

Isolation nourishes sadness.

(Paris, May, 1968)

Millions of grains of sand in the world . . . why such a lonely beach?

(Me-Shack Coffee House, West Palm Beach, Fla., 1970)

People who live in Lonelytown think sunshine is sentimental.

(Mr. Waffles Ice Cream Parlor, New York City)

"Sue Wilson and nobody as yet."

(Among amorous scrawls on a construction fence)

We lie down
because we are tired
we sleep
because we are alone.

(Lion's Head, New York City)

What train would come to bear me back across so wide a town?

(Subway, New York City—cited in The New Yorker*)*

LOVE

Agatho, slave of Herennius, asks Venus for his life . . .

UNDERNEATH

I ask her to let him perish.

(Pompeii, 79 A.D.)

Ah! if I should ever wish to be a god without thee, may I die!

(Pompeii, 79 A.D.)

Art is Love is God.

(Engagé Coffee House, New York City)

As Glass obdurate no Impression makes,
But what the radiant piercing Diamond makes;
Just so my Heart all other Pow'rs defies,
But those of fair Venilla's brilliant Eyes.

(On a window, Ardenham-House, Hertfordshire, England)

The blonde makes me scorn all brunettes
she's so far set above them.
I'll turn them down if I can.
If I can't, I'll reluctantly love them.

(Pompeii, 79 A.D.)

Boy named Cupid, wanted for questioning by local police.

(Men's toilet, London, 1967)

Celadus [a gladiator] glory of the girls, sigh of the girls.

(Pompeii, 79 A.D.)

Celia, the Joy of all my Parts,
I kiss'd, and broke ten thousand Hearts:
There's ne'er a Man the Girl will see,
But dearest, dearest, dearest me.
I.H. Esq; I can boast,
The greatest Conquest o'er the greatest Toast.

UNDERNEATH

Proud Puppy, who pretend'st to find,
A Woman with a constant Mind,
Surely denotes that Love is blind.
For I have kiss'd her myself,
Or else I'm an Elf,
R.C. Fellow-Commoner, Oxon.

(Mitre, Hampton, England, 1708)

A Liliputian Ode.
Charming Molly,
Cease your Folly;
Learn to ease me,
No more teaze me.
Love's but Reason
When in Season:
Nay, 'tis Duty,
Youth and Beauty
To improve
In happy Love,
Therefore, Molly,
Cease your Folly,
And instead of being coy,
Give, O give your Lover Joy!

The Faire Lady's Answer. In the same Measure:
Rhiming Billy,
Soft and silly,
Are the Verses,
Muse rehearses,
When straining
You're obtaining
Her Assistance
'Gainst Resistance,
Made by Mistress
To your Distress.
Therefore early
Quit them fairly,
If you'd be rid of Woe,
Prithee, Prithee, Coxcomb, do.

(Tunbridge, England)

Chloe is fair as Fields in Autumn seen,
Her Temper gentle as the purling Stream:
That's true; but then with those the rest conspire,
Lighter she is than Air, and hot as Fire.

(Tunbridge, England)

Cinedus, the physician of my needs.

(On wall, Ancient Rome; Cinedus, whose name means "son of a bitch," was a popular gladiator)

Come hither, dearest, sweetest Turtle-Dove;
You are my Goddess.—You alone I love.
At Night, whene'er I close my Eyes to Rest,
I dream of laying in your snow-white Breast.
But oft oppress'd with Grief and pensive Care,
I to enjoy such Happiness despair.
O wretched me! Celestial Pow'rs above!
O mighty Jove! what must I die for Love!
If you're inclin'd to cure the Wound you gave,
Come quick, relieve, and save me from the Grave.
Her answer.

Unhappy Youth, pray trouble not your Mind,
By mighty Jove, I swear I will be kind.
I swear by Venus, and the Pow'rs above;
By Cupid's Darts, and all the Joys of Love,
To thee, my Youth, my Swain, I'll ever constant prove.

(On a window, The Ram, Newmarket, England)

Come lovers all, I want to crack Venus' ribs and cripple the goddess's lewd loins with clubs. If she's allowed to break my tender heart why can't I break her head now for a start?

(Pompeii, 79 A.D.)

Coquets will always merry prove;
But Prudes are those give down their love;
And love and move, and move to love.

UNDERNEATH

A Prude for my Money, by G–d.
T.S. 1711.

(Red-Lion, Egham, England)

Could fairest dear Eliza know how much I love,
My story might, at least, her gen'rous Pity move;
Her Pity's all my Hope, nor durst I more implore,
With that I still might live, and still her Charms adore.

UNDERNEATH

Poor Wretch, alas! I pity Thee with all my heart,
Since that, it seems, alone will cure thy Love-sick Smart:
For he that has not Courage further to implore,
May surely have our Pity, but deserves no more.

(On the wall of one of the summer houses in Gray's Inn Walks, England, 18th century)

Devil may care.

UNDERNEATH

I love you Pierre.

(Ladies' room, Lion's Head, New York City)

Dolly with Beauty and Art,
Has so hemm'd in my Heart,
That I cannot resist the Charm.
  In Revenge I will stitch
  Up the Hole near her Breach,
With a Needle as long as my Arm R.

(On a window at Charing-Cross, England—written about a beautiful seamstress)

Don't fuck with love.

(Ladies' room, Lion's Head, New York City)

Dorothy vs. Johnny.

(Among the usual love messages)

Enjoy without shackles.
Live without dead time.
Love without lies.

(Nanterre, May, 1968)

Even dirty old men need love.

(On various walls, also on a button)

Figulus loves Ida.

(Pompeii, 79 A.D.)

For you teach me.
Love held my pen and told me what to say.
I wouldn't be a god with you away.

(Pompeii, 79 A.D.)

Fortunatus you sweet little darling you great fornicator, someone who knows you writes this.

(Pompeii, 79 A.D.)

Free love isn't free.

(Florida State University)

The Lover's Retreat.
From meaner Pleasure I retire,
  Yet real Happiness pursue;
Friendship and Love my Breast inspire,
  And I have met them both in you,

Whatever in my Wish had Place,
  In thee, my lovely Fair, I find;
All that's beauteous in thy Face,
  And all that's virtuous in thy Mind.

(On a window at Parson's Green, England)

  Go you false and faithless Fair,
Gods above forbid my Fate,
  First me Joys do you prepare,
Then you Sorrows do create;
For 'tis the Nature of your Sex,
First to pleasure, then perplex,
  Happy's he without your Smiles.
Ever-blest he lives content;
  In exorbitant Exiles,
Never can his Fate repent;
All his Wishes and Desires,
To destroy Love's burning Fires.
R.C. June 14, 1731.

(On a window at the Old Crown at Ware, Hertfordshire, England—supposed to have been written by a slighted lover)

God is love.
Love is blind.

(Ladies' room, Ninth Circle Restaurant, New York City)

Some Love Verses being first written on a window in Brook-Street, and scratched out, occasioned the following:

Good grave Papa, you hope in vain,
  By blotting this to mend her;
She who writes Love upon the Pane,
  Will soon leap out a Window.

(England, mid-18th century)

Hamillus loves Nothe.
[*This was written backwards to try for further anonymity.*]

(Pompeii, 79 A.D.)

Hate ain't worth the energy it takes.

(San Diego State College, 1970)

He who hates, loves.

(Pompeii, 79 A.D.)

He will come like the sun to warm my sadness.
—Sarah

(Ladies' room, Greenwich Village Restaurant, New York City)

Help me, ye Pow'rs, to sing my Sylvia's Praise;
Nor P–pe, nor Sw–ft can do it now a-days.
But you, nor I, or them, can ever boast,
There ever was in Europe such a Toast;
All we can say, is, Lucy rules the Roast.

Michael Hunt's Health.
Here's a Health to Mich. Hunt,
And to Mich. Hunt's Breeches;
And why may I scratch Mich. Hunt,
When Mich. Hunt itches.

(The Darindal's Cap, Windsor, England)

The Clock goes as swift as the Hours that fly.
When together in Bed are my Chloe and I;
But when she is gone, I bemoan my hard Fate,
It is Millions of Years till she knocks at my Gate.

UNDERNEATH

D—n the Clock for its Inconstancy; to give me Moments and Ages in the same Time! O my Chloe!
R.W. 1720.

HOLLAND

(Wall, West Side, New York City, 1970—an example of an acronym which is found in the graffiti of the young—"Hoping our love lasts and never dies")

How do I fear my Lover will not come,
And yet I bid him not: But should he come,
Then let him read —
Let Man—r—ing love on, I will requite thee,
Taming my wild Heart to thy loving Hand.
If thou dost love, my Kindness shall incite thee,
To bind our Loves up in a holy Band.
Anne Oph—lia, 1708

(The White-Hart, Windsor, England)

How sad is my soul.
Until I see that certain party!

(On a ruined inside patio wall of the Cortez Palace in Cuernavaca, Mexico, 1522 or 1523)

How wonderful love is if it were not so dangerous.

(Men's room, Germany)

I am a Dog—
In true Fidelity:
I am a Sun—
In faithful Constancy:
I am a Stote,—
To please a listful Lass;
I am a Hog,—
And you may kiss my A–se.
But if my Celia comes within my Ken;
Than I shall be again like other Men.

(On a window, Hampstead, England)

I do not complain of my Phillis,
Because I know what her proud Will is;
For I know how she'll rant,
And I know what I want;
G–d d—n her old Aunt;
I stand here, and wait for her, THAT still is.

I kiss'd her standing,
Kiss'd her lying,
Kiss'd her in Health,
and kiss'd her dying;
And when she mounts the Skies,
I'll kiss her flying.

UNDERNEATH

Well said, my Boy. R.S.

(Bath, England)

I love Betty, and Betty loves me:
And it shall not be long before marry'd we be.

UNDERNEATH

If you make a Rhime upon your lass,
I'll make another—Rhimer kiss my Asse.

(Peacock, Northampton, England, early 18th century)

I love Jon.

UNDERNEATH

That's funny!! I love Jon too. One of us has a problem.

(Ladies' room, Lion's Head, New York City)

I love Liam—so does Liam.

(Ladies' room, Lion's Head, New York City)

I love Steve.
—Mary

UNDERNEATH

Tough luck, Mary.
—Steve

(University of Florida)

I love you—you better love me.

(Written within a drawn heart)

I need no sunshine save the light within your eyes
With all the souls deep knowledge glowing.
I love you Kiwi.

(Written in the dust on a window at 132 W. Houston Street, New York City)

I wish I had the urge to make love (or the nerve).

UNDERNEATH

Tsk. Tsk.

I'm tired of empty sex, why can't I love somebody and not be afraid of rejection? Eros, where are you?

UNDERNEATH

Because you're insecure—your id sucks!

(Goddard College, Plainfield, Vt., 1971)

It always rains on the unloved.

I've met my love—
I'll never ask for more,
She's deaf and dumb, over sexed
And owns a liquor store.

(Men's room, San Francisco, 1964)

I've now a Coach and Six before me,
Each female court'sies to adore me:
But from my dearest I can't part,
Without returning her my Heart:
Tell her I am gone a Month or longer,
While she may gain more Love, and I grow stronger.
S.M. Oct. 17, 1720.

(Tavern, Royal Exchange, England)

Joey loves Mary.

UNDERNEATH

Too bad he's married to Maggie.

(Sidewalk—cited by Norton Mockridge, columnist, Boston Herald, *December 2, 1966)*

J.F. is fifteen, and so charming her mien,
Her eyes are like brilliants,
Her looks are serene,
And one kiss from her lips
is worth ten from a queen.

(The Cardinal's Cap, Windsor, England, 1726)

John loves Sarrah [*sic*].

UNDERNEATH

John must be a dropout.

(Greenwich Village—cited by Norton Mockridge, columnist, Boston Herald, *December, 1966)*

Larry has me always.

(IND subway, New York City)

Let Jove his Juno, and his Nectar boast,
Champain's my Liquor, and Miss R—g my toast.

(On a window, Mainwaring's Coffee-House, Fleet Street, London)

Let the lovers flourish and let the unloving perish.
But a double death if he uses his breath for reproving our loving.

(Pompeii, 79 A.D.)

Lie down, I think I love you.

Like Mars I'll fight,
  like Antony I'll love,
I'll drink like Bacchus,
  and I'll whore like Jove.

(Common graffito, England, early 18th century)

Love and diarrhea cause much pain,
diarrhea in your belly, love in your heart.

(Halle, Prussia, 1903)

Love him only if you can basically tolerate him.

(Ladies' room, Café Figaro, New York City)

Love is a many gendered thing.

Love is a many splintered thing.

(Cornell University)

Love is, as some physicians say,
A fever bred by too high feeding:
To cure it then by the speediest way,
Would be by purging and by bleeding.

(England, early 18th century)

Love is blind
with sex in mind
  but
Don't be resigned
It always takes
two of a kind.

(Ladies' room, Limelight Restaurant, New York City)

Love is like blindman's buff, where we pursue,
We know not what we catch, we know not who;
And when we grasp our wish, what price is won?
Our eyes are open'd, and the play is done.

(On a window at Busby-Hall, Herfordshire, England, early 18th century)

Love is the answer.

UNDERNEATH

What is the question?

The Effects of Love.

Love is the sweetest softest Passion,
That can warm the human Soul;
'Tis a gentle Inclination
Which doth ev'ry Care controul:

Thro' our Bosom Love diffusing,
Tender Thoughts is ever choosing;
Softest Words its Flame expressing,
Towards the Dame our Heart possessing.

Love still gentle makes and easy,
Soft in ev'ry Thing we do;
Bent on all Things that may please ye,
Men are Angels when they Woo.

Love pats are basic human kneads.

Love people use things.

UNDERNEATH

better vice versa.

(Me-Shack Coffee House, West Palm Beach, Fla., 1970)

Love, 'tis said, his Arrows shooting,
Wounds is ever distributing;
But before I felt, I knew not,
That in Poison dipp'd they flew hot.

(On Mrs. Cowser's Window, in Russell Street, Covent-Garden, London)

To Jenny I owe
That this Secret I know,
For her I felt Smart
At first in my Heart;

Which quickly she cur'd: But alack and alas!
I now feel a Throbbing in a much lower Place.
To Jenny I went; but, alas! it was in vain.
Though she gave me the Wound, she can't cure me again.

Lovers, like bees, enjoy a life of honey.

UNDERNEATH

Wishful thinking.

(Pompeii, 79 A.D.)

Make haste! Make love!

UNDERNEATH

Haste is passé and for amateurs.

(Men's room, Lamont Library, Harvard University)

Make love and if you want to make war, enjoy yourself.

(IND subway, New York City)

Make love and revolution.

(University of California at Los Angeles, 1970)

Make love, not Irishmen.

(Ladies' room, Lion's Head, New York City, 1972)

Make love, not litter.

(San Francisco State College, 1970)

Make love, not peace.

Make love not promises.

(Me-Shack Coffee House, West Palm Beach, Fla., 1970)

Make love, not war.

(Nanterre University, May, 1968—written in English; one of the most frequent wall messages of the last few years, also on a button)

Make luv, not catalog cards.

(Arlington County Public Library, Va.—cited in American Library Association Bulletin, *April, 1969, also cited in* Library Journal, *January 1, 1969)*

May you perish, sweet love, for I love you so much that I too perish, Taine, my sweetest darling.

(Pompeii, 79 A.D.)

Might all my Wishes but propitious prove,
And all my Wants supply'd by mighty Jove;
Give me dear W—rs, and I'll ask no more,
But think her dearer than the golden Shower.
C.M.

(On a drinking glass at Pontack's-Head Tavern, Fleet Street, London)

The more I make love, the more I want to make revolution. The more I make revolution, the more I want to make love.
—One of the outraged.

(Sorbonne, May, 1968)

My God, I have never believed in you, but I have always loved you.

(Men's room, Under The Stairs Bar & Restaurant, New York City)

On Miss J—s.
My Good or Ill in her alone is found,
And in that Thought all other Cares are drown'd.
R.G.—11.

(The Bull-Inn, Ware, England)

My Loisl is a sweet boy
He never gets enough of kissing.

(Vienna, late 19th century—cited in Leben, Meinungen und Wirken, *by Wetti Himmlisch, 1906)*

My life, my darling, to play for a while let me beckon, this couch is our field and you as the horse we'll reckon.

(Pompeii, 79 A.D.)

No one's a handsome fellow unless he has loved.

(Pompeii, 79 A.D.)

Nothing can endure with an endless motion.
When the sun's beamed his best, he sets in ocean.
The Moon, but lately full, wanes by degrees,
and the storms of Venus fade to a gentle breeze.

(Pompeii, 79 A.D.)

Now anger is recent, now is the time to depart.
If tears appear (trust me) love revisits the heart.

(Pompeii, 79 A.D.)

Now my Sun is retired;
My Heart is all fired;
My Sylvia's lost
And I am toss'd,
Into Love's Flames,
What shall I do to gain her?
Sure something must restrain her,
Or else she'd come.
Then I'm undone.
Help me, dear Cupid,

Or I shall grow stupid;
And if you won't help me,
Then Bacchus protect me.

(The Cardinal's-Cap, Windsor, England)

Oh I wish I was a diamond upon my Lulas hand, then every time she'd wipe her ass I'd see the promised land.

(Men's room, Banff, Alberta, 1928)

Put a little love in your sex life.

Resist and love.

(New York University)

Romula tarried here with Staphylus.

(Pompeii, 79 A.D.)

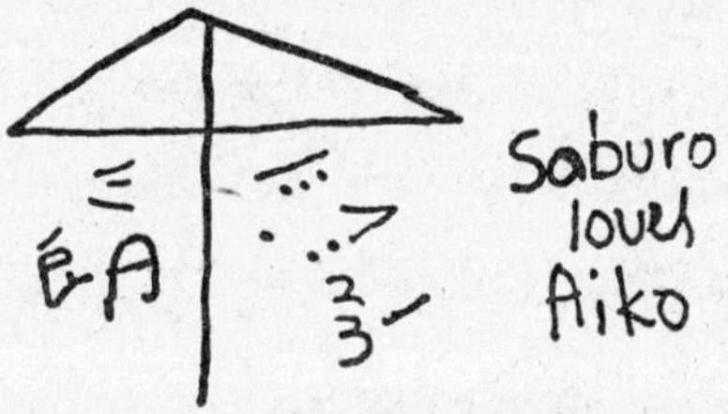

(The names of two sharing an umbrella is the Japanese equivalent of the heart and names)

Salley's my Toast from Head to Tail;
Not half so good is Toast and Ale.
J.S. Esq; of Oriel-College, Oxon.

(On a window at the Catherine-Wheel, High-Wickham, England)

Written in a woman's hand:
Since cruel Fate has robb'd me of the Youth,
For whom my Heart had hoarded all its Truth,
I'll ne'er love more, dispairing e'er to find,
Such Constancy and Truth amongst Mankind.
Feb. 18. 1725.

UNDERNEATH

I kiss'd her the next Night, and she's one of the Walkers Family.
Feb. 18. 1725.

(Tavern, Fleet Street, London)

Tea is a groove
and AMT (Amphetamine) is really boss,
LSD is a trip,

Hash is too much, but
being high on love is the most precious because you don't buy it or con it or substitute.

(Ladies' room, Limelight Restaurant, New York City)

To fuck is to love again.

To the lovely Ann for one more night.

(On a lampshade in a night club called The Apartment, New York City, 1968)

To Victoria: Greetings, and may you sneeze sweetly wherever you are.

(Pompeii, 79 A.D.)

Touch not, except in love.

(Wall at 8th Street, Greenwich Village, New York City)

Understanding is the growing.
Love is the fruit.

(New York University, 1972)

Vivius Restitutus slept here all on his own and longed for his Urbana.

(Pompeii, 79 A.D.)

What do you do if you love someone who does not give a damn about you?

UNDERNEATH

Knee him in the balls, he'll soon care.

UNDERNEATH

Girls the only way to get over him is to contract a fatal disease.

UNDERNEATH

Find someone 10 years younger than he and you.

(Ladies' room, Ninth Circle Restaurant, New York City)

What might happen to the world if for one generation we did not teach our children to hate?

(California Rehabilitation Center for female drug addicts, Norco, 1970)

What's this, my Eyes? You draw me into Fire.
And its not water down your cheeks you pour.
Tears cannot quench my flaring-up desires

They waste my soul and burn my bones the more.
Tiburtinus composed these.

(Pompeii, 79 A.D.)

When Daizies gay, and Violets blue,
And Cowslips with their yellow Hue,
And Lady's Smocks of Silver white,
Paint all the Meadows with Delight,
Then shall I meet my charming Fair,
On ouzy Banks to take the Air;
There shall we taste delicious Love,
Equal to what is known Above.
R.T. April 14. 1716.

(The Crown, at Harlow, England)

The Imorato

When dull and melancholy,
I rove to charming Dolly,
Whose Sweetness doth so charm me,
And wanton Tricks so warm me,
That quite dissolv'd in Love,
No Trouble then I prove,
But am as truly blest
Upon her panting Breast,
As if to me she brought
All for which Caesar fought:
For I, like Anthony,
With Beauty would be free,
Altho' again't shou'd cost
The Price of Empire lost.

(On a window, Twickenham, England)

When with Phillis toying,
Eager for enjoying,
What Muse can say
How sweet our Play,
What Numbers tell
The Joys we feel?
Happy Lovers only know
Bliss unmix'd with any Woe.

(On a window of a certain lady of pleasure's lodgings in Bow Street, England)

The Ambitious when rais'd to the Summit of Power,
In the Midst of their Joy fear that Fortune may lower;
The Miser, who Thousands has heap'd in his Chest,
In the Midst of Riches is never at rest.
And the Heroe, whose Bosom his Glory still warms,
In the Midst of his Conquests fears the Change of his Arms.
But the Lover, whose Fondness his Hours doth employ,
In the Midst of her Charms knows no End of his Joy.

Then quit Hopes of rising,
And Riches despising,
Leave the Camp and the Court
For Love's pleasing Sport;
By experience you'll know,
Love's Pleasures still flow.
Un-embitter'd with Care, and untinctur'd with Woe.

AN ANSWER:

You sure were full of Folly,
When in the Praise of Dolly,
You wrote your am'rous Ditty,
Which sure deserves her Pity.
Since plainly it doth prove,
Your Brain is crack'd with Love;
Who else would talk of giving
An Empire for a —
When Twenty will down
Each for a Silver Crown,
And thank you when they've done.

(On adjacent window panes in a brothel in London)

Whoever has a mind to hinder lovers' way
Let him the Zephyrs bind or running water stay.

(Pompeii, 79 A.D.)

Whoever speaks of love destroys love.

(Nanterre, May, 1968)

Why does free love cost so much?

Would I could clasp you, with small arms round your neck,
and press my kisses on your tender lips,
Go then, poppet, confide your joys to the winds.
Believe me, the nature of men is light.
Often I've woken in the desperate depths of night thinking things over with a sigh.
Many whom Fortune has thrust up on high
she suddenly harries, they slip and fall in pain
So Venus, mingling the sudden bodies of lovers,
parts them again.

(Pompeii, 79 A.D.)

You've the power but not the wish; why in joy delay?
You lean on hope and bid back yesterday?
You force me live without you, force me to die?
Someday you'll be glad you didn't crucify me.
What hope has snatched, hope surely returns the lover . . .

(Pompeii, 79 A.D.)

LUCE, HENRY R. (1898–1967)

The wages of Luce living is death.

(Men's room, Time & Life building, New York City)

LUTHER, MARTIN (1483–1546)

(Note: Luther was afflicted with constipation and addressed himself to that subject in his writings)

He who has trouble defecating should call Martin Luther.

(Men's room, Langenau in Silesia—cited in Anthropophyteia, *Vol. 6, 1909)*

The patron saint of him who shits, this role Dr. Martin Luther fits.

(Men's room, Breslau—cited in Anthropophyteia, *Vol. 6, 1909)*

LYND, STAUGHTON C. (1929–)

Lynd not Lyndon.

M

McCARTHY, EUGENE (1916–   )

Bobby Kennedy is sex, but Eugene McCarthy is love.

McCARTNEY, PAUL (1942–   )

I am 33 years old, I love John Lennon.
I wish I had eyebrows like Paul McCartney.

(Ladies' room, Ninth Circle Restaurant, New York City, 1965)

McGOVERN, GEORGE (1922–   )

Don't blame me, I'm from Massachusetts.

(Various walls in Boston, December, 1972; comment on snarled peace negotiations with Hanoi; McGovern promised immediate peace and Massachusetts voted for him in Presidential Election)

McGovern cannot govern
Nixon cannot cope
Wallace in a wheel chair
Is still the nation's hope.

(Construction fence, Trenton, pre-Election, 1972)

MACHIAVELLI, NICCOLO (1469–1527)

Machiavelli is a goddam neo-classicist.

McLUHAN, MARSHALL (1911–)

Marshall McLuhan is print-oriented.

McNAMARA, ROBERT (1916–)

Back Mac.

UNDERNEATH IN LIPSTICK

Lock up McNamara and throw away the Ky.

(Boston, 1967)

Mac the knife.

(Someone closed the letter c and it "became "Mao the Knife")

MAGAZINES

Billy Graham is the religious editor of Time.

(Lion's Head, New York City)

Collier's lives!

(Subway, New York City)

God is dead.
—Time
Time is dead.
—God
God and Time are dead.
—Bill Graham
God is Time.
—Dead

(Ladies' room, Lion's Head, New York City)

The following was written on Time *magazine advertising poster:*
The Literary Digest was RIGHT!

MAHLER, GUSTAV (1860–1911)

Mahler was a great painter.

MAILER, NORMAN (1923–)

Norman Mailer can't make the middleweight limit.

(Cited by Jim Moran, columnist, Chicago Daily News, *May 27, 1967)*

Norman Mailer is the master of the single entendre.

(Ladies' room, Limelight Restaurant, New York City)

MALE CHAUVINISM

Damn Molley H—for her pride,
She'll suffer none but Lords to ride:
But what the devil should I care,
Since I can find another mare.

(Hampton Court, England, 1708)

My father was openminded. He gave my mother permission to vote for liberals.

(Wall, Helsinki, 1969)

Princeton women are just men who worked their balls off!

UNDERNEATH

This is just another case of P.U. male chauvinism.

UNDERNEATH

Typical co-ed reaction.

(Laundry room, Princeton University, 1971)

Woman is like a pig,
All the parts are good,
It goes well with all sauces.

(Café, Paris, 1966)

A woman's like a piano, if she's not upright she's grand.

(De Pauw University, Greencastle, Ind.)

Women should be obscene and not heard.

(Cedar Tavern, New York City, also on a button)

MALEDICTION

Book you.

(On various walls)

Chius, I hope your piles are chafed once more that they may burn worse than they've burnt before.

(Pompeii, 79 A.D.)

Crescens, if someone lures my girl to meet him, on far-off mountaintops a bear will eat him.

(Pompeii, 79 A.D.)

Deck Morris if you see this . . . am after you for the dirty deal you pulled on me in K.C. Joe.

(Railway station, Grinnell, Ia., 1931)

Dirty is only in the mind, so fuck you.

(Men's toilet, Newport Jazz Festival, 1967)

F.T.Q. [*Fuck the Queen*]

UNDERNEATH

F.T.P. [*Fuck the Pope*]

(Various walls, Belfast, Ireland, 1971)

Fuque you.

UNDERNEATH

Class huh?

(Wall, New York City)

I don't mean to be old-fashioned or sentimental but fuck you.

(IRT subway, New York City, 1971)

If you can read this . . . Fuck you!

(Men's room, University of California at Berkeley—written in extremely fine print)

May you be nailed to the cross.

(Baths, Pompeii, 79 A.D.)

Need a lift? Stick a jack up your ass.

(Men's toilet, Men's faculty lounge, Hunter College, New York City)

Phuque ewe.

Servilius loves another girl, may he never have the means of doing anything.

(Pompeii, 79 A.D.—written by a former sweetheart who wishes Servilius to be impotent)

Servillus is in love, I hope he doesn't get a chance at all—
Servillus, you low-down kisser.

(Pompeii, 79 A.D.)

Up against the wall, Fathersucker.

(Men's room, Engineering building, University of Maryland, 1972)

Who wants my girl to do me a bad turn—
let him with love on desert mountains burn.

(Pompeii, 79 A.D.)

MAN

What is man? A clod of earth
colored with red ink;
his hole is big as a dollar
and in front hangs his rifle.
Under it hangs the powder bag,
filled with two cartridges,
and behind is the shooting place,
where the cannon thunders.

(Germany, 1894)

MAO TSE-TUNG (1893-)

Don't dispare [*sic*]
Mao's there.

(The Exit Coffee House, New York City)

How now brown Mao?

(Co-ed toilet, Alternate U., New York City)

Mac the knife.

(Someone closed the letter c and it became "Mao the Knife")

Mao's wife is an Oriyentah.

Mao Tse-tung plays Monopoly.

MARIJUANA, *see also* DRUG ADDICTION

All flesh is grass.
—Isaiah

UNDERNEATH

Smoke a friend today.

Antioch is going to pot.

UNDERNEATH

It's a grass root problem.

(Antioch College, Yellow Springs, Ohio)

Be all you can be . . . WEED!

(Library staff lounge, Fort Belvoir, Va.—cited in American Library Association Bulletin, *April, 1969)*

Burn pot, not people.

(On various walls, also on a button)

Buy Pot Art.

(Men's room, Blind Lemon Pub, Berkeley, Cal.)

The Devil says: legalize abortion, pot, homosexuality.

(IRT subway, New York City)

Equal rights for heads.

(Ladies' room, Max's Kansas City Restaurant, New York City, also on a button)

Fly half fare—cut rate grass.

(Wall, St. Mark's Place, New York City)

For me it's the green grass of home.

UNDERNEATH

The grass is greener in Tiajuana.

UNDERNEATH

Who wants *green* grass.

(Men's room, Columbia University)

Free Pot . . . TH 5-8000 Ext. 201

(The Mediterranium Trattoria, Berkeley, Cal.—the number is for the Berkeley Police Department Vice Squad)

A friend in need is a pest get rid of him.

UNDERNEATH

But a friend with weed is a friend indeed.

(IRT subway, New York City—the second statement is also on a button)

Give the grass a chance.

God grows good grass.

(University of Michigan)

Grass is a gas.

Grass is nature's way of saying, 'high.'

(IND subway, New York City, 1970)

Head power.

(On various walls, also on a button)

Jesus was a "head."

(Lexington Avenue subway, New York City)

John the Baptist was a head.

LSD is the best. Pot and Hatch are the second best.

UNDERNEATH

I think you mean "hash."

(Ladies' room, Max's Kansas City Restaurant, New York City)

Legalize pot!
legalize heroin!
legalize outlaws!
legalize me!
and legalization.

(Ladies' room, Limelight Restaurant, New York City)

Let's get naked and smoke.

(On various walls, also on a button)

Love is essence.

UNDERNEATH

But pot is best.

UNDERNEATH

Essence stinks.

(Ladies' room, Max's Kansas City Restaurant, New York City)

Marijuana may be settled by a joint meeting of Congress.

Mickey Mouse smokes pot.

No cannabism!

Peanut butter is better than pot.

(Free Store Theatre, New York City, also on a button)

People who live in grass houses shouldn't be stoned.

(Cornell University, 1970)

Please hemp me.

(On various walls, also on a button)

Pot—don't knock it unless you've tried it.

(Men's room, University of New Hampshire)

Pot is a hobby not a habit.

(Ladies' room, Max's Kansas City Restaurant, New York City)

Pot, peace, pussy, perversion.

Sunshine and very many mosquitoes.

High grass but nothing to smoke.

(Men's room, Germany, 1968)

There is a plot against pot.

The Unicorn Tapestry smokes pot.

(Washington Square Arch, Greenwich Village)

Viva Sativa.

The whole world is going to pot.

MARRIAGE

Abolish marriage!

(Wolfie's Restaurant, Brooklyn, 1969)

This was wrote somewhere; and means something, if you can find it out:

A Beauty like her's whose Charms I now sing,
Ne'er sparkled in vain in the Box or the Ring;
No Youth of Distinction who gaz'd on her Eyes,
E'er retir'd, but he left her his Heart as her Prize.
Vain are all their Endeavours, for still the coy Maid.
At the Mention of Marriage, look'd strangely afraid.
Nor e'er thought of yielding—until not long since.
Eluding dull Ties—she was join'd to a P—

Boys marry virgins, men marry women.

(Ladies' room, New York University)

Contracts are agreements between businessmen who don't trust each other, so what's marriage?

UNDERNEATH

Against women's nature.

On a Butcher's marrying a Tanner's Daughter at Reading:

A fitter Match there never could have been,
Since here the Flesh is wedded to the Skin.

Fuck marriage, not men.

(Wall, New York City)

A good Wife is like a Turtle that bills and cooes,
and turns up her T—l to her Husband.

(On a window in a great house in Lincoln's-Inn-Fields, England)

Here in their last Bed.
The loving Alice rests with her Love Ned.

UNDERNEATH (BY A CAMBRIDGE SCHOLAR)

Viator fifte! ecce miraculum!
Vir & Uxor, hic non litigant.
[*Which in English may stand thus:*]
Behold a Bed, where without Strife,
There rests a Man, and eke his Wife.

(On a Tomb, England, early 18th century)

On Marriage:
If 'tis to marry when the Knot is ty'd,
Why then they marry, who at Tyburn ride.
And if that Knot, 'till Death is loos'd by none,
Why then to marry, and be hang'd's all one.

(On a window, Tunbridge, England)

Marriage in Days of old has liken'd been
Unto a public Feast, or Revel Rout,
Where those who are without would fain get in,
And those who are within would fain get out.

(Tuns, Cambridge—written in pencil on the wall)

Marriage is a weird trip. You have to let yourselves love and live together.

(Ladies' room, Boston, 1972)

Marriage legalizes rape.

Tom of Bedlam's Sentiments on Marriage:

One ask'd a Madman, if a Wife he had,
A Wife! quoth he,—No!—I'm not quite so mad.

There are three crosses at your door, hang up your wife and you'll count four.

(On a window of the Three Crosses Inn, England—Written by Jonathan Swift, 1667–1745)

This Dance foretells that Couple's Life,
Who mean to dance as Man and Wife;
As here, they'll first with Vigour set,
Give Hands, and turn whene'er they meet;
But soon will quit their former Track,
Cast off, and end in Back to Back.

(The Apollo, the large dancing room in the Devil Tavern, written when some were engaged in a particular country dance)

Wives are unpaid labor.

MARX, KARL (1818–1883)

For Hegel contradiction was a moment in totality. For Marx totality was a moment in contradiction.

(Men's room, New York University, 1969)

On a poster that read "Trust in God, read the Bible and go to Heaven," the following was written:
Trust in Mao, read Marx and go to China.

MASOCHISM

Come on over to the S and M side.

(S and M stands for sadism and masochism)

I am a masochist—please spindle, fold or mutilate.

Masochists: you're only hurting yourselves.

Slave needs master—call 333-.

Who will make me bleed till I shoot?

(Toilet, London)

MASTURBATION

Aristoteles Onanis.

(Wall, Helsinki, 1970)

Be a man, not a fool
Pull the chain, not your tool.

Confucius say 'he who masturbates pulls boner.'

(Men's room, 125th Street ferry, N.J. side, 1940)

Do not climax in this bathroom.

(Ladies' room, Brooklyn College)

Don't play with the rifle, it might go off too easily.

(Men's room, Riesengebirge—cited in Anthropophyteia, *Vol. 6, 1909)*

Hands across the sea is a long way to COME.

(Vietnam, 1970)

The hell with whores and tramps, we'll keep on rubbing.

(Men's room, Germany, 1965)

Here anyone may masturbate but don't smear the semen on the door knob.

(Men's room, Germany, 1910)

Here was a 'Pothecary's Wife,
Who never lov'd her Spouse in all her Life;
And for want of his Handle,
Made use of a Candle;
—Light as a Feather
To bring Things together.
S.C. 1710.

UNDERNEATH

Thou Fool, 'twas done for want of Sense,
I tickl'd her Concupiscence:
And that is enough to save her Credit.
S.B. 1712.

UNDERNEATH

From the Story above,
The Girls that love,
Have learn'd the Use of Candles;
And since that, by Jove,
And the God of Love,
We have lost the Use of Handles.
W.S.—pe, Feb. 2. 1714.

(Wall, The King's Arms, Salisbury, England)

Here's to the girl who was afraid of men
Fucked herself with a fountain pen
The pen broke and the ink went wild
And she gave birth to a colored child.

(Grants Pass, Ore., 1928)

I come here to get ahold of myself.

(Men's room, University of Colorado)

I masterbated here 12/15/69.

UNDERNEATH

Shame on you, a post-graduate student and unable to spell.

UNDERNEATH

I'm a faculty member.

(Men's room, Post-Graduate Center, New School for Social Research, New York City)

I think I've fallen in love with my hand.
Don't you wish you were ambidextrous?

(Vietnam, 1971)

If love gives you trouble turn to manual labor.

(Men's room, Germany)

A commercially printed sign read, "Instructions for removing toilet seat covers: First pull up, then pull down." The words "removing seat covers" were crossed out and substituted was the word:
Masturbation.

(Penny's Department Store, Phoenix, February 1, 1965)

J— plays with himself when he shits.

UNDERNEATH

Plays with his what?

UNDERNEATH

With his clit, what else?

(Co-ed toilet, East Village Other, *1970)*

Jack off and get more pimples.

(Cedar City, Utah, 1928)

The law forbids boys. Sixtus forbids bawdy houses.
What then is to be done? Your hand
will have to be your girl friend!

Little Miss Moffett plays with herself.

(Scholtz's Beer Garden, Austin)

Masturbate on Master Charge.

(In a sperm bank in Arizona where Master Charge cards are honored for the fee for storage, 1972)

Masturbation makes the body weak, but fucking is another matter.

(Men's room, Riesengebirge— cited in Anthropophyteia, *Vol. 6, 1909)*

Minorbation is good during a depression.
(Co-ed toilet, Alternate U., New York City)

More than three shakes is masturbation.
(Toilet, Buenos Aires)

More than two shakes and you're playing with it.

Never pull off tomorrow what you can pull off today.
(Lion's Head, New York City)

The new cinematic emporium, is not just a super sensorium,
But a highly effectual, heterosexual mutual masturbatorium.
(Men's room, Princeton University, 1970)

No beating in this area.
(Men's room, Hunter College, New York City, 1972)

Now I'm going to take the thing in hand.
(Cited in Anthropophyteia, *Vol. 9, 1912)*

One orgasm in the bush is worth two in the hand.

One thing about masturbation, you don't have to look your best.

Only to satisfy my lust do I masturbate but without knowing how much harm I do to my poor brain.
(Trujillo, Peru, 1890)

Other degenerates sign here
Jack Hoff, shithouse poet
Ivan Jackoff.
(Cedar City, Utah, 1928)

Play the music slowly
And softly shut the door
For many a jack-off baby
Lies dead upon the floor.
(Tower Falls Camp, Yellowstone National Park)

Roses are red, violets are blue
I've had a finger, but never a screw.
(Ladies' room, White Pine, Ontario)

Self-love is first, so masturbate.

(University of California at San Diego, 1971)

Sonnet Written in a Bathroom:
Some come here to urinate
And some come here to difecate [*sic*]
But I sit down upon this seat
And then I start to beat my meat
When I come within this stall
I splatter sperm upon the wall
And then it slips upon the floor
And seeps from underneath the door.
Some people tell me that I'm foul,
That I should splatter in a towel;
But I just tell them that their gall
Will not keep my sperm off the wall.

UNDERNEATH

This is really not a sonnet,
Till you add a couplet on it.

UNDERNEATH

Should be spelled defecate but what do you
want good grammar or good taste?

(Men's room, Princeton University, 1970)

Some come here to sit and think
Others come here to shit and stink
But I come here to pull my dink
Cause Sacramento's fucking is on the blink.

(Sacramento, Cal., 1928)

They laughed when I sat down to play—how did I know that bathroom door was open.

This is a teepee
For you to peepee
Not a wigwam
To beat your tomtom.

Wer't not for Whims, Candles, and Carrots,
Young Fellows Things might ride in Chariots.
Tom Long, July 17.

UNDERNEATH

Thank Heaven for all those Helps to Nature,
Or else poor P— could get no Quarter.

(Three Pigeons, Brentford, England, early 18th century)

What kind of nonsense are you
doing with your thick one?
Do it rather with your paw.
That is now the style.

(Ladies' room, Thüringen—cited in Anthropophyteia, *Vol. 7, 1910)*

Whoever masturbates in church will soon be ordained a priest.

(Men's room, Prussia-Silesia—cited in Anthropophyteia, *Vol. 7, 1910)*

MATHEMATICS

$$\text{s.d.s.} = ds^2 = \tfrac{1}{2}\ as^2 = \tfrac{1}{2}\ \text{ass.}$$

$$(\text{ice})^2 = d\ (\text{ice}) = \text{ice}^3$$

$$\frac{d(\text{cabin})}{\text{cabin}} = \log \text{cabin}$$

(Men's room, Princeton University, 1970)

The square root of 69 is 8 something.

(Men's room, Bernard Baruch College, New York City, 1970)

There's is absolutely no cause for alarm.

$$Se^x = f(u^n)$$

(Laundry room, Princeton University, 1971)

MATURITY

Maturity is the process of exchanging an old idea for a young one.

(San Francisco State College, 1970)

You are fast becoming what you are going to be.

MAXIMS, see PROVERBS

MEGALOMANIA

Taki 183.

(Written all over New York City; The New York Times *on July 21, 1971 wrote a story unraveling the mystery of Taki, a youth who lived on 183rd Street; his notoriety was a contributing factor to the ensuing blight of names scrawled with spray cans)*

Taki 181—I moved.

MEIR, GOLDA (1898–)

Golda—get out of Arab Land.

Golda the Terrible.

MELVILLE, HERMAN (1819–1891)

Herman Melville eats blubber.

(Stuyvesant High School, New York City, also on a button)

Moby Dick was a honkie.

(Library staff lounge, Fort Belvoir, Va.—cited in American Library Association Bulletin, *April, 1969)*

MENSTRUATION

The apple is sour, the apple is sweet,
The girl has nosebleeds between her feet.

(Café-Haus Mohr, Ostrau, 1910)

I don't think much of fucking. I do it with pleasure only during menstruation.

(Ladies' room, Prussia-Silesia—cited in Anthropophyteia, *Vol. 7, 1910)*

MENTAL HYGIENE

Birdie, Birdie on the sill,
With the pretty yellow bill,
First I fed you crusts of bread,
Then I smashed your fuckin' head.

UNDERNEATH

You need a psychologist before it's too late.

(Men's room, Rutgers University)

Call again and bring your butterfly net.

Chico has mental health.

(Wall near New York Academy of Medicine, 1957)

Dingbat Power!

(Ladies' room, Lion's Head, New York City, 1972)

Freak freely.

Have a fit today.

(Men's room, The Flick Restaurant, New York City, 1968)

Honor thy analyst.

I don't want to be normal.

In an insane world the only sane men are crucified, shot, jailed or classified as insane themselves.

(Le Metro Caffe Espresso, New York City)

It's hard to see the picture when you're inside the frame.

(Mental Institution, Chicago)

Make your psychosis work for you.

Oh to be out of my catatonic trance, now that April's here.

Repeal inhibition.

Stamp out mental health.

(Also on a button)

Support mental health like Crazy!

Support mental health or I'll kill you.

(The Riviera, New York City, also on button)

MENTALLY HANDICAPPED

Help retarded children or I'll kill you.

Help support retarded unicellular animals!

UNDERNEATH

What about multicellular organisms, you idiot you.

(Men's room, New York University, 1969)

The following was written on a poster that said, "If the President finds time to help the mentally retarded, what are you doing that's so important?":

Working to get them out of Washington.

METAPHYSICS

Me within all,
All within me.

UNDERNEATH

Are you pregnant?

(Kettle of Fish Bar & Restaurant, New York City)

There are no answers, only mysteries.

(Le Metro Caffe Espresso, New York City)

We are all one, unite with outer and inner space.

UNDERNEATH

Only on the subway.

(Paradox Restaurant, New York City)

We are all too much.

(Paradox Restaurant, New York City)

Why?

UNDERNEATH

Why not?

(Ladies' room, Mt. Sinai Hospital, New York City, 1968)

Yang and Yin shall be one.

Yes is the ultimate answer to all questions.

(Le Metro Caffe Espresso, New York City)

MEXICO

Long live Mexico, sons of the one who has been fucked.

(Mexico City)

MILLER, HENRY (1891-)

Henry Miller is a virgin.

(Free Library of Philadelphia, 1968)

MILNE, A. A. (1882–1956)

The only thing worse than Winnie's Pooh is Gomer's Pyle.

(Mooney's, San Francisco, 1970)

MINORITIES

Equality for all minorities!

UNDERNEATH

You dunce—by equalizing all minorities, you thereby destroy their identities as minorities, thereby making them no longer minorities.

UNDERNEATH

Semantic bullshit and fourth term fallacy.

UNDERNEATH

You anti-Semantic motherfucker.

UNDERNEATH

Semen tick bullshit.
Some maniac bullshit.

UNDERNEATH

Register all puns.
Semantic Bullshit.

UNDERNEATH

You anti-semantic mother-fucker.

UNDERNEATH

Semen tick bullshit.

UNDERNEATH

Some manic bullshit.

UNDERNEATH

Just bullshit: all of it.

UNDERNEATH

Register all puns.

UNDERNEATH

Puns don't kill people, people kill people.

UNDERNEATH

Everybody must get stoned—now.

(Co-ed toilet, East Village Other, *1970)*

What man is not a member of a minority?

(San Francisco State College, 1970)

MINORU, YAMASAKI (1912–)

Yamasaki is strictly Shinto Gothic.

(Yale University—written in Japanese; refers to a piece of architecture on the campus designed by Yamasaki)

MISANTHROPY

"Ain't you ugly."

(On gum machine mirror in IRT subway, New York City)

Fuck everybody! Why discriminate?

(IND subway, New York City)

George Orwell was an optimist.

(Men's room, East Village Other, *1969)*

Hi ugly world!

Homo homini lupus.
[*Man is a wolf to his fellow man.*]

UNDERNEATH

And I'm the Big Bad Wolf!

UNDERNEATH

Just remember that Walt Disney created you.

(Wall, Helsinki, 1969)

The human race is fixed.

I hated my siblings so why the fuck should I call anybody brother or sister.

I protest everything including my existence and especially yours.

(IRT subway, New York City, 1971)

The more you cultivate people, the more you turn up clods.

(Wall, Ann Arbor, Mich., 1970)

Retain your humanity. Cash it when the price goes up.

(Bates College, Lewiston, Me.)

Stamp out poverty, not people.

UNDERNEATH

Stamp out poverty and people.

Stupidity is alive and well in humanity.

This morning I stuck my cock out of the window and fucked the world.

(Subway toilet, New York City)

True Hate.

(Wall, Chicopee Falls, Mass.)

We hate all people, regardless of race, creed or color.

The World is full of Fools and Asses,
To see them not—retire and break your Glasses.

(Written on a looking glass in the Rue Boucharie, Paris)

MISCEGENATION

All white women worship afro cock.

UNDERNEATH

Fuck you nigger ape.

(Back of seat on 6th Avenue bus, New York City, 1969)

I love black cocks.

(Ladies' room, West End Bar & Grill, New York City)

I want a big black dick.

UNDERNEATH

It's quality not quantity that counts.

(Ladies' room, City College of New York City, 1969)

If you think black is unique and white is right, wait until you have a Puerto Rican.

(Ladies' room, West Side, New York City—cited by Lindsy Van Gelder in New York Post, *March 28, 1972)*

MITCHELL, JOHN (1913–   )

Nixon's army, Mitchell's law ain't gonna stop the people's war.

(Subway, New York City, 1970)

MONDRIAAN, PIETER (1872–1944)

Mondriaan is square!

MONEY

Cinderella married for money.

(On various walls, also on a button)

Don't wait to be told . . . you need gold.

(Antioch College, Yellow Springs, Ohio—takeoff on the ad: "Don't wait to be told, you need Palmolive Gold")

Earn, Baby, Earn.

(Men's room, brokerage house, Palm Beach, Fla.)

The golden age was the age when gold did not reign. The golden calf is always mud.

(Paris, May, 1968)

Here's my advice. Share out the Common Chest for in our coffers piles of money rest.

(Pompeii, 79 A.D.)

Money can't buy happiness or very much of anything else today.

Various religions, several tenets hold;
Yet all one God acknowledge, which is *Gold.*

(Uxbridge, England, 1719)

When full of Pence, I was expensive,
And now I've none, I'm always pensive.

UNDERNEATH

Then be at no Expence
And you'll have no suspence.
W.T.

(On a window, Rumford, England)

MOONEY, TOM (1883–1942)

Independence for Puerto Rico.

UNDERNEATH

Free Tom Mooney.

(IRT subway, New York City, 1970)

MOSES

God is dead
—Nietzche [*sic*]
Nietzche is dead
—God

UNDERNEATH

Who cares?
—Moses
Me.
—God
Jesus saves, but Moses invests.

(Popular wall inscription and often quoted)

Jesus saves; Moses invests; but only Buddha pays dividends.

MOSES, GRANDMA (1860–1961)

Grandma Moses loves Picasso.

MOTHERHOOD

All that I am my mothers made me.

UNDERNEATH

I made them, too.

(Engagé Coffee House, New York City)

Children—beat your mother while she is young.

(Wall, London)

Machines are made by men and thee.
But only Moms can make a me.

(Men's room, The Blue Unicorn Coffee House, San Francisco)

Motherhood is too unprofessional.

(Children's room, Teaneck Public Library, N. J., 1971)

Parents are fuck-ups, especially Aquarian mothers.

(Co-ed toilet, Free Store Theatre, New York City)

Songs I've learned at my mother's knee and other low joints.

(Ladies' room, Greenwich Village restaurant)

Visit your mother today, maybe she hasn't had any problems lately.

You'll never be the man your mother was.
signed A Negro.

(The Exit Coffee House, New York City)

MOVING PICTURES

Long live the Cisco Kid.

(Engagé Coffee House, New York City)

The new cinematic emporium is not just a super sensorium,
But a highly effectual, heterosexual mutual masturbatorium.

(Men's room, Princeton University, 1970)

Ratso Rizzo will rise.

(New York University, 1969—refers to Dustin Hoffman's role in Midnight Cowboy*)*

Rose-bud lives!

(The name of the sleigh in the movie Citizen Kane*)*

Today Hollywood tomorrow the world!

MOZART, WOLFGANG AMADEUS (1756–1791)

The following was written on a poster advertising an art school that said, "At 35 Gauguin worked in a bank. It's never too late":

At 35 Mozart was dead.

Don Giovanni loves

Mozart forever.

Mozart refreshes best.

(Construction fence near Juilliard Music School, New York City)

MUSIC, *see also* OPERA

The flower generation has a tin ear.

Folk you.

Hummingbirds never remember the words to songs.

I deny all the gods, all of em. He wins, He wins in the All-out Musical Contest, Tal does, the lute-player he plays like Apollo. I'm only a flute-player, of course I lose. But he's a camelopard (a giraffe. He must have had a long neck) (She added something of him being) an Achilles for renown. But me I'm in a passion. Well, Vulcan is the medicine.

(Pompeii, 79 A.D.)

Muzzle Muzak.

Painting, love-making and singing are three things which cannot be forced.

(Cited in Anthropophyteia, *Vol. 9, 1912)*

MYTHOLOGY

Aphrodite sucks.

(Paradox Restaurant, New York City)

Apollo loves Artemis.

("55" Bar, New York City)

Beware of the Chimera.

Clytemnaestra lives in Agamemnon.

(Lexington Avenue subway, New York City)

I am an atheist. I don't believe in Zeus.

(Construction wall, Philadelphia, 1969)

Leda loves swans.

Leda was for the birds.

(Ladies' room, Boston, 1972)

Old Orpheus tickled his Harp so well,
That he tickled Eurydice out of Hell,
With a Twing come Twang, and a Twing come Twant; but
Some say Eurydice was a Scold,
Therefore the Devil of her took hold,
With a Twing come Twant, &c.
S.S. 1714.

(On a Window in Hell, near Westminster Hall, London)

St. George to save a Maid, a Dragon Slew,
A gallant Action, grant the Thing be true.
Yet some say there's no Dragons.—Nay, 'tis said,
There's no St. George—Pray Heav'n there be a Maid.

(Under the George-Inn Sign at Farnham, England)

Sisyphus ~~digs~~ pushes rocks.

(Limelight Restaurant, New York City)

Zeus gave Prometheus the bird.

(University of Michigan)

Zeus loves Ganymede.

(Lion's Head, New York City)

N

NAPOLEON I (1769–1821)

There is where Napoleon tore his Bonaparte.

NARCOTICS, see DRUG ADDICTION

NASSER, GAMAL ABDEL (1918–1970)

Long live Nasser.

UNDERNEATH

The only Arab Zionist.

(West End Bar & Restaurant, New York City)

NATIONALISM

Copper for the people of Chile

(Wall, Santiago, Chile, 1970)

Quebec will be free!

(Subway, Boston)

Up the Queen. No Pope here.

UNDERNEATH

No Queen here. Up the Pope. Up Celtic.

(Wall, Belfast, 1969—written, alternately, by Protestant and Catholic partisans in Northern Ireland; Celtic is the name of a Catholic soccer team)

NAVY, *see* ARMED FORCES

NAZISM

Don't believe the words of the Germans; they are liars.

(Prison, Dijon, 1944, during German occupation in France)

Don't let your courage fail you,
Stick your ass out of the window,
Shows eggs, sausage and ham!

(Various toilet walls in Nazi Germany when Goering promised the people many things)

The landlady also had an S.A. man
Who stood close to Captain Röhm
In order to please him
He had himself tattooed "Heil Hitler"
On his ass hole.

The men from hard Bavaria have swastikas on their testicles.

(Men's room, Germany)

My dear Victor Lutze
Fuck a cunt
Never fuck an ass
Otherwise you'll end up in a sarcophagus.

(Hitler had Röhm executed, based on charges of homosexuality; Viktor Lütze was his successor)

NECROPHILIA

Legalize necrophilia.

NEW YORK CITY

Brooklyn is alive and somewhere in New York.

Canarsie is a hot bed.

(IND subway, New York City)

The following was written on a poster that said, "Did you make New York dirty today?":
New York makes ME dirty every day.

Free the Panther 21.
UNDERNEATH
Free the 8 million New Yorkers.
(Construction fence, New York City, 1970)

Greenwich Village has moved to Williamsburgh.

John Lindsay for President in 1972.
UNDERNEATH
He ruined New York City he can do the same for the country.
(Construction fence, New York City, 1971)

La Guardia ruined N.Y.C.
(Club Lunch Restaurant, New York City, 1967)

N.Y.C. Spic Coon jungle.
(Stanley's Bar, New York City)

New York is a summer vegetable.
(Takeoff on a Lindsay Administration slogan: "New York is a summer festival")

New York is fucking itself to death.
UNDERNEATH
Not to mention New Yorkers.
(Lion's Head, New York City)

Staten Island lives!!
(Kettle of Fish Bar & Restaurant, New York City)

NEWSPAPERS

The following was written on a poster advertising The New York Times:
Coons read kike N.Y. Post

The following was written on a poster that said, "I got my job through The New York Times":
So did Castro.

The Journal-American is a Commie newspaper.

(Subway, New York City, 1956)

The following were written on a poster that said, "Some people don't read The Daily News":

Thank God!
They wipe their as–es with it.
That's why they buy the NEWS.
They make love instead.
They just look at the pictures.
They line their garbage cans with it!

NEWTON, ISAAC (1642–1727)

Isaac Newton had pull.

NIETZSCHE, FRIEDRICH (1844–1900)

God is dead.
—Nietzche [*sic*]
Nietzche is dead.
—God

God is dead.
—Nietzche [*sic*]
Nietzche is dead.
—God
They're both dead.
—Odin

God is dead.
—Nietzche [*sic*]
Nietzche is dead.
—God

UNDERNEATH

Who cares?
—Moses
Me—God.

Nietzche is pietzche.

NIGHTINGALE, FLORENCE (1820–1910)

Florence Nightingale was a pan handler.

NIXON, RICHARD M. (1913–)

Dick and Spiro add up to zero.

(Men's room, Bates College, Lewiston, Me.)

Dick Nixon, before he dicks you.

(On a bank building, Bethesda, Md., 1971)

Do you realize that if Kissinger was shot today Nixon would become President.

(Library, New York University, 1972)

Don't change dicks in the middle of a screw
Vote for Nixon in '72.

(Men's room, Palomar State College, Cal., 1971)

Every now and again Nixon is unable to conceal any longer his internal death and absence of sanity even in posed newspaper pictures!

(Fence, New York City, 1970)

Face it Nixon, insanity never has been a pleasant affiliation.

(University of California at Los Angeles, 1970)

Give Nixon time with his withdrawal program.

UNDERNEATH

Withdrawal is something Nixon's father should have done 58 years ago.

UNDERNEATH

You shithouse philosophers have all the answers.

UNDERNEATH

Better than you non thinking lifers.

(Vietnam, 1970)

How can anyone hate a President with a name like Dick?

(Men's room, Rutgers University)

How come everyone hates Nixon so much?

UNDERNEATH

1. Because he is a bum.
2. His political smile.
3. Because they know he is going to be elected again.

(Bathroom, Art Gallery, New York City, October, 1972)

The liberals got us into Vietnam, Nixon will get us out.

(Wall near Union Square, New York City, 1971)

Lick Dick.

(Ladies' room, Bernard Baruch College, New York City, 1969)

Nix on Nixon.

NI卐ON FOR DOGCATCHER

Nixon has pentagonorrhea.

(Men's room, Harvard University)

Nixon is the first president to have an ass-hole for a vice president.

UNDERNEATH

No, Eisenhower was.

(University of Michigan)

Nixon is to peace as penis is to pussy.

UNDERNEATH

No, Mary, Fucking is good!

UNDERNEATH

No—wrong analogy. Penis fucks pussy and Nixon fucks peace.

(Co-ed toilet, Alternate U., New York City)

Nixon is XYY.

(Subway, New York City, 1970—XYY [extra male chromosome] has been found to be the genetic makeup of many criminals)

Nixon to the Tombs,
People to the streets.

(Fence, 18 West 11th Street, New York City, 1970—site of building that was blown up accidentally, killing three young political bomb makers)

Nixon's army, Mitchell's law ain't gonna stop the people's war.

(Subway, New York City, 1970)

Nixon's chief contact with the real world is Spiro Agnew.

(San Francisco State College, 1970)

Richard Nixon the evil of two lessers.

(On a billboard in subway during the 1968 Humphrey-Nixon campaign)

Richard Nixon will have two cabinets—one to hide Spiro Agnew.

Shit + Beauty = Nixon + Constitution.

(University of California at Los Angeles, 1970)

Vote for Dick, he's up and coming.

(Men's room, Electric Circus, St. Mark's Place, New York City)

Whatever happened to Rosemary's baby?

UNDERNEATH

He's in the White House.

(Construction wall, Philadelphia, 1969)

Willy Brandt: don't give Nixon or Agnew political asylum in Germany.

(Deli-Plaza, New York City, 1970)

You are what you eat and Nixon eats shit.

(University of California at Los Angeles, 1972)

NIXON, TRICIA (1946–)

Tricia Nixon is a virgin.

UNDERNEATH

So is Pat.

(Ladies' room, Bernard Baruch College, New York City, 1970)

NUCLEAR POWER, see ATOMIC POWER

NUNS

I'm so horny, I'm joining a convent.

UNDERNEATH

Watch out for the lesbians there.

(Ladies' room, Bernard Baruch College, New York City, 1970)

Nuns are rarely pious,
they make out of lard and onions
a coarse peasant dish,
they stumble about in the hole.
Nuns are rarely pious.

(Convent, Germany, 1905)

Nuns—kick the habit.

(Grand Central Station, New York City, 1970)

Nuns, nuns! they're not so dumb!
If they don't get a piece from the priest
they cut off a piece of sausage and use that.
Nuns, nuns, they're not so dumb.

*(Men's room, Vienna—
Cited in* Anthropophyteia, *Vol. 5, 1908)*

Whoever wants to taste the highest delight of all should fuck a nun at least once.

*(Men's room, Prussia-Silesia—
cited in* Anthropophyteia, *Vol. 7, 1910)*

NYMPHOMANIA

Hester Prynne was a nymphomaniac.

My Dear, like a Candle,
Lights every one's Handle,
Yet loses no Bit of her own;
She will piss, and she'll kiss
Until every one hiss,

And she better had stay'd at Home.
As she lost nothing by it, she may still
remain a Light to the World.

(On a window, Salisbury, England)

A nymphomaniac is a girl who likes every man to be in different.

(Alvin's Finer Delicatessen, Detroit, 1971)

A Ramp of very noted Name,
I need not say, for all Men know her Fame,
Lascivious, as the human Race could be,
She could not see a Man, but fell in Extasy.

(The Mitre, Hampton-Court, England)

Tell me why, ye gen'rous Swains?
Tell me, ye Nymphs upon the Plains?
Why does Sylvia leave the Green?
Has she done any Thing obscene?
They all reply'd Your Sylvia's gone;
For she will do't with ev'ry one.

(The Flask, Hampstead, England)

What signifies your chattering, dearest Nancy,
And swearing d—n your Blood, to please your Fancy;
For if your Scruples find that one won't do,
Z—ds, cock, and prime, and then take two.
Captain J.F. 1729.

(On a window, York, England)

O

OBESITY

Fat will finally be in!

(New York University, 1969)

Obesity is the high-priced spread.

Obesity is *too much.*

Screwing, balling, fucking
I only do it to the fat ones.

(Germany, 1904)

OBSCENITY, *see also* PORNOGRAPHY

A dirty mind is a perpetual solace.

Fuck scatology.

Help bring F*ck into polite usage.

Let's talk dirty.

Obscenity is the crutch of the inarticulate mother-fucker.

(University of California at San Diego, 1971)

Take the four letter word out of the classroom and restore it to its rightful place. Here.

(Men's room, Greyhound bus depot)

Think dirty.

This wall is ready for any budding scatologist.

(Men's room, Rutgers University, 1969)

ODIN

God is dead.
—Nietzche [*sic*]
Nietzche is dead.
—God
They're both dead.
—Odin

OEDIPUS COMPLEX

Electra loves daddy.

(Ladies' room, Ninth Circle Restaurant, New York City)

Jesus had an Oedipus complex.

(Men's room, Telephone Company, New York City, 1969)

Oedipus was a mater violater.

(Ladies' room, Limelight Restaurant, New York City, 1965)

Oedipus was the first man to plug the generation gap.

(Men's room, Princeton University, 1970)

Public Notice: Oedipus come home, all is forgiven, Mother loves you.

(Ladies' room, Under The Stairs, Bar & Restaurant, New York City, 1972)

You think Oedipus had a problem, Adam was Eve's mother.

(Construction wall, Philadelphia, 1969)

OLD AGE, *see* AGING

OPERA

Despite many appeals such as letters, telegrams, day and night vigils, the old Metropolitan Opera House in midtown New York could not be saved. In the middle of January, 1967, demolition began. The fences around all four sides of the building were covered with graffiti. "Rock," "Rocky" are nicknames for Governor Nelson Rockefeller. The following are statements written there:

Bug the Mayor and Rocky.

Bug Rocky now!

Save the Met, call out the reserves.

Stay the execution.

Rock the Rock.

First the Met—now the Astor and Paramount $$$.

Why must everything historical and beautiful be destroyed for modern devices in this city?

Slaughter of the arts.

Your Maker will strick [*sic*] you dead if you destroy the Old Met.

The "Old Met" will not die.

UNDERNEATH

You wanna bet.

Turn Lincoln Center into an Induction Center.

Laugh Pagliacci, this is the final tragic hour.

Should we lose it—we are to blame, miracles happen when you ask for one.

I am a Philistine—who cares.

We have nothing to lose but Society.

Classic example of American dilemma.

Tho Jeanette and Nelson's voices have been silenced their memory will live on forever.

If the Old Met dies, so will a lot of the culture that has grown around this House!

The great God Tishman moves in mysterious ways.

UNDERNEATH

Not to mention devious ones too.

[*Tishman is a construction company which has put up many large office buildings.*]

We destroy the 'Soul' in order to get money with which to buy back the 'Soul.'

What is an opera?

UNDERNEATH

Opera is the combination of music and drama.

UNDERNEATH

Not a good definition otherwise comic opera would be musical comedy.

UNDERNEATH

That's what it is!

(Men's room, University of Minnesota, 1972)

OPTIMISM

As you ramble on through life, brother
Whatever be your goal
Keep your eye on the doughnut
Not upon the hole.

(Men's room, Market Diner, New York City—
a traditional wall inscription)

I am an incurable optimist who daily raises my head to the beat of human existence.

ORAGENITALISM, *see also* CUNNILINGUS, FELLATIO

Balloons are for blowing.

UNDERNEATH

Balloons who?

(Greyhound bus station, Springfield, Massachusetts)

Call Sp-1 - - - If I like your voice I'll go down on you.

The gentry prefer double entry.
The proletariat like to bury it.

Gravity is a myth; the Earth sucks.

(Men's room, Grumman Aviation, Long Island, New York)

I am a cunning linguist. I don't suck pricks.

(59th Street station, IRT subway)

I bowled a 69.

(Melrose Bowling Alleys, Phoenix, Arizona, 1965)

I like sucking.

UNDERNEATH

Get a popsicle.

UNDERNEATH

How about a dick-si-cup.

(Ladies' room, Bernard Baruch College, New York)

Joe's bicycle pump sucks!!!

Kiss it or kiss it goodbye.

Love makes the world go down.

Love sucks.

Mary Poppins sucks!

Oxygen sucks.

Polystoma sucks.
[*Polystoma (many mouthed) is a type of worm.*]

(University of Michigan, Ann Arbor)

The square root of 69 is 8 something.

(Men's room, Bernard Baruch College, New York, 1970)

Suck, don't fuck. If you're in love, oral copulation can be beautiful.

(Ladies' room, Blind Lemon bar, Berkeley, California)

Suck my idd [*sic*], kiss my ego!

(Construction fence, New York City, 1969)

Up with going down.

Vacuum cleaners suck.

(Ladies' room, Lion's Head, Greenwich Village, New York City)

White man sucks with forked tongue.

'You make out better at both ends' 69.

UNDERNEATH

Silly.

ORGY

Daisies of the world unite; you have nothing to lose but your chains.

(Ladies' room, Vassar College)

The more the merrier.

Let me suck you and your wife. I'll fuck your mother for nothing.

(Men's room, 125th Street IRT subway station, New York City, 1940)

My wife and I picked up a hitchhiker here. He fucked her in the back seat and then I fucked him in the ass. We like to travel around and pick up people for a good time.

(Route 95, Maine, 1971)

ORWELL, GEORGE (1903–1950)

George Orwell was an optimist.

(Men's room, East Village Other, *1969)*

OSWALD, LEE HARVEY (1939–1963)

The following was written on recruitment poster that said, "The Marine Corps Builds Men":
Marine Corps builds Oswalds.

(Also on a button)

Oswald lives!
Ruby sucks!

(Max's Kansas City Restaurant, New York City)

Where is Lee Harvey Oswald now that we really need him?

(On various walls, also on a button—during Johnson Administration)

OUTER SPACE

Forget about the moon and lets get down to earth.

Free space.

(University of Michigan)

The giant Martians landed, thought Los Angeles was a men's room and left.

(Cited in column in the Sacramento Union, *1967)*

My sons are extraterrestrials.

Pray for extraterrestrial intervention.

(Cited in The Spoilers, *Boston)*

Space is a vacuum because the Earth sucks.

(University of New Hampshire)

P

PAINTING

Have a soft palette but carry a hard edge.

Momism is groovy.

Painting is fine and dandy.
but not in this spot,
Where the finger serves as brush
And the ass as color pot.

(Breslau, 1859)

Painting, love-making and singing are three things which cannot be forced.

(Cited in Anthropophyteia, *Vol. 9, 1912)*

PALINDROMES

Roma summus amor.

(Tavern wall, Imperial Rome; translated—Rome supreme love)

Roma tibi subito motibus ibit amor.

(Cabaret window, Paris; translated—Suddenly, with passionate affection, Rome will turn out to be, for you, Love)

PARANOIA

Even paranoids have real enemies.

(On back of the seat of bus, New York City, also on a button)

Help! the paranoids are after me.

(Arlington County Public Library, Va.—cited in American Library Association Bulletin, *April, 1969)*

Paranoia is heightened awareness.

(Free Church, Berkeley, Cal., 1971)

Paranoid—someone is watching you thru the keyhole. Plug it with toilet paper.

(Co-ed toilet, Alternate U., New York City)

PARENT AND CHILD, *see also* MOTHERHOOD

Call your mother Laura, it's very important.

UNDERNEATH

Don't do it Laura, it's a trick.

UNDERNEATH

It was.

The generation gap is between the ears.

Mom—would you believe me now?

(Yale University)

Tuula is a whore.

UNDERNEATH

Tuula doesn't even exist.
—Tuula's mother

UNDERNEATH

But you just said you're her mother.

UNDERNEATH

Yes, but I had an abortion.

(Wall, Helsinki 1970)

We are the people our parents warned us about.

(Engagé Coffee House, New York City)

You'd rebel too if your mother made you part your hair down the middle.

UNDERNEATH

That's right, blame everything on your mother you ass-hole.

(Ladies' room, University of Michigan)

PARKER, CHARLIE (1920–1955)

Bird lives!

(On many walls in jazz clubs in England and United States)

Birdland lives!

(Birdland, now defunct jazz club in New York City, was named after Charlie "Bird" Parker, so this inscription is a tribute to him)

Bird's Gone.

(Cited in Graffiti *by Richard Freeman, London)*

Vogel lives!

*(Stanley's Bar, New York City—*vogel *is German for bird)*

PATIENCE

Grief is overcome by patience.

(Beauchamp Tower, Tower of London, 1586—written by reputed spy George Gyfford)

The most unhappy man in the world is he that is not pacient in adversities; For men are not killed with the adversities they have, but with ye pacience which they suffer.

(Beauchamp Tower, Tower of London, 16th century—written by Charles Bailly)

There are no problems to be solved without patience.

(Ellis Island, N.Y.—written in Greek on a wall in the main building, Oct. 23, 1953)

PATRIOTISM

Make patriotism legal now.

Patriots with feet under the table and noses glued to the radio set—we don't need any more of your kind.

(Prison, Dijon, 1944—during German occupation of France)

Suck American, fuck American, buy American.

(Greenwich Village, 1940)

Why did God allow Hitler to die? I'm not a nazi. I'm just against punks who do nothing for country and wreap [*sic*] its wealth.

(Subway, New York City, January 21, 1967)

A young kid from Toucy who is going to die without lowering his head.

(Prison, Dijon, 1943—during German occupation of France)

PEACE

Amo—not ammo.

Beware Christians.
This is the sign of the anti-Christ. Believe not the devils and whoremongers who profess peace but who display the witches foot. For their paths lead aught to destruction and eternal damnation in the everlasting fires of hell. Man is incapable of spreading peace across the land, and is doomed to constant war on earth. True peace is obtainable only through our savior So do not strieve [*sic*] now to bring peace among us, but repent now, that you may know peace in the afterlife. J.C.

(University of California at San Diego)

Brahms, not bombs.

(Wall, New York City, also on a button)

Burn flags, not people.

Burn pot, not people.

(On various walls, also on a button)

Cruise for peace.

Deface for peace. ☮

(Ladies' room, Hunter College, New York City)

Die for peace.

(University of California at Los Angeles, 1970)

Dow shalt not kill.

(Construction fence, New York City)

Effete snob for peace.

(On various walls shortly after a November, 1969, speech by Vice President Agnew in which he referred to certain peace demonstrators as effete snobs)

Escalate minds, not war.

Fighting for peace is like fucking for chastity.

(Men's room, Rutgers University)

Kill for peace

UNDERNEATH

Is like fornicating for Chastity.

(Men's room, Bates College, Lewiston, Me.)

Footprint of a chicken. ☮

(Men's room, Grumman Aviation, Bethpage, N.Y.)

Fuck for peace.

(The Dom, St. Marks Place, New York City)

Fuck the war, please.

(University of California at Los Angeles)

God in the form of a white dove, came before the Americans and said kill, kill, kill all unfree, undemocratic people in my name.

God is not on our side.

(On various walls; also on a button)

If we could see what others seem to see
when others seem to see it,
Then scores of wars would never
have been fought,
And hundreds of alliances would never
have been sought,
And millions of graveside flowers would never
have been bought
If we could see what others see
when others seem to see it.

If we kill man with whom shall we live?

Is that a bunny?
No, ya dumshit, it's the peace symbol. 

(Vietnam, 1971)

A just peace in '69.

UNDERNEATH

Just a piece by 69.

(Chelsea, Mass.)

Kill for Lent.

Lysistrata had a good idea.

(Ladies' room, Brooklyn College, 1970)

Make love, not war.

(Nanterre University, May, 1968—written in English; one of the most frequent wall messages of the last few years, also on a button)

Make peace—not woe.

Napalm peaceniks!

Negotiate don't escalate.

Our world is one big jigsaw puzzle with a "peace" missing!

Pacifists of all countries thwart all military enterprises by becoming citizens of the world.

(Sorbonne, May, 1968)

A pax on both your houses.

(Ladies' room, "55" Bar, New York City)

Peace Bug

Take my country
Bug my flag
Rape my sister
But please
Leave me alone.

(IND subway, New York City)

Peace for everyone.

UNDERNEATH

Get it!

(Wall, New York City)

Peace is a
Casualty of war

(Vietnam, 1971)

Peace is a cool scene.

Peace is for the dead.

(Ladies' room, John Adams Luncheonette, 1968)

Peace on you.

Peace to all and to all a good piece!

(Men's room, Central Falls, R.I.)

Peacing is the active verb for peace!

(Ladies' room, New York University)

Pot, peace, pussy, perversion.

Power to the Peaceful.

(Wall near People's Park, Berkeley, Cal.)

Shalom amigos.

(Norfolk Street, New York City)

Smash the peace creeps.

(IRT subway, New York City, 1970)

Support peace or I'll kill you.

*(Written on Moratorium day, October 15, 1969,
Blimpie Base, New York City, also on a button)*

Supposing they gave a war and nobody came.

(This graffito became so popular a variation was made into a poster)

There will be peace in 1978—with or without people.

(Subway bulletin board)

Things go better with peace on earth.

(Courthouse, Mineola, N.Y., 1970)

When the power of love overcomes the love of power, then there will be peace.

(Free Church, Berkeley, Cal., 1971)

Would Christ carry a draft card?

PEALE, NORMAN VINCENT (1898-)

Norman Vincent Peale takes mood-elevators.

(Cited by Jim Moran, columnist, Chicago Daily News, *May 27, 1967)*

PEDOPHILIA

He who fucks children surely deserves the rope.

(Breslau—cited in Anthropophyteia, *Vol. 6, 1909)*

I have seduced my own child and I didn't feel a nickel's worth of remorse.

(Men's room, Riesengebirge—cited in Anthropophyteia, *Vol. 6, 1909)*

Molesting minors is child's play.

(Men's room, University of Maryland, 1972)

Screwing a beautiful child is no sin.

(Men's room, Konstanz am Rhein—cited in Anthropophyteia, *Vol. 5, 1908)*

PERIODICALS, see NEWSPAPERS; MAGAZINES

PERSONAL HYGIENE

Brunetta, I grant you, can give her swain death;
But 'tis not with her eyes,
but with her ill breath.

(Lady's dressing-room, England, early 18th century)

Dear Pat, 'tis vain to patch or paint,
Since still a fragrant Breath you want;
For though well furnished, yet all Folks
Despise a Room whose Chimney smokes.

(Launder's Coffee House, in the Old Play-House Passage, England)

Employees must wash ~~hands~~ cocks before leaving.

(Max's Kansas City Restaurant, New York City)

The following were written on signs that said, "Employees must wash hands before leaving washroom":

Better management should.
Rather they should wash their assholes.
Guilt complex.
No one must wash hands before leaving, do it after!!
Pontius Pilate says.

Employees must wash their hands before leaking.

(Ladies' room, Max's Kansas City Restaurant, New York City)

Employees must wash walls before leaving.

Here's to the hole that never heals
The more you rub it the better it feels
All the water this side of hell
Can't wash away the codfish smell.

(Camp Maxey, Paris, Tex., 1945)

Save water, bathe with friends.

PESSIMISM

Bullshit, bullshit I've known it all,
It just precedes the cosmic fall.

(Men's room, Princeton University, 1970)

Chicken Little was right.

Don't look back, the lemmings are gaining on you.

(Thames-side pub, London)

Fuck the future and hope that tomorrow will be a miscarriage.

(University of Michigan)

One day it will begin to rain, and rain, and rain . . .

Some day
the day will come
When the day won't.

There is no tomorrow.

UNDERNEATH

How about tonight?

When in doubt, worry.

PHILOSOPHY, *see also* ETHICS; EXISTENTIALISM; FATALISM; HEDONISM; METAPHYSICS; REALITY

All the world's a stage and the people on it are poorly rehearsed.

UNDERNEATH

No, just poorly directed.

UNDERNEATH

No, just poorly cast.

(American Academy of Dramatic Arts, New York City, 1969)

Ambiguity is a bitch.
Uncertainty kills the mind.
Yes and no's are cool.
So's sometimes
But maybe's for shit.

(Men's room, New York University, 1972)

Any destruction is creative.

Awareness is misery.

(Men's room, New School for Social Research, New York City, 1972)

A circle is perfect but the world is not round.

The cost of a thing is the amount of life required to be expended for it.

UNDERNEATH

For those who live life rather than expend it, everything is free.

(Men's room, Telephone Company, New York City, 1969)

Divorce fear, you are no more than now.

(Paradox Restaurant, New York City)

Do and you shall be.
—Sartre
Be and you shall do.
—Camus
Do be do be do.
—Sinatra

Hang on.

(Ladies' room, Limelight Restaurant, New York City)

Have you done enough today to absolve yourself of blame for tomorrow's doom?

(Men's room, Men's faculty lounge, Hunter College, New York City)

In today's screwed society you should never ask a three dimensional question like—Why?

(Free Store Theatre, New York City)

The infinite has no accent.

(Medical School, Paris, May, 1968)

Live in the present.

(Paris, May, 1968)

The longest journey ends with one step to go.

(San Francisco State College, 1970)

Love with passion.

UNDERNEATH

Study with passion; think with passion;
accept with passion; understand with passion.

UNDERNEATH

Dispassionate life is not worth living.

UNDERNEATH

Since we are incapable of understanding or accepting, let our futile attempts be done in a passionate way.

UNDERNEATH

Abstractions are meaningless. Including that one.

(Antioch College, Yellow Springs, Ohio)

My utopia is an environment that works so well I can run wild in it.

UNDERNEATH

My utopia is an environment that works so well it can run wild in me!

(New York University, 1969)

1. Subject and object are the essential tic-toc.
2. What is your trouble? Mistaken identity.
3. All subjects are necessarily untouchable.
4. Mind is the dynamic aspect of matter.
5. How do we know the world is transitory? We could not know that our river is flowing unless we put our foot on the bank!

(Stockholm official graffiti wall [Kotterplank], *1969)*

Nothing so certain as the Uncertainties of this Life, says one of the Greek Philosophers.

(The Flask, Hampstead, England)

O mortal Man that's made of Clay,
Is here to-Morrow, and is gone to Day.

(On a window in Castle Street, Dublin, 18th century)

Obligation stay, don't surrender.

(Siena College, Loudonville, N.Y., 1972)

Phenomenon is based upon one's limitations of observance.

(University of Michigan)

Quid me vexatibus?

(Cornell University—Latin version of "What, me worry?" credo of Mad *magazine character Alfred E. Neuman)*

Reflection of life is only the transparency of the lived.

(Sorbonne, May, 1968)

The road of excess leads to the palace of wisdom—Crash.

Some of us are going to come through. Man isn't big enough to destroy man. Take it like you find it and leave it like it is.

(O'John Restaurant, New York City, 1969)

To yield a little is to capitulate a lot.

(Paris, May, 1968)

Turbulence is the end product of all thought.

A: Verbally justify your own existence.
B: My existence is contained in my essence.
C: Cogito ergo sum.
(Coitus ergo sum?)
(Does this mean "all men are fools")
D: Existence is my essence. Your philosophy shits.

(Ladies' room, Le Metro Caffe Espresso, New York City)

We complain that roses have thorns, but let's praise God that thorns have roses.

(Prison, Dijon, 1944—during German occupation of France)

We have only one life to live and this is no dress rehearsal.

(California Rehabilitation Center for female drug addicts, Norco, 1970)

We must systematically explore chance.

(Paris, May, 1968)

PHYSICALLY HANDICAPPED

The following were written on a poster that said, "The future belongs to the fit!":

Whatever happened to the program to hire the handicapped.

The future belongs to the fit so us spastics better swing now!

The following was written on a poster that said, "Hire the Handicapped":

They're fun to watch.

PHYSICIANS

The doctor more than illness we should fear;
Sickness precedes, and Death attends his coach,
Agues to fevers rise, if he appear,
And fevers grow to plagues at his approach.

(Chamber window of a lady who, on a slight indisposition, sent for S.J.S., early 18th century, England)

On an Eminent Physician's being called out of Church:
Whilst holy Prayers to Heaven were made,
One soon was heard, and answer'd too,
Save us from sudden Death, was said,
And strait from Church Sir H— withdrew.

(On a church door, England, mid-18th century)

PHYSICS

The angle of the dangle is in direct proportion to the heat of the meat and the mass of the ass.

(Men's room, Engineering building, University of Maryland, 1972)

Gravity is a myth, the Earth sucks.

(Men's room, Grumman Aviation, N.Y.)

100% of all students who take physics pass it.

UNDERNEATH

Students who take Physics deserve it.

Repeal the law of gravity.

PICASSO, PABLO (1881–1973)

Grandma Moses loves Picasso.

PLAGUE

The beginning of the plague was in 1350 minus one . . . wretched, fierce, violent. The dregs of the population live to tell the tale [*the inscription goes on to note a terrible storm on St. Maurus's Day on January 5, 1361*]. At the end of the [*pestilence*] a mighty wind. This year Maurus thunders in the heaven.

(Written in Latin on a wall in Ashwell Church, Hertfordshire, England)

POETRY

Daniel Berrigan's poetry rhymes.

(On cover of The Critic, *which was a picture of a wall covered with graffiti, December, 1966–January, 1967)*

I can't help thinking
That at this moment, a poet's place
Is in the street
That you poets should storm and capture
The Ivory Towers. Raze them
Proclaim
A state of emergency
If I give in
To mawkishness about my misery
And this misery isn't also
Yours

Reader
Punch me good and hard
Let's put an end
to poetry in absentia.
[*Trans. by Joachim Neugroschel*]

Poetry is in the street.

(Paris, May, 1968)

Seven foot poets of the world, arise!

(Men's room, Amarillo, Tex.—written high on the wall)

Support your local poet.

POLICE

A cop sleeps within each of us, he must be killed.

(Paris, May, 1968)

Cops eat flowers.

(San Diego State College, 1970)

Defrock John Birch cops.

(On a button)

Help send Commissioner Murphy and 'New York's Finest' to their Bullshit Jesus.

(IRT subway, New York City—during the Harlem riots of 1964)

Kill a cop.

(Mr. Waffles Ice Cream Parlor, New York City)

Kill a cop gently.

(Men's room, Coffman Memorial building, University of Minnesota, 1971)

New York's finest; the best that money can buy.

Off the pig.

(New York University, 1970)

Police protect the rich and beat and oppress the poor.

(Watts, Los Angeles, 1970)

Put a cop under your motor.

(Paris, May, 1968)

Report your loco police.

(The Exit Coffee House, New York City)

Support New York's finest; bribe a cop today.

Support your local fuzz.

Support your local police—help kill.

Support your local police victims.

Teach a cop to fuck.

This must be police headquarters because all the dicks hang out here.

(Men's room, Under The Stairs Bar & Restaurant, New York City)

Today's pigs is tomorrow's bacon.

(University of California at Los Angeles, 1970)

Warning—your local police are armed and dangerous.

POLITICS, see *also* ELECTIONS

All reform is characterized by the utopianism of its strategy and the opportunism of its tactics.

(Sorbonne, May, 1968)

All the reactionaries are paper tigers.

(Nanterre, May, 1968)

Attention, comrades, the republican order will be reestablished.—A defeatist.

(Sorbonne, May, 1968)

Bread and circuses now.

(Wolfie's Restaurant, Brooklyn, also on a button)

Conservatism is synonymous with putrefaction and ugliness.

(School of Medicine, Paris, May, 1968)

Down with the objectivity of parliamentary groupings.
Intelligence is on the side of the bourgeoisie
Creativity is on the side of the masses.
Don't vote anymore.

(Sorbonne, May, 1968)

He took 3 weeks to announce in 5 minutes that he would undertake in one month what he had been unable to accomplish in 10 years.

(This graffito refers to de Gaulle. Paris, May, 1968)

Human institutions are a part of human life, and not superior to it.

If your heart is on your left, don't have your billfold on your right.

(Paris, May, 1968)

Let's all get together and fight for individual rights.

Marxist repression is no better than any other kind.

(Co-ed toilet, Alternate U., New York City)

Royalists amuse us, fascists bug us.

(Paris, May, 1968)

The Silent Majority has nothing to say about it.

(University of Michigan, 1970)

The Silent Majority is a nice way to speak to a nation of sheep.

(Ann Arbor, 1970)

The VID proves that liberalism sucks.
In a socialist America the VIDs will be street cleaners.

(Lion's Head, New York City—refers to Village Independent Democrats, a liberal group)

We have a prehistoric left.

(Paris, May, 1968)

What's RYM 73?

UNDERNEATH

RYM 73 broke off from RYM 72 because RYM 73 disagreed with page two, paragraph three, and page four, paragraph one of the constitution. RYM 72's are too politically-oriented. People who are too political are 'rotting water-buffalo corpses' any more questions?

UNDERNEATH

Dirty cunt! Someday we'll put you up against the wall for your counter-revolutionary activities . . . A Communist.

UNDERNEATH

My cunt is clean! We'll give you a good job, some money, nice clothes and a nice home and you'll see how you feel then.

(Ladies' room, City College of New York, 1971—refers to Youth Revolutionary Movement)

POLK, JAMES (1795–1849)

I am the rightful heir to President Poke [*sic*], yet no one will listen to me.

(Café Figaro, New York City)

POPULATION, *see also* BIRTH CONTROL

Crowded Tube?
in 29 years
the population will have doubled
To breed is greed

(Southern Region train at London Bridge—cited in New Scientist and Science Journal, *April 8, 1971)*

Familiarity breeds.

More deviation, less population.

(On various walls, also on a button)

The population bomb is everybody's baby.

Population × copulation = too many fucking people.

UNDERNEATH

Let copulation thrive.
—King Lear. Act 4, scene 6.

(Men's room, Princeton University, 1970)

PORNOGRAPHY, *see also* OBSCENITY

Beware of the 'porno bomb.'

(Wall, New York City)

Fuck smut.

Pray for obscene mail.

Support your local pornographer.

POVERTY

Blessed are the poor in piss.

(Ladies' room, Le Metro Caffe Espresso, New York City)

Dep't of Slum Maintenance.

(On the door of the Welfare Center, Bronx)

Fuck, fuck, fuck and nothing to eat in the house.

(Public toilet for workers, Schuckl's Cannery, Sunnyvale, Cal., 1938)

I fight poverty! I work.

Rich people kiss each other, poor people piss on each other.

(Toilet, Berlin, 1910)

Stamp out poverty, not people.

UNDERNEATH

Stamp out poverty and people.

When you're rich it's malnutrition. When you're poor, it's starvation.

POWELL, ADAM CLAYTON (1908–1972)

Adam Clayton Powell uses Man-Tan.

(Cited by Art Buchwald, columnist, Washington Post*)*

Black Powell!!

NAACP stands for Negroes Are Always Colored People.

UNDERNEATH

No, it stands for Never Antagonize Adam Clayton Powell.

PRIESTS, *see* CLERGY

PRISONS, *see* IMPRISONMENT

PROMISCUITY

And on the landlady's grave there stood
a man—his pecker in his hand
and he said to him: my lad
now weep a little tear for her
now she is being fucked by the angels.

(The last of the Frau Wirtin verse series which appeared frequently in German toilets)

Do you believe in sexual fidelity?

UNDERNEATH

Yes—after old age.

UNDERNEATH

Only when it's worth it.

UNDERNEATH

To no more than 4 men at a time.

(Ladies' room, The Idler Coffee House, Cambridge, Mass., 1972)

How have I strove to gain the Fair?
And yet how little does she care?
But leaves me starving with Despair.
'Tis now full Eight, I fear her Spouse
Has given her a Rendezvous.

Those five Lines were crossed out; but then follows:

D–mn the first Lines, they are not mine,
T'abuse a Lady so divine;
Altho' I waited for her Hours,
I have enjoy'd her lovely Powers,
Her Wit, her Beauty, and her Sense,
Have fully made me Recompence.

Captain R.T. July 10. 1710.

UNDERNEATH

Friend Captain T,

If thou can'st C,
Mind what I have to say to thee,
Thy Strumpet Wh–re abominable,
Which thou didst kiss upon a Table,
Has made thy manly Part unable.
Farewel, &c. Z.B.

(The Mitre, Hampton Court, England, 1718)

How, says the Proverb, can it e'er be thought,
What's bred i'th' Bone can out o'the Flesh be brought:
Her Mother kiss'd with every one, and Moll does plainly shew her;
For Molly kind is kiss'd by none, but only all that know her.
I.S. 1718.

(On a window, Carlisle, England)

If it be true each Promise is a Debt,
Then Celia will her Freedom get;
Yet she, to satisfy her Debts, desires
To yield her Body as the Law requires.

(On a window, Lebeck's Head, England)

My Chloe is an Angel bright,
But Chloe's common—so is Light.
And who with Phoebus Fault shall find,
Because his Beams to all are kind.

(On the window of a coffee house, Richmond, England)

The following graffiti were all dedicated to a young lady named Primigenia, a resident of Nuceria, a suburb of Pompeii. This girl apparently was quite generous with her favors.

How Happy we are to have known Primigenia.
Goodbye Primigenia, keep well.
Sabinus was here with Primigenia.
By the Roman Gate at Nuceria you may seek out Novella Primigenia, in Venus Street.
Primigenia, Primigenia, goodbye.
Secundus with Primigenia met here.
Cornelius sends the biggest possible bundle of good wishes to Primigenia.

Welcome to Primigenia the sweetest and most darling of all the girls in the world, our best wishes.
Good wishes to Primigenia of Nuceria.
Hermeros wishes all the best to Lady Primigenia. Come to Puteoli and in the Timian Street at the place of the banker Messius, ask for Hermeros freedman of Phoebus.

(Pompeii, 79 A.D.)

PROPHECY

In the future world only the children will be privileged.

(Wall, Santiago, Chile, 1970)

In the new society, people will ask. "What will the NEW SOCIETY BE LIKE?"

(New York University, 1969)

PROSTITUTION

Arphocras had a good fornication with Drauca for a denario.

(Pompeii, 79 A.D.)

Brothel can you spare a dame.

(Champagne Gallery, New York City—Pun on an old depression song, "Brother Can You Spare a Dime")

Cunt $1.50. See porter.

(Men's room, bus terminal, 42d Street, New York City, 1940)

A d——d confounded Bitch
Ugly and cunning as a Witch.
Her Bill shall be preferr'd by Law;
The House we wish we'd never saw.
One Pound five and ten Pence;
Grant her Repentance;
We'll never come here again;
And let her alone remain.
J.S.
R.S. 17 July
1722. very truly.

(England, early 18th century)

Dear Doll is a Prude,
  And I tumbled her down;
And I tickled her Fancy
  For half a Crown.
R.M.—r, July 17. 1714.

(Greyhound, Maidenhead, England)

Euche, slave; available for use at 2 coppers a time.

(Pompeii, 79 A.D.)

Euplia loosely broad and prominently sexed.

(Pompeii, 79 A.D.)

Eutychis a Greek girl 2 coppers she is all that could be desired.

(Pompeii, 79 A.D.)

Gammer Sprigins had gotten a Maidenhead,
And for a Gold Guinea she brought it to Bed;
But I found by embracing that I was undone;
'Twas a d—n'd p–ck–y Wh–re, just come from London.
R.L. 1710.

(On a window, Hampstead, England)

Helsinki girls go for a Finn.
Her Step delivers those her Eyes enslave,
She looks to conquer, but she treads to save.

(Angel, Marlborough, England)

  Chloe's Character.
Her Voice is as clear as the Stream;
Her Character light as the Sun;
Her Dealings are hard as a Stone;
But her Promise as sure as a Gun.
A.P—pe, 1712.

Here did I lay my Celia down;
I got the pox and she got half a crown.

(On a window in Chancery Lane, London, 1719)

Here I lie properly enjoyed.

(Brothel, Pompeii, 79 A.D.—in a girl's hand)

Here I stand alone and confused
Tried to hustle but was only cruised.

(Wall, 54th Street and Lexington Avenue, New York City)

I am yours for two coppers.

(Pompeii, 79 A.D.)

I become all Things to all Men, to gain some,
  or I must have starved.
Moll. Friskey.

(Wall, tavern near Covent-Garden, London)

I fucked Mariette for three mangos.

UNDERNEATH

Stupid, you were cheated out of two.

(Toilet, Buenos Aires—
mangos is Argentinian slang for dollars)

I watch and pray for dearest Nancy,
Because I always love her Fancy:
  But then there comes,
  Like Bailiff Bunts,
The Watch with Lights we can see;
  And then she'll pray,
  And I must pay,
And retreat as clean as a Tansey.

UNDERNEATH

For Money one may whore,
And I'll say no more.—R.T.

(Red Lion, Egham, England)

Let prostitutes work.

UNDERNEATH

Do you call what they do work?

(Wall, New York City)

The miners came in 49
The hores [*sic*] in 51
They jumbled a mess together
And called it the Native Son

(Winona, Ariz., 1928)

Molley came up to Town precise,
Demure, yet fire in her eyes;
So did she look confounded civil;
With Grace and Beauty like a Devil;
But soon her Eyes drew in some Hearts,
And some Things else like Cupid's Darts,
Which gave her Pains, and many Smarts.

UNDERNEATH

Thou Puppy,—
The Fire of her Eyes occasioned the Flame of her Heart,
And drew the Fire to her lower Part.
R.L.

*(The Crown, Uxbridge, England—
in the literature of this period the name Molly
was usually associated with a loose woman)*

Molly the gay, the black, the friskey,
Would kiss like any wanton Gipsey;
Nor was her Mouth alone the Case,
A Man of Worth might kiss her A–se.

(Star-Inn, Coventry, England)

My father is a butcher,
My mother cuts the meat
My sister runs a whore house
Just across the street.

(Wall, main building, Ellis Island, N.Y., 1953)

My maidenhead sold for a guinea,
A lac'd head with the money I bought;
In which I looked so bonny,
The heart of a gamester I caught:
A while he was fond, and brought gold to my box,
But at last he robbed me, and left me the pox.

UNDERNEATH

When you balance accounts, it sure may be said,
You at a bad market sold your maidenhead.

*(On a panel at the Faulcon in St. Neot's,
Huntingdonshire, England, 18th century)*

My wife's cunt, truly! It brings in money daily.

(Men's room, Prussia-Silesia—cited in Anthropophyteia, *Vol. 7, 1910)*

Nanny Meadowes has undone me,
From myself her Charms have won me.
With Love's blazing Flames I die,
Whither, whither shall I fly!

UNDERNEATH

Prithee, Coxcomb, without Whining,
Say thou hast a mind to Sinning
With a Guinea, do but ask her,
Love you'll find—is no hard Task, Sir.

(On a panel, The Rose, England)

O cunt, sweet hole!
If only I still had my dollar!

(Elberfeld, Germany, 1905)

Orgasms for sale, rent or trade.

A pimp is a snatch purser.

(Alvin's Finer Delicatessen, Detroit, 1971)

Says Nan B—ch to Sir John, you're a scandalous Villain;
D'ye think I would do what I did for a Shilling?
In good Truth, says Sir John, when I find a Girl willing.
Let her take what she finds, and give Willing for Willing.
But if you insist upon Money for that,
I need not speak plainer, you know what is what,
I shall always look on you as a money-wise Cat.
J.E. July 17. 1713.

(Corwin, Basinstoke, England)

So early Con began the wanton trade,
She scarce remembers when she was a maid.

(On a window, Rose Tavern, Catherine Street, England, early 18th century)

Stop screwing around—patronize your local brothel.

Support free enterprise, legalize prostitution.

There was a young whore visited Devon
And thought she was in a male heaven
Imagine her fright
When there was no night
And her red light went out at eleven.

(Men's room, Arctic Institute's Devon Island Research Station, Lat 75°40′ North, 1972—the electric generators stop there at 2300 hours)

21st November. Epaphra, Actus and Auctus brought the woman Tyche to this place, her charge was 5 coppers per man.—M. Mesalla and L. Lentulus, Consuls.

(Pompeii, 79 A.D.)

Two pitiful Dukes at our Race did appear;
One bespoke him a Girl, the other new Geer,
And both went away without paying I hear,
For the Cheat lov'd his Money, and so did the Peer.

UNDERNEATH

You Rogue, Taylor shan't catch me, while your
Legs they are cross'd.
Don't cry my dear Girl, since you have got more
than you lost.

(Boghouse, Ludlow, England)

W. . . . . lay at the Angel in Marlborough Town,
And an angel lay with him all night;
He tipp'd her an angel before she lay down,
Which you know was but decent and right.
But an angel of darkness she proved to be sure;
For scarce twenty angels would pay for his cure.

(On a window at The Angel, Marlborough, England, 18th century)

What do you do till the call girl comes?

(W)horse power!

Wipe out male prostitution—adopt a hustler today. Get murdered tonight.

(Free Store Theatre, New York City)

Within this Place
Lives Minerva and Grace,
An Angel hangs out at the Door;
If you rise in the Night,
And call for a Light,
Then presently down comes a Wh——.

(On the door of two celebrated milliners, England)

Wou'd you know the true Road that to Pleasure doth lead,
Then this Way, ye Swains, your Footsteps must tread.
And then for the Piece which this Pleasure doth cost,
Why, 'tis only a Guinea, you can't think it lost.
Since Supper and Lodging, and Mistress and all,
Nay, and Maid, if you like her, are ready at Call.

(Written by Mr. —— in Chloe's Bed-Chamber, England, early 18th century)

You can bring a horticulture but you can't make her think.

PROUST, MARCEL (1871–1922)

Marcel Proust is a yenta.

*(*Yenta *is a Yiddish word meaning gossip or busybody)*

Rememberance [*sic*] of things Pabst.

(Men's room, Greenwich Village)

PROVERBS

A bird in the hand can be messy.

Cold hand, warm ass.

(Men's room, Germany)

Don't count your chickens before they hatch,
There's many a slip twixt the cock and the snatch.

(Men's room, University of California at Berkeley)

Evil spelled backwards is live.

(Subway, New York City)

Excuses are like assholes—everybody's got one!

(Engineering Society of Detroit, 1971)

If you don't want to be crucified, don't hang around crosses.

If you want to waste your time, scatter millet and pick it up again.

(Pompeii, 79 A.D.)

The open mouth invites the foot.

Start the day with a smile and get it over with.

To save face keep lower-half shut.

Tomorrow is the first day of the rest of your life.

(This graffito became so popular a variation of it was made into a poster; the slogan was also picked up by Madison Avenue for use in commercials)

The world is your oyster, so EAT IT!

A yong rewler wytles
A pore man spendar haveles
A ryche man bif nedeles
A old man lecher lwue (les
A woman rebolde sameless.

(Ridgewell Church, Essex, England—written in middle English)

PSYCHIATRY

Psychiatrist is whore.

(On office building on Park Avenue South, New York City—cited by Norton Mockridge, columnist, Boston Herald, *October 11, 1966)*

People are no damned good.

UNDERNEATH

Psychiatrists are worse.

UNDERNEATH

Psychiatrists aren't people.

(On Park Avenue apartment house—cited by Norton Mockridge, columnist, Boston Herald, *December 2, 1966)*

Psychiatry the new inquisition.

Who ever heard of a toilet seat as a substitute for a psychrists [*sic*] couch?

(Men's room, Men's faculty lounge, Hunter College, New York City)

PSYCHOLOGY

Anyone who worships the accomplished fact is incapable of preparing for the future.

(Ladies' room, Ninth Circle Restaurant, New York City)

As I walk'd by myself,
I said to myself,
And myself said again to me:
Look to thyself,
Take Care of thyself,
For nobody cares for thee
Then I myself
Thus answer'd myself,
With the self-same Repartee:
Look to thyself,
Or look not to thyself,
'Tis the self-same Thing to me.
John Careless.

(The Cranes, Edgeworth, England)

Better to be pissed off than pissed on.

(Stonybrook College, N.Y.)

An evil conscience makes men fear even security.

(Beauchamp Tower, Tower of London, 1586—written by reputed spy George Gyfford)

For those who think life is a game—do you like the part you are playing?

(New York University, 1969)

Get yourself together.

(East Harlem, New York City, 1970)

The happiest day is that day in the past that you always run back to when the present proves unbearable.

(California Rehabilitation Center for female drug addicts, Norco, 1970)

How far *In* can you get before you begin to suspect someone is putting you on?

I want to be what I was when I wanted to be what I am now.

(Ladies' room, Ninth Circle Restaurant, New York City)

It's banal to be anal, but far worse when you're polymorphous-perverse.

(Ladies' room, Max's Kansas City Restaurant, New York City)

Maintain your cool.

Motions kill emotions.

(Paris, May, 1968)

There's no problem so big or complicated that it can't be run away from.

(California Rehabilitation Center for female drug addicts, Norco, 1970)

You've got to be able to stand alone to be worth anything to anyone.

(Ladies' room, Lion's Head, New York City)

PUBERTY

I am 12 years old and can come a little.

Lower the age of puberty.

(New York University)

Stop the war.

UNDERNEATH

On poverty.

CHANGED TO

Stop the war on puberty.

PUBLIC UTILITIES

Con Ed is the chemical branch of the Viet Cong.

Dig we must—for holes in your pocket.

UNDERNEATH

Con ed tried to gas us.

(Chalk on the sidewalk near where Con Edison men were working, New York City)

Power to the people.
—Con Ed.

(Men's room, Princeton University, 1970)

Support striking telephone operators.

UNDERNEATH

And ugly ones too.

(Ladies' room, San Francisco Public Library, 1971)

R

RACE CONFLICT, *see also* ANTI-SEMITISM

All Caucasians back to Caucases [*sic*]. They can't fuck.

(Ladies' room, Ninth Circle Restaurant, New York City)

All Jews and Niggers are one and the same.

(Men's room, Rutgers University, 1969)

white
All power to the^people.

Anybody who fucks a Vietnamese
Is too lazy to masturbate.

(Vietnam, 1971)

Asian flu for Asians only.

Barbados Negroes are Uncle Toms in the U.S.A.

(IND subway, 1970)

Be a man, join the Klan.

(Hudson tubes, Jersey City stop, 1968)

Be kind to Chuck the spade, he's the official Negro.

(Lion's Head, New York City)

Black African Misfits.

(University of Michigan)

BLACK
ass
&
shity
POWER

(Lion's Head, New York City)

Black girls are better. They're not hung up like Jewish princess virgins.

(Men's room, Brooklyn College, 1970)

Black go back. Africa needs you.

(London, England. From "Graffiti" by Richard Freeman)

Black is beautiful.

UNDERNEATH

Death is black
Is death beautiful?

(Trailways bus station, Pittsburgh)

Black is whats happening.

UNDERNEATH

As long as it doesn't happen to me!

(Men's room, John Jay College of Criminal Justice, New York City, 1972)

Black power.

UNDERNEATH

Back to the cotton fields.

Black Power—Fuck a white woman.

(In various subway stations, New York City)

Bring back white slavery.

UNDERNEATH

What about the Blacks, you damn bigot.

Burn baby, burn.

(Engagé Coffee House, New York City, also on a button)

Congo coons rape nuns.

(Pete's Tavern, New York City)

The following was written on ads for The New York Times:
Coons read kike N.Y. Post.

(Subway, New York City)

Do niggers live longer?

UNDERNEATH

We fuck longer.

UNDERNEATH

What else do you do?

For Sale, Cheap: Beer Bar in Watts called Whitey's.

(Norwalk, Cal.)

Fuck all Porto [*sic*] Ricans not that you haven't done it already.

Fuck your ethnic group.

UNDERNEATH

Yassuh!

(Wells Garden Supper Club, New York City)

Harlem is Mecca, blood brothers only.

(Harlem, New York City, c. 1970)

Hitler should have killed 19,000,000 crackers of whites instead of Jews.

(Subway, New York City)

A honky ain't shit, especially Wallace.

(Men's room, Gitlitz Delicatessen & Bar, New York City, 1969)

I am a nigger, at least this is what you have named me, and that name shall be the death of you white bastards and bitches. This is an oath not a threat.

(The Dom, St. Mark's Place, New York City, 1966)

I fuck your mother for a solid hour.
The baby came out screaming BLACK POWER.

(Men's room, John Jay College of Criminal Justice, New York City, 1972)

I love Hitler.

UNDERNEATH

Because your nature is like his.

UNDERNEATH

No, because he kills Jews. Jews are disgusting but then again so are niggers. All whites are created equal. Niggers are made inferior and lowly to God, whites, wasps.

UNDERNEATH

If any N.Y.U. student wrote any of this shit, then your education has not helped your intellect. If you wish to voice your opinions in a protest group, start a Race war. If not stop this shit and get yourself together.

(New York University, 1972)

If black is beautiful, I've just shit a masterpiece.

(Men's room, airport, New Orleans, 1972)

I'm a mother fucker—I fuck white mothers.

(Wall, Amsterdam Avenue, New York City, 1970)

Is a black boy better than a Frito-Lay?

(Men's room, Hunter College, New York City, 1972)

J— has nothing against colored people—he thinks everyone should own one.

(Co-ed toilet, East Village Other, *1970)*

Jew is nigger turned inside out.

K.K.K. Welcome.

UNDERNEATH

Nig forever.

(IND subway, New York City)

Keep America Wasp.

Kill all niggers
Kill all ofays
But leave me alone.

(Men's room, Slugs', New York City)

King leaves, riots follow.

(IND subway, New York City—written a week after the King assassination, which occurred April 4, 1968)

LBFM's never come
Whats an LBFM?
A little brown fucking machine.

(Vietnam, 1971)

Magyar bastards!

(Men's room, delicatessen, Sunnyside, Queens, N.Y., 1969)

My destiny lies in the death of racist pigs
Kill black pig devil.
Hate white people, beast of the earth.

(New Orleans, 1973—written on wall of Mark James Robert Essex's apartment, police say he killed 6 people and wounded 15 others)

NAACP stands for Negroes Are Always Colored People.

UNDERNEATH

No, it stands for Never Antagonize Adam Clayton Powell.

The Nature of Men
To a Red Man read thy Read;
To a Brown Man break thy Bread;
At a Pale Man draw thy Knife,
From a Black Man keep thy Wife.

(Summer house near Richmond, England)

N.Y.C. Spic Coon jungle.

(Stanley's Bar, New York City)

Negroes just *subtract* from the culture, they *add* nothing and just *divide* the people.

UNDERNEATH

But they sure can *multiply!*

(Building on Lower East Side, New York City, 1969)

The niggers in Dixie are planning your execution.

(Men's room, New York Public Library, 42nd Street, 1971)

9/10ths of whores are BLACK of course.

(Ferry terminal, New York City, 1972)

No white wanted, this is our community.

(Harlem, New York City, c. *1970)*

Othello was a bigot.

Pink men you can't keep your women.

(Cited in Graffiti *by Richard Freeman, London)*

Please flush the toilet, we want the niggers to starve to death.

(Café, Missouri, 1965)

Porto [*sic*] Rican babies are brought up on Dr. Spick.

The stands collapsed at a soccer game in Northern Ireland, killing seventy-seven fans. Scrawled above scoreboard was the following:

Rangers 77 Celtics O

Reprimand White racists but kill Black racists.

(Men's room, Rutgers University)

Snow White is a nigger.

(Scholtz's Beer Garden, Austin)

Soul Nation, Brothers Only.

(Harlem, New York City, c. *1970)*

Spread tolerance—kill a Polelock [*sic*].

(Men's room, New York University)

Stay seated. This is a Core shit-in.

(Men's room, library, University of California at Berkeley, 1964)

Support Black Power—buy coal.

Supremacy is doomed.

(Carved on back seat of Lexington Avenue bus, New York City—cited in The New Yorker, *January 11, 1941)*

Today is a new day for all black people. Today we kick ass.

(IND subway, New York City—found day after the murder of Martin Luther King, which occurred April 4, 1968)

The U.S. government is the main enemy of the Blacks!

(Watts, Los Angeles, 1970)

We use to have pity for the white bitches. Today our feelings have left us, so beware, kick ass—black power.

(IND subway, New York City—found two days after the murder of Martin Luther King, which occurred April 4, 1968)

White is reliable.

(Construction fence, Midtown, New York City)

White people are pink flower bitches. The shaded flower is dead.

(IND subway, New York City—found a day after the murder of Martin Luther King, which occurred April 4, 1968)

Whitey has had it Baby.
Why try to blot it out.

UNDERNEATH

Face it, Blacky is not too bright!

(Limelight Restaurant, New York City)

Whitey lacks confidence.

(Limelight Restaurant, New York City)

Why does everyone hate Jews, homosexuals and blacks?

UNDERNEATH

Were you ever circumcized, blown or mugged?

(Men's room, Hunter College, New York City, 1972)

You people are sick, white bastards.
—An Indian

(Ladies' room, Limelight Restaurant, New York City)

RACE DISCRIMINATION, see RACE CONFLICT

RAPE

Disarm all rapists.

UNDERNEATH

It's not their arms I'm worried about.

(Ladies' room, Greenwich Village pub, New York City, 1971)

Marriage legalizes rape.

Show a little kindness—rape an old maid.

Warning: trespassers will be violated.

To Mr. D—b, on his being very hot upon Mrs. N.S. 1714.

When the Devil would commit a Rape.
He took upon him Cupid's Shape:
When he the Fair-One met, at least,
They kiss'd and hugg'd, or hugg'd and kiss'd;
  But in amorous Desire,
Thought she had Cupid's Dart,
  But got Hell Fire,
  And found the Smart.
N.B. And then the Surgeon was sent for.

(Sun behind the Exchange, London)

RALEIGH, WALTER (1552–1618)

Cowards fear to die, but courage stout,
Rather than live in snuff, will put it out.

(Written by Sir Walter Raleigh, with the snuff of a candle, the night before he died)

RASPUTIN, GRIGORI EFIMOVICH (1872–1916)

Rasputin lives! He is in the kitchen.

(Max's Kansas City Restaurant, New York City)

REAGAN, RONALD (1911–)

Governor Reagan, call your studio.

Impeach Reagan.

(On various walls, also on a button)

Reagan can't *act* either.

Ronald Reagan eats peanut butter.

Reagan—save our Republic.

REALITY

Be realists, demand the impossible.

(Paris, May, 1968)

Do not adjust your mind—there is a fault in reality.

(Balliol College, Oxford University, 1972)

The dream is reality.

(Paris, May, 1968)

Enjoying your dream?

(University of Michigan)

I just turned real.

(Engagé Coffee House, New York City)

My wishes are the reality.

(Nanterre, May, 1968)

Reality is a crutch.

(Lamont Library, Harvard University, also on buttons)

Reality is an obstacle to hallucination.

(Ladies' room, Top of the Gate Restaurant, New York City)

Reality is good sometimes for kicks, but don't let it get you down.

Reality is no obstacle.

Reality is the shifting face of need.

(Le Metro Caffe Espresso, New York City)

Stamp out reality.

(In various toilets, also on a button)

Subjective reality is not all its cracked up to be.

(Men's room, Princeton University, 1970)

There's more to life than meets the mind.

REBUSES

Rebus on Miss S. Bell

The greatest Noise on Sundays made,
Tells us her Name is Masquerade,
Whom I must kiss, —— or be a Shade.

Rebus for Miss M. Cotton

One of the softest Things in Nature,
Beareth the Name of my dear Creature.

Rebus on Miss Ann Oliv-er
A Pickle of excellent Growth.
And to *Sin against the Truth,
Tells the Name of a Virgin of Beauty and Youth.
*i.e. To Err.

Miss Hutch-in-son
The Place where Rabbits are confin'd.
The Place where Strangers are refresh'd;
And what best pleas'd my Mother's Mind,
Tell you the Charmer of my Breast.

Rebus on Miss Har-ring-ton
The Pleasure of the Sportsman's Chace;
The Pledge in Matrimonial Cafe,
With Twenty Hundred Weight beside,
Name her I wish to make my Bride.

Miss Weathers
Tell me her Name, whose Looks serene
Shew her a Goddess, or a Queen;
Who, if in turbulent Disguise,
Will make you shudder at her Eyes:
For her, all others I despise.

On Miss Partridge of Ely
That of the pretty feather'd Race,
Which most doth courtly Tables grace,
And o'er the Mountains bends it Flight,
Or lurks in Fields with Harvest bright
For whose Destruction men with Care,
The noblest Canine Breed prepare,
Bestows a Name on that fair Maid
Whose Eyes to Love my Heart betray'd.

Miss Shuttle-worth
What a Weaver will toss about all the Day long,
And a Value, whose Praise can't be nam'd in my Song,
Tells the Name of my Charmer who's witty and young.

On Miss Green
What gives the pleasant Mead its Grace,
What spreads at Spring Earth's smiling Face,
What jolly Hunters chuse to wear,
Gives Name to her whose Chains I bear.

Rebus on Miss Bell-a-dine
What in a Steeple bears a Sound?
What in the Horn-Book first is found;
And eat the Meal of glorious Noon;
Give me, Great Jove, this Lady soon,
Whose Name the first three Lines explain:
Her Love's my Life, my Death in her Disdain.

RECHY, JOHN (1934–)

(Note: Avant-garde writer on sexual themes)

John Rechy: Where are you now?

(Men's room, Mama's Chicken 'n Rib, New York City, also on a button)

REINCARNATION

Bridey Murphy Lives!

I wish I could come back as a bug, to bite an ass.

(Le Metro Caffe Espresso, New York City)

Reincarnation is a pleasant surprise.

(Men's room, East Village Other, *1969)*

When I'm reincarnated, I hope I'm Queer. At least the problems and frustrations will be different then.

(Ladies' room, Lion's Head, New York City)

RELIGION, *see also* BIBLE

All that we know of what is done above,
Is, that the Blessed sing, and that they love.

(Queen's College, Oxon, England)

As much suffering for Christ in this world
So much the greater glory with Christ in the world to come
Thou has crowned him Lord, with glory and honour;
The just man shall be forever.

(Beauchamp Tower. Tower of London, 16th century—written by Philip Howard, First Earl of Arundel, who died of food poisoning)

Written by Sir Thomas Moor.
At last I've found a Haven where,
I'll ride secure from Hope or Fear.
Thy Game is, Fortune. o'er with me,
And thou to others now may'st flee
To cheat them with Inconstancy.

Be frend to one—Be ennermye to none.

(Beauchamp Tower, Tower of London, 16th century—written by Charles Bailly)

Be thou faithful unto death and I will give thee a crown of life.

(White Tower, Tower of London, 1553—written by T. Fane, who took part in Wyatt's rebellion)

Bless, O Lord, your servant Theodore, and Kassia, and Auxon, and Nonna, And Stefanos, and John.

(On rock, Wadi Haggaj [Ravine of the Pilgrims], Sinai Desert, 6th century A.D.*)*

Blessed ar they that suffer persecution for righteusnes.

(Salt Tower, Tower of London, 16th century)

Blind faith belongs to the Dark Ages.

Bomb a church tomorrow!

(University of Florida)

Bring back paganism.

Christianity will live as long as there's anti-Semitism.

(Rutgers University, 1971)

Do you know that some Christians still exist?

(Sorbonne, May, 1968)

Enough churches.

(Paris, Boulevard Saint-Germain, May, 1968)

Evil works.

The following were written on a poster that said, "The family that prays together stays together":
The family that shoots together loots together.
The family that flays together stays together.

The fear of the Lord is the beginning of wisdome.

(Beauchamp Tower, Tower of London, 16th century written by Charles Bailly)

Feare fortuns flateri, fraile of felicitie,
dispayre not in danger, God is defender.

(Salt Tower, Tower of London, 16th century)

He that endureth to the end shall be saved.

(White Tower, Tower of London—written by Robert Rudston of Dartford)

He who scorns life mocks easily at God.

(Pompeii, 79 A.D.)

He who will take a good pious shit must visit the Pope in Rome.

(Men's room, Breslau—cited in Anthropophyteia, *Vol. 6, 1909)*

How can you think freely in the shadow of the chapel?

(Chapel of the Sorbonne, May, 1968)

If you're looking this far, you're looking for something, try Catholicism.

(Village Gate, New York City, also quoted in Commonweal*)*

I'm a square I drive a Rambler and I go to church.

(IRT subway, New York City, 1969)

Inasmuch as it is a disgrace to be bound because of sin, so, on the contrary to suffer the bonds of captivity for Christ's sake is the greatest glory.

(Beauchamp Tower, Tower of London, 1587; written in Latin)

King Kong—he died for our sins.

(The Forum Coffee House, New York City)

Let us not prey.

(Wall next to Trinity Church, New York City)

Love thy neighbor but don't get caught

(The Riviera, New York City)

Man created god in his image.

(On a religious poster)

The mark of primitive religion (or big Gov't.) is sacrifice.

Neither master, nor God. God is I.

(Paris, May, 1968)

O God, who sojourns at the place, help and redeem your servant Stefanos and the architect of this monastery Aelisios and Nonna.

(St. Catherine's Monastery on Mt. Sinai, Sinai Desert, 6th century A.D.*)*

O Lord, give me redemption for my sins.

(Sinai Peninsula)

One God the highest.
—Abraham, the son of Sarutha

(On rock, Wadi Haggaj [Ravine of the Pilgrims], Sinai Desert, 6th century A.D.*)*

Regulate your "drive" on earth because in heaven there is nothing to fuck.

(Men's room, Germany)

Religion is for idiots—The Ludicrous Missfit
Let us help the human race.
I'll believe anything you say for $10,000.
To Ludicrous Missfit—Are you sure you know what you're talking about?—Wendy the Witch
Ludicrous Missfit! We all have problems. Don't be ashamed to accept help.
Ludicrous Missfit! Go to hell.
Ludicrous Missfit! Have seen your messages all over subway walls—Just wanted to let you know that they are being read—Keep up the good work—Am going back to my own planet soon and may contact.

(On poster for Paulist Fathers Services)

Religion is the answer.

UNDERNEATH

There are no answers.

UNDERNEATH

Is this the answer?

Religious faith is merely an excuse for man's moral weaknesses.

(Wall, Wagner College, Staten Island, N.Y.)

Revive fertility rites.

(The Village Gate, New York City, also on a button)

Sainthood is an Ego trip.

(Subway, New York City)

Shmuel, son of Hillel, asks to be blessed and remembered.

(On rock, Wadi Haggaj [Ravine of the Pilgrims], Sinai Desert, 6th century A.D.)

Sin now—pay later.

Tax the churches.

To serve God, to endure penance, to obey the fates, is to reign.

(Beauchamp Tower, Tower of London, 1564—written by Arthur Poole)

Typping stand and bere thy cross for thou art catholyke but no worce and for that cause this 3 yeer space thou hast conteanewed in great disgrac yet what happ will hitt I cannot tel but be death or be wel content swet Good.

(Beauchamp Tower, Tower of London, 16th century)

Various Religions, several Tenets hold;
Yet all one God acknowledge, which is Gold.

(Uxbridge, England, 1719)

We didn't invent sin, we're just trying to perfect it.

Whensoever you go by me
Whether man, woman or boy you be,
Bear in mind you do not fail
To say in passing "Mary Hail."

(St. Margaret Church, Cowlinge, Suffolk, England, Middle Ages)

Where the ass of a priest blows, there smell good Catholic noses.

(Breslau—cited in Anthropophyteia, *Vol. 6, 1909)*

The following were written on a poster that said, "Worship Together This Week":

Is it your business?
Don't advertise religion.
Keep our God free of churches.
Just a universal conspiracy for idiots.

The following was written on a religious poster that said, "You can lift your life":

With a jock.

REVERE, PAUL (1735–1818)

Paul Revere was a tattle tale.

(Me-Shack Coffee House, West Palm Beach, Fla., 1970)

Paul Revere was an alarmist.

REVOLUTION

Action permits us to surmount divisions and find solutions. Action is in the streets.

(Paris, May, 1968)

The aggressor is not he who rebels but he who affirms.

(Nanterre, May, 1968)

Already 10 days of happiness.

(Paris, May, 1968)

Arm your imagination for revolution.

(Wall near People's Park, Berkeley, Cal.)

At Nanterre as in other places, the angry ones shit on you (illustrated catalog to appear).

(Sorbonne, May, 1968)

The barricade closes the street but opens the way.

(Paris, May 3, 1968)

Battle Zone Ahead.

(University of California at Berkeley)

Be quick and cruel cannibals.

(Nanterre, May, 1968)

Blow up your mind.

(Nanterre University, May, 1968—written in English)

Choose your weapons—flowers or guns but remember flowers don't shoot and guns make shitty flower pots.

(University of California at Los Angeles—1970)

Count your resentments and be ashamed.

(Paris, May, 1968)

Crush the Oppressor.

(Wall near People's Park, Berkeley, Cal., 1970)

Death is necessarily counter-revolutionary.

(Sorbonne, May, 1968)

Death to the tepid.

(Paris, May, 1968)

Destroy political masturbation. Demand Revolution.

(Wall near People's Park, Berkeley, Cal., 1970)

Don't make a revolution in the image of your confused and sclerotic university.

(Sorbonne, May, 1968)

Embrace your love without dropping your gun.

(Paris, May, 1968)

Expropriate the banks, crush the banker octopuses.

(Wall, Santiago, Chile, 1970)

Free yourself from the Sorbonne (by burning it).

(Sorbonne, May, 1968)

From now on there will be only two types of people, the sheep and the revolutionaries.

(Sorbonne, May, 1968)

Give the guns to the people not the gangsters.

(Co-ed toilet, Alternate U., New York City)

Green night
Night of the barricades . . . ?
Green night or red or blue or black
What does it matter, comrades?
The hope of victory
Is what matters, comrades!

(Sorbonne, May, 1968)

How can you free me, when you can't free yourself.

(Free Church, Berkeley, Cal., 1971)

I am an agitator.

I am an enemy of the state.
UNDERNEATH
I am an enema of the state.

(Wall, Lower East Side, New York City—the first statement also appears on a button)

I come on the paving stones.

(Nanterre, May, 1968)

I decree the state of permanent happiness.

(Paris, May, 1968)

I love you! ! ! Oh! say it with paving stones! ! ! !

(Nanterre, May, 1968)

I suspect you God of being a left-wing intellectual.

(Paris, May, 1968)

If it is necessary to resort to force, don't sit on the fence.

(Sorbonne, May, 1968)

Imagination is seizing power.

(Paris, May, 1968)

Imperialism, fascism, racism ÷ workers' and students' strikes, people's war = revolution—here and in the third world.

(University of California at Los Angeles, 1970)

In the caverns of order our hands will forge bombs.

(Sorbonne, May, 1968)

In the paths that no one has trodden, risk your steps.
In the thoughts no one has thought, risk your head.

(Paris, May, 1968)

It's not a revolution, sir, it's a mutation.

(Nanterre, May, 1968)

Join the conspiracy.

Let's not change masters, let's become the masters of our lives.

Let us not consummate Marx.

(Paris, May, 1968)

Let us open the doors of asylums, prisons and other Faculties.

(Music Amphitheatre, Nanterre, May, 1968)

Let us refuse to talk to those who beat us up.

(Nanterre, May, 1968)

Let's forget the unforgettable!

(Nanterre, May, 1968)

Let's participate in the sweeping up, there are no maids here.

(Beaux-Arts, Paris, May, 1968)

Live like Vietcong.

(Berkeley, Cal., 1970)

Make love and revolution.

(University of California at Los Angeles, 1970)

Make love, not bombs.

(Fence at site of building that was destroyed by young bomb makers, who were killed in the explosion, New York City, 1970)

The Mandarin is in you.

Millionaires of all countries unite; the wind is changing.

(Paris, May, 1968)

The more I make love, the more I want to make revolution.
The more I make revolution, the more I want to make love.
(One of the enraged)

(Sorbonne, May, 1968)

Neither guerillas, bankers nor Yankees will be able to stop the Chilean Revolution.

(Wall, Santiago, Chile, 1970)

No class today, no ruling class tomorrow.

(University of California at Los Angeles, 1970)

No. 1 Rule of Revolution: Do not get caught.

(Wall near People's Park, Berkeley, Cal., 1970)

No replastering, the structure is rotten.

(Sorbonne, May, 1968)

One more war—Revolution!

(Fence near Brooklyn College, 1970)

Only revolution ends war!

ON OPPOSITE WALL

Only revolution ends poverty!

(Lower East Side, New York City, 1970)

Our hope can only come from the hopeless.

(Paris, May, 1968)

Our humble task is to organize the apocalypse.

(Men's room, Goddard College, Plainfield, Vt., 1971)

The people who are afraid will be with us if we remain strong.

(Paris, May, 1968)

Permanent confrontation.

(Paris, May, 1968)

Permanent revolution, 'death to the right.'

UNDERNEATH

All death is left and right.

(Men's room, New York University, 1969)

Power to all Blacks by any means necessary.

(Watts, Los Angeles, 1970)

Rain, rain and wind and carnage do not disperse us but weld us.

—Committee of Cultural Agitation

(Sorbonne, May, 1968)

Rather cease to be than cease to be revolutionary.

(Watts, Los Angeles, 1970)

Resist and love.

(New York University)

Revolution allows the revolutionary to sublimate his sado-masochistic, neurotic, anal tendencies into a concern for the working class.

(Subway, Columbia University stop, New York City, 1970)

Revolution ceases the moment it is necessary to sacrifice oneself for it.

(Paris, May, 1968)

Revolution/Evolution.

(University of California at Los Angeles, 1970)

Revolution is unbelievable because it is true.

(Paris, May, 1968)

Revolution must take place within people before it can come to pass in the outside world.

(Sorbonne, May, 1968)

A revolutionary is a tightrope dancer.

(Paris, May, 1968)

Run comrade, the old is chasing you.

(Sorbonne, May, 1968)

Seize the time.

(Watts, Los Angeles, 1970)

Shame is counter-revolutionary.

(Nanterre, May, 1968)

A single non-revolutionary weekend is infinitely more bloody than a month of permanent revolution.

(Paris, May, 1968)

Speeches are counter-revolutionary.

(Nanterre, May, 1968)

Take what you want.
—Sartre
Take what you need
—Jesus
There's plenty to go around
Everything is Free
—US

(Wall near People's Park, Berkeley, Cal., 1970)

There is no such thing as revolutionary thought.
There is only revolutionary action.

(Nanterre, May, 1968)

They will demand nothing.
They will request nothing.
They will seize and occupy.

(Sorbonne, May, 1968)

Those who make revolutions half-heartedly, are only digging their grave.

(Paris, May, 1968)

To be free in 1968 is to participate.

(Paris, May, 1968)

To expropriate from the rich is no crime.

(Wall, Santiago, Chile, 1970)

To shout death means to shout life.

(Nanterre, May, 1968)

To think together no. To push together yes.

(Paris, May, 1968)

Today East Village, tomorrow the world.

(Engagé Coffee House, New York City, 1967, also on a button)

Underneath the paving stones is the beach.

(Sorbonne, May, 1968)

Up the people.

UNDERNEATH

Up your ass.

UNDERNEATH

Up the people's ass.

(University of Michigan, 1970)

Guerilla urbaine.

Very soon there will be charming ruins.

(Nanterre University, May, 1968)

A Vietnam Girl
Taking in her hand
a gun is an armed
flower the wrath
of the people
flowers gather
for war

(Wall near People's Park, Berkeley, Cal., 1970)

We are the rats (perhaps) and we bite.
—The Angry Ones

We have only accomplished the insurrection of our revolution.

(Sorbonne, May, 1968)

We shall overthrow.

We shall steal the new society from the old one.

(New York University, 1969)

We will burn the Merchandise.

(Paris, May, 1968)

Weather people live.

(Fence at site of brownstone that was destroyed by three young bomb-makers, who were killed in the explosion, New York City, 1972)

Weather is vanguard.

(University of California at Los Angeles, 1970)

When law is tyranny, revolution is order.

(University of California at Los Angeles, 1970)

When the National Assembly becomes a bourgeois theatre, all the bourgeois theatres must become National Assemblies.

(Paris, May, 1968)

White students: unite, think violent, motherfuck capitalism.

(University of California at Los Angeles, 1970)

Without a people's army the people have nothing.

(Wall near People's Park, Berkeley, Cal., 1970)

Workers of the world unite, or we shoot you!

(Wall, Helsinki, 1970)

RIDDLES

If an armpit is a place to throw old arms, what is a cockpit?

(Ladies' room, The Soho Strawberry, New York City)

What do you give a wall that has everything?

UNDERNEATH

A firing squad?

(Men's room, Vietnam, 1972)

What is white and crawls up your leg?
1. Uncle Ben's perverted rice.
2. Homing sperm.

(Men's room, University of Maryland, 1972)

What similarity is there between a toilet and a bank business?
In the toilet you get a crash and then the papers fall; in the bank it is the other way around.

(Cited in Anthropophyteia, *Vol. 4, 1907)*

What's harder than stone and gentler than water flowing?
Yet the hard stone is hollowed by flowing water.

(Pompeii, 79 A.D.—written by a man who feels that a woman's resistance can be worn down by his tears)

RIMBAUD, ARTHUR (1854–1891)

Rimbaud slept here.

UNDERNEATH

Who with?

(Men's room, Goddard College, Plainfield, Vt., 1971)

ROCKWELL, GEORGE LINCOLN (1918–1969)

George Lincoln Rockwell is a robot.

George Lincoln Rockwell lives!

ROLLING STONES

Stones are sex.

ROMNEY, GEORGE (1907–)

Governor Romney—Would you buy a new car from this man?

(Cited by Art Buchwald, columnist, Washington Post*)*

ROTH, PHILIP (1933–)

I'd rather do it myself.
—Alexander Portnoy

Portnoy's mother is a shikse.

ROUSSEAU, JEAN JACQUES (1712–1778)

Concentrate on Rousseau instead of your trousseau. Sorry I Kant.

(Library staff lounge, Fort Belvoir, Va.—cited in American Library Association Bulletin, *April, 1969)*

RUDD, MARK (1948–)

(Note: Mr. Rudd was a noted campus radical)

Mark Rudd is a virgin.

(Columbia University)

RUSK, DEAN (1909–)

Dean Rusk is a recorded announcement.

RUSSELL, BERTRAND (1872–1970)

Bertrand Russell is a peacemonger.

S

SADE, MARQUIS DE (1740–1814)

Fold me, spindle me, mutilate me.
—Marquis de Sade.

The Marquis De Sade is a pervert! !

That Marquis De Sade, he sure knew how to hurt a guy.

SAINT-EXUPÉRY, ANTOINE DE (1900–1944)

Le Petit Prince is a fairy.

(University of Florida)

ST. PETER (*d.* 67? A.D.)

St. Peter likes cloves.

(Men's room, Goodale's Restaurant, New York City, 1969)

The Thief and the Doctor:

A Thief a Parson stopp'd on the Highway,
And having bid him stand, next bid him pay.
The Parson drew his Sword, for well he durst,
And quickly put his Foe unto the Worst.
Sir, (quoth the Thief) I by your Habit see,
You are a Churchman, and Debate should flee,
You know 'tis written in the sacred Word,
Jesus to Peter said, Put up thy Sword:
Truth, (quoth the Parson,) but withal then hear,
St. Peter first had cut off Malchus's Ear.

SANTA CLAUS

If you can believe in Tiny Tim, Santa Claus should be easy.

Santa Claus is a fascist pig!

Santa sucks.

(On various walls, also on a button—this legend incurred the wrath of the law and was the subject of a court case)

What is the difference between God and Santa Claus? *Answer.* There is a Santa Claus.

SANTAYANA, GEORGE (1863–1952)

George Santayana is a dirty old man.

SARTRE, JEAN-PAUL (1905–)

Jean Paul Sartre isn't.

SATYRIASIS

I'm a fucker I cannot help myself.

Stop me before I fuck more.

SCHIZOPHRENIA

Kitty the strangest Girl in Life,
For any one to make a Wife:
Her Constitution's cold, with warm Desire,
She kisses just like Ice and Fire.

(The White Hart, Acton, England)

Neurosis is red
Melancholia is blue
I'm schizophrenic
What are you?

(Lion's Head, New York City)

You're never alone with schizophrenia.

SCHULZ, CHARLES (1922–)

Charles Schultz [*sic*] is getting fat on "Peanuts."

SEALE, BOBBY (1936–)

Free Bobby Seale.

UNDERNEATH

Free the people.

UNDERNEATH

Free me.

(Watts, Los Angeles, 1970)

Light a fire for Bobby.

(Watts, Los Angeles, 1970)

Stop the slaughter of seals.

UNDERNEATH

You mean Bobby Seale, you dummy.

(IRT subway, New York City, 1971)

SEDUCTION

Familiarity breeds attempt.

I am a young Thing, just come from my Mammy.
S.D.

UNDERNEATH

Then you want to be kiss'd. G–d d—n ye.
Captain R.T.

(Red Lion, Egham, England)

In a Window, In a Window,
I saw a Cat lick her Ear in a Window,

(On a window, Maidenhead, England)

Nay, Sir, — she cry'd I'll swear I won't.
I vow I never yet have don't!
Lord I Pray, Sir, do not press me so;
I'll call for all the Folks below.
Good Lord! what is't? You're very rude?
And then she acted like a Prude.
And then,
Like Birds of a Feather.
They flock'd together.

S.T.
To kiss is human; to seduce, divine.

SEGAL, GEORGE (1924–)

Ten seconds from now you will be encased in plaster for George Segal's latest work—"Man in the toilet stall."

(Men's room, Museum of Modern Art, New York City, 1970)

SEX

Above all else fuck.

UNDERNEATH

Above all else—sky.

(Ladies' room, Le Metro Caffe Espresso, New York City)

According to the rule of the law
every young man as a hunter
must fuck three times a day.

(Men's toilet, Erfurter, 1906)

Ashes to ashes and dust to dust
if it wasn't for cunts your cock would rust.

(El Centro, Cal., 1928)

Assume the missionary position.

Be creative, invent a sexual perversion.

(Ladies' room, Ninth Circle Restaurant, New York City —also on a button)

Be modern—Fuck.

(YMCA, New York City)

Birds do it and fly
Girls do it and dry
dogs do it and stick to it
so why don't you and I.

(Waterloo, Iowa, 1928)

A bush in the hand is worth two birds.

(Men's room, Dorrian's Red Hand Restaurant, New York City, 1971)

Coito ergo sum.

(Greenwich Village, New York City)

Confrontation. But first cunt.

(Nanterre University, May, 1968)

Don't judge a girl by her looks
For her eyes may be black as charcoal
For her beauty lies between the thighs
Two inches from her ass hole.

(Yosemite National Park, Cal., 1928)

Friend, the beautiful girls are indeed nice things. Even if you see one only half naked the eleventh finger stiffens.

(Men's room, Germany)

Fuck, Fuck, Fuck, Fuck, what else?

UNDERNEATH

Eat, Eat, Eat, Eat.

(State Street Tavern, Bellingham, Wash.)

Fucking is the best thing and has been such for a thousand years.

(Men's room, Konstanz am Rhein, 1908)

Gilt without sex.

(Engagé Coffee House, New York City)

Hail Priapus!

(University of New Mexico, Albuquerque)

Happiness is a warm puppy.

UNDERNEATH

No! it's a warm pussy.

(Men's room, Boston University—first legend is also on a button)

Help stamp in sex.

Help stamp out hymens.

(Construction fence, also on a button)

"A hole is a hole" said the cook and fucked the gaspipe.

(Men's room, Germany)

Horray, horray, It is the first of May,
Outdoor f——ing starts today.

(Ladies' room, Lion's Head, New York City)

I am!
I exist!
For what!

UNDERNEATH

For a piece of ass!

I Fuck is a many-spendored thing.

(Toilet, Fair Park, Dallas)

If it moves, fondle it.

(The Village Gate, New York City—also on a button)

If you want to get laid call Mrs. Murphy at CH 0-110—if her husband answers he's pretty good too.

(Fence, Alfred University, N.Y.)

Large cats can be dangerous but a little pussy never hurt anyone.

(IRT subway, New York City)

Last sperm in is a rotten egg.

Let's fug.

Liberate a cunt today.

(Men's room, Men's faculty lounge, Hunter College, New York City)

More congress, less legislation.

Omne Animal Post Coitiem Triste Est.

UNDERNEATH

You're typing people.

(Village Gate, New York City)

Orifice—not artifice.
The risen flesh commands, let there be love.

(Pompeii, 79 A.D.)

Sex is beautiful but unsanitary.

UNDERNEATH

So wash.

(Ladies' room, Hunter College, New York City, 1970)

The sex life of a camel is stranger than anyone thinks,
For in moments of amorous passion he's been known to make love to the Sphinx.
But the Sphinx's posterior channel has been closed by the sands of the Nile,
Which accounts for the hump on the camel and the Sphinx's perpetual smile.
[*Quite common in England and has been set to music.*]

VARIATION:

Oh, the sexual life of a camel is stranger than anyone thinks;
In the height of the mating season it tried to bugger the Sphinx.
But the Sphinx's celestial orifice was blocked by the sands of the Nile,
Which accounts for the hump on the camel and the Sphinx's inscrutable smile.

Sex proves all men are not equal.

(Ladies' room, Lansdale, Pa., 1972)

Sex takes the drudgery out of housework.

Wrap your loins around me as softly as a kiss on a babies cheek.

(On subway column)

SEXUAL QUANDARY

Girls, what do you do when you find your cat with another cat?

UNDERNEATH

Let the cats be happy together and find a MAN.

Girls—What do you do when your cat finds you with another cat?

UNDERNEATH

Buy some catnip at the A & P. Your cat will forget all about both of you.

(Ladies' room, Limelight Restaurant, New York City)

I have a problem. I am 21 and I have never been with a man. I masturbate a lot but it's not the same. Can you help me?

UNDERNEATH

Improve your figure and personality or both.

UNDERNEATH

Forget it, men are nothing, keep masturbating.

UNDERNEATH

You're probably shy, don't be—go out and enjoy.

UNDERNEATH

It's no problem—it keeps one out of trouble—How are you sure it's not the same if you haven't tried?

UNDERNEATH

Search yourself—you probably have hang-ups about sex—you're afraid. Relax and don't shun it. It's great.

UNDERNEATH

Wait—your time will come.

(Ladies' room, Hunter College, New York City, 1970)

What's the matter with me? Every time someone talks about women my tits get hard instead of my cock.

(Men's room, Hunter College, New York City, 1972)

SHAKESPEARE, WILLIAM (1564–1616)

Othello was a bigot.

Shakespeare eats Bacon.

UNDERNEATH

It can't be Donne.

(Lion's Head, New York City)

To be or not to be is not the question, it's what was.

(Old Vic Theatre, London)

To pee or not to pee!

(Coed toilet, Alternate U., New York City)

SHEEN, FULTON (1895–)

Consult Bishop Sheen for revocation of the 10 Commandments.

(Ladies' room, Community College of New York, 1969)

SITWELL, EDITH (1887–1964)

Edith Sitwell is a transvestite.

UNDERNEATH

She's dead, you dope!

UNDERNEATH

OK, Edith Sitwell is a dead transvestite.

(Chumley's Restaurant, New York City)

SLANDER, *see also* INSULT

Clelia's Epitaph, who was slander'd to Death:

Death, to vindicate her Wrongs,
Gives her Fame which never dies;
So the Life that died with Shame,
Lives in Death with glorious Fame.
R.S. Oct. 17. 1708.

(Catherine-Wheel, Henley, England)

Gaius Marius wife sleeps with anybody.

(Wall, Ancient Rome)

There's none but the Vicious, or the Base,
That false Reports can trouble or disgrace:
The virtuous Man must ever stand secure
'Gainst all the Lies which Falsehood can procure:
For a sound Mind or Conscience gives a Peace,
Which to Eternity can never cease.
E.K.

UNDERNEATH

D—n your conscientious Rascals; there's so few of them in this Age, that a Man appears singular who is govern'd thereby.

Capt. T.R. 1730.

The Four Swans, Uxbridge, England)

Tim Kirby, Peter Harrod, and Will Hall,
Are three fit Pieces for a Bog-House Wall.

UNDERNEATH

But Old Nick has got them all.

(Boghouse in St. Michael's Parish, Norwich, England)

SMOKING, see TOBACCO

SOCIAL CHANGE

The B.B.C. has always been 50 years old.

(British Broadcasting Corporation offices, London, Nov. 14, 1972, on the occasion of its 50th anniversary)

Down with Matriarchal Society!

(Toilet, BMT subway, New York City)

Nostalgia isn't what it used to be.

Our Rulers are dinosaurs fearing extinction.

(Wall near People's Park, Berkeley, Cal.)

Someday we'll look back on all this and shudder.

Tear down your walls.

(Wall near People's Park, Berkeley, Cal., 1970)

The world is going through a great big menopause.

(Wolfie's Restaurant, Brooklyn)

This is the dawning of the Age of Aquarius—and the sunset of the corporate state Fascism.

(Free Church, Berkeley, Cal., 1971)

What strange Vicissitudes we see
  In Pleasure, as in Realms take Place
For nothing here can constant be,
  Where springing Joys the old efface.
The Theatre of Yore the Field
  Of Conquests, gain'd by blooming Maids,
Now must to modern Operas yield,
  As they, to courtly Masquerades.
Nor better fares those sweet Retreats
  Which they in sultry Summer chose:
Since Scarb'rough, Paradise of Sweets!
  On ruined Bath and Tunbridge rose.

(On a window of the Great Room, Scarborough, England)

SOCIAL CLASSES

The gentry prefer double entry.
The proletariat like to bury it.

A mark of quality is still a mark.

(Lion's Head, New York City)

The Poor have little, Beggars none,
The Rich too much, enough, not one.

(Boghouse, Putney, England)

Rich people kiss each other, poor people piss on each other.

(Toilet, Berlin, 1910)

Send the wasps back to the English debtors prisons where they belong.

(Railroad Station, Riverdale, N.Y., 1972)

Social advantages are death.

(Sorbonne, May, 1968)

Sunshine for the little man is to fuck and get drunk.

(Men's room, Germany)

They eat beans then they belch chicken.

(Mexico City—said of those who pretend to be of a higher social class)

You will all end by croaking of comfort.

(Nanterre, May, 1968)

SOCIAL ISOLATION, *see also* LONELINESS

Concrete breeds indifference.

Industrialization is threatening us. Rubber nipples are turning us into a carnivorous society.

(Paris, May, 1968)

SOCIAL VALUES

Clean box write something clean here.	Dirty box write something dirty here.
an unused rubber a douched vagina a recently blown prick	apple pie motherhood the girl next door officers of the law

(Men's room, Rutgers University)

I love: Greed, sexual lust, violence, hate, defecation, war, New York Athletic club, Pentagon, wrestling, rollar [*sic*] derby, Police Benevolent Association, Proccacino, money, napalm, General Hershey, Ike, stock market, God, Frank Sinatra, Las Vegas, Daily News, Flag, democracy and freedom, pink Cadillac Convertibles, missiles, ABM.

(On a religious poster, 14th Street Station, IND subway)

I'm a square I drive a Rambler and I go to church.

(IRT subway, New York City, 1969)

Long live love, wine and drinking, adulterous intercourse, the Pope and fucking.

(Men's room, Germany)

Production and consummation are the two mammary glands of our society.

We remain faithful to our fate: perversity, anxiety and laziness.

(Men's room, Germany)

SOCIALISM

Communism: Socialism at its highest potency.
Capitalism: Democracy at its lowest impotence.

(Stockholm official graffiti wall [Kotterplank], *November 7, 1968)*

Copper for the people of Chile.

(Wall, Santiago, Chile, 1970)

Down with socialist realism. Long live surrealism.

(Paris, May, 1968)

I am a creeping socialist.

Socialism: forwardness, humanism, "what one is."
Capitalism: backwardness, egoism, criminality, "what one has."

(Stockholm official graffiti wall [Kotterplank], *November 7, 1968)*

SOCRATES (469–399 B.C.)

Acquit Socrates.

Sockitome, Socrates!

(Arlington County Public Library, Va.—cited in American Library Association Bulletin, *April, 1969)*

Socrates drank no-cal Hemlock.

Socrates eats Hemlock.

(Lion's Head, New York City, also on a button)

SODOMY

The following was written on an ad for the medication Preparation H for hemorrhoids:

Greek Toothpaste.

If I have only one life to live,
let me live it as a Greek.

(IND subway, New York City)

Lend your ear to many—
Your voice to few—
Your butt to none.

(Paradox Restaurant, New York City)

Up love!
Up penis!
Up your ass!

(The Exit Coffee House, New York City)

SONTAG, SUSAN (1933–)

Renata Adler is smarter than Susan Sontag.

SOUTHERN STATES

Save your Dixie Cups. The South will rise again.

The South will rise again because shit floats.

(Men's room, New York University, 1969)

SPANIARDS IN AMERICA

Here was the General Don Diego de Vargas who conquered for our Holy Faith, and for the Royal Crown all of New Mexico at his own expense, year 1692.

(El Morro National Monument, New Mexico)

His Lordship the Governor here made a call
Since, now, the impossible (the truth to relate-o)
His trusty arm and courage holds in thrall
With the chariots of our sovereign lord (of all);
A thing: which he alone brought to this state (-O-)
Of August, 1629, that he (need no more tarry)
(But) well may to Zuni proceed and the Faith hither carry.

(El Morro National Monument, New Mexico)

I am the Captain General of the Province of New Mexico for the King our Lord, passed by here on the return from the pueblos of Zuni on the 29th of July the year 1620 and put them at peace at their humble petition, they asking favor as their vassals of his Majesty and promising anew their obedience, all of which he did, with clemency, zeal and prudence, as a most Christianlike (gentleman) extraordinary and gallant soldier of enduring and praised memory.

(El Morro National Monument, New Mexico)

Passed by here the Governor Don Juan de Arnate, from the discovery of the Sea of the South (Gulf of California) in the 16th of April, 1605.

(El Morro National Monument, New Mexico)

SPARTACUS

(Note: A gladiator who led a slave revolt against Rome in 73 B.C.)

Serfs up—Spartacus.

SPECK, RICHARD B. (1941–)

(Note: A convicted mass murderer)

Johnson & Speck in '68.

SPELLMAN, FRANCIS (1889–1967)

(Note: Archbishop of New York, Cardinal of the Catholic church)

Cardinal Spellman you should be ashamed and ask God's forgiveness.

UNDERNEATH

You're forgiven.
—Bobby

SPINOZA, BARUCH (1632–1677)

If it wasn't for Spinoza we'd all be in Pittsburgh.

(Men's room, Princeton University, 1970)

Spinoza eats bagels.

(Lion's Head, New York City)

SPOCK, BENJAMIN (1903–)

Dr. Spock wears rubber pants.

Porto [*sic*] Rican babies are brought up on Dr. Spick.

SPORTS

Free the Indianapolis 500.

Graham Hill was a speed freak.

(Free Store Theatre, New York City)

The philosopher Amnaeus Seneca is the only Roman writer to condemn the bloody games.

(Pompeii, 79 A.D.)

Severus, Freedman, 55 fights, has just won again.

(Pompeii, 79 A.D.)

Spare the rod and spoil the drag race.

(Library staff lounge, Fort Belvoir, Va.—cited in American Library Association Bulletin, *April, 1969)*

That's okay, Casey, a year from now nobody will remember you struck out.

(Wall, Sacramento, 1967—refers to "Casey at the Bat" by Ernest Lawrence Thayer)

STALIN, JOSEPH (1879–1953)

Long live Stalin! Without him the Soviet Union would be an American colony.

(Stockholm official graffiti wall [Kotterplank], *November 7, 1968)*

STANDISH, MILES (1584?–1656)

If Miles Standish had shot a cat instead of a turkey we would all be eating pussy for Thanksgiving.

STEIN, GERTRUDE (1874–1946)

Alice B. Toklas loves Gertrude Stein.

(Toilet, North Beach, San Francisco)

STORM, GALE (1922–)

Gale Storm lives!

UNDERNEATH

It's about time.

STUDENTS FOR A DEMOCRATIC SOCIETY

If SDS closes down the school you won't be able to get your diploma and graduate.

UNDERNEATH

Too bad! No diploma to Plasticland.

(San Francisco State College, 1968)

New SDS banner. 

(Men's room, Rutgers University)

s.d.s. = $ds^2 = \frac{1}{2} as^2 = \frac{1}{2}$ ass.

(Men's room, Princeton University, 1970)

S.D.S. = SS.

(Cornell University)

Support the strike; don't shit—SDS.

(Men's room, University of Michigan, 1970)

SUBWAYS

Cast your vote for free subways, put your chewing gum in the token slot.

(IND subway, New York City)

Dear T.A.
I can keep it up as long as you can.

(IND subway, New York City, 1970)

Dirty train stations cause terminal illness.

(Subway, New York City)

Don't pay the unfare.

(Various subway stations, New York City, 1970—in protest against the fare raise)

Ride the subways free—fuck the fare.

(IND subway, New York City, 1970—one of many irate messages because of the subway fare raise from 20 to 30 cents)

Subways will be stricken.

("55" Bar, New York City)

30 cents to ride in a crowded, accursed vehicle of transportation.

(IRT subway, New York City, 1971)

SUICIDE

The greatest high is suicide.

(Ladies' room, Hofstra College, N.Y.)

The most sincere form of criticism is suicide—do it.

(Men's room, Goose & Gherkin Ale House, New York City, 1969)

My Swan Song

I go to a better world
Now there will be wild goings-on
And full plates eternally
I have always been hungry on earth,
Yonder I will eat and drink
And one thing will be particularly beautiful,
One doesn't have to go to the toilet.

(Vienna, late 19th century—cited in Leben, Meinungen und Wirken, *by Wetti Himmlisch, 1906—this was a suicide note left by a starving poet in a toilet stall)*

A young Lady, who hang'd herself, left the following Lines upon the Table:

O Death! thou pleasing End of human Woe!
Thou Cure of Life, thou best of Things below!
May'st thou for ever shun the Coward Slave,
And thy soft Slumbers only ease the Brave!

SULLIVAN, ED (1902–)

Life without love is a living death.

UNDERNEATH

Ed Sullivan must be loveless, then.

SUPERNATURAL

Some nights the wolves are silent and the moon howls.

Trees at night have voices which call the lost children to their sides.

(Ladies' room, Limelight Restaurant, New York City)

SUSANN, JACQUELINE (1926–)

Give a damn—Jacquelyn Susann does.

(New York University, 1969)

SWIFT, JONATHAN (1667–1745)

There are three crosses at your door, hang up your wife and you'll count four.

(On a window, Three Crosses Inn, England—written by Jonathan Swift)

T

TAXATION

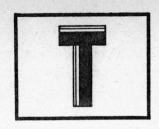

Help the Government stamp out take home pay!

Tax the churches.

TENNYSON, ALFRED (1809–1892)

Better to have failed your Wassermann test than never to have loved at all.

(Ladies' room, Limelight Restaurant, New York City—takeoff on Tennyson's "In Memoriam": "Tis better to have loved and lost, Than never to have loved at all.")

Into the valley of death rode the sex hungry.

It is better to have loved and lost than never to have lost at all.

(Ladies' room, McBell's Restaurant, New York City, 1969)

'Tis better to have loved an hermaphrodite—Than never to have loved at all.

(Chumley's Restaurant, New York City)

TEXAS

Dallas still lives, God *must* be dead.

(Men's room, Southern Methodist University, Dallas)

Directions to get to Texas: Go west until you smell shit, that's Oklahoma. Then go south until you step in it—that's Texas.

(Manchester, N.H., c. 1953)

Texas T shirts.

(Bathroom, Callas, Tex.—written on a receptacle that contained toilet seat covers)

THEATER

Actius, darling of the people, come back quickly.

(Pompeii, 79 A.D.—this is a tribute to C. Ummidius Actius Anicetus, actor of pantomime; he was the Sir Laurence Olivier of his time)

All the world's a stage and the people on it are poorly rehearsed.

UNDERNEATH

No, just poorly directed.

UNDERNEATH

No, just poorly cast.

(American Academy of Dramatic Arts, New York City, 1969)

Vive The Living Theater.

(Nanterre, May, 1968—The Living Theatre is a nomadic American avant-garde theater group that played in France in 1968)

THOREAU, HENRY (1817–1862)

Henry Thoreau talks to himself.

(Cited by Jim Moran, columnist, Chicago Daily News, *May 27, 1967)*

Thoreau was a hippie.

UNDERNEATH

But at least she [*sic*] could read and write.

(Fedora restaurant, New York City)

THURMOND, STROM (1902–)

Strom Thurmond sniffs drainpipes.

(Men's room, Rutgers University)

TIME

Here Time is bought and sold; 'Tis plain, my Friend,
My Clocks and Watches shew what I intend;
For you I Time correct,
My Time I spend;
By Time I live,
But not one Inch will lend,
Except you pay the ready down or send:
I trust no Time,
Unless the Times do mend.

(On a watchmaker's window, Fleet Street, London)

I have no Legs,
And yet I go and stand:
And when I stand, I lie;
Witness my Hand;
Mentiri non est meunt.

(On a clock in Tavistock Street, Covent Garden, London, 1712)

I've shot the morning, time is dead.

(Men's room, Princeton University, 1970)

On a Watch-Case in a Gentleman's Pocket, given him by a Lady.
The Wretched pray to make more Haste,
The Happy say we fly too fast;
Therefore impossible to know,
Whether I go too fast or slow.
S.M.

Why worry about tomorrow when today is so far off?

TINY TIM (1923?-)

If you can believe in Tiny Tim, Santa Claus should be easy.

Tiny Tim is just another pretty face.

TOBACCO

Alcohol and tobacco do away with half of mankind but without alcohol and tobacco the other half would die.
(Men's room, Germany)

Cancer cures smoking.
(On various walls, also on a button)

Cigarette coupons pay for cancer operations.

Not only are you getting cancer you're polluting MY air.
—Mr. American Tobacco Co.

UNDERNEATH

Cancer, emphazema [*sic*], yellow teeth, death.

UNDERNEATH

Yes, but we're helping ease the population explosion.
(IND subway, New York City, 1971)

Of course I smoke, it's safer than breathing.

Smoke—Choke—Croak.

Tobacco, that outlandish weed,
It dries the brain, and spoils the seed
It dulls the spirit, it dims the sight,
It robs a woman of her right.
(Trinity Church, England, 18th century)

TOILETS, *see* WATER CLOSETS

TOKLAS, ALICE B. (1877–1967)

Alice B. Toklas loves Gertrude Stein.
(Toilet, North Beach, San Francisco)

TOLKIEN, J. R. R. (1922–)

Come to middle earth.

Frodo has been busted.

(Men's room, Back Fence Bar, New York City)

Frodo is God.

Frodo lives.

(On various walls, also on a button)

Help feed my hobbit.

(Café Figaro, New York City, also on a button)

Gandalf for President.

Sauron lives!

Tolkien spokien here.

TOLSTOY, LEO (1828–1910)

Leo Tolstoy drinks tea from a glass.

(Cited by Jim Moran, columnist, Chicago Daily News, *May 27, 1967)*

TOTALITARIANISM

R.A. 1700, writ suspension, martial law—Marcos' tools to stifle dissent!

(University of Philippines, 1972)

On a poster which said "The Iron Curtain Isn't Soundproof," the following was written:
Some truth gets out.

TRANSVESTISM

Clark Kent is a transvestite.

Edith Sitwell is a transvestite.

UNDERNEATH

She's dead, you dope!

UNDERNEATH

OK, Edith Sitwell is a dead transvestite.

(Chumley's Restaurant, New York City)

John Lennon is Jesus in drag.

Judge Crater is a transvestite.
[*Interesting supposition as to why he was never found.*]

Morris is a transvestite, he wears a lace yamulka.

O! would I go in a woman's clothes—
And had a cunt of pig leather,
Then I would travel around the world
And let myself be fucked for free.

(Copenhagen, 1910)

Virginia Slims are Silva Thins in drag.

(IRT subway, New York City)

TREACLE

Let me smile as I pass you by. I may never walk this street again.

(Ladies' room, Limelight restaurant, New York City)

A smile increases ones face value.

Today is the first day of the rest of your life—celebrate now.

Want him to be more of a man? Try being more of a woman.

UNDERNEATH

How much more?

UNDERNEATH

Of this shit can we take.

(Union Bulletin Board, Antioch College, 1968)

You are me . . . happy birthday.

*(Men's room, Princton University, 1970)

TROTSKY, LEON (1877–1940)

All Trots [*Trotskyites*] should break out in a fast one.
(Co-ed toilet, Alternate U., New York City, 1969)

To sell some Guevara, to slip in some Trotsky, is to be a traitor two times.

Trotsky will return.
(Café Figaro, New York City)

TRUCKS, *see* AUTOMOBILES

TRUMAN, HARRY (1884–1972)

I miss Ike.

UNDERNEATH

Hell, I miss Harry.
(Cited in Norton Mockridge, columnist, Boston Herald, *December 2, 1966)*

TRUTH

Novelty is revolutionary, so is truth.
(Paris, May, 1968)

Only the truth is revolutionary.
(Nanterre, May, 1968)

On a poster which said "The Iron Curtain Isn't Soundproof," the following was written:
Some truth gets out.

The truth is the safest lie.
(IRT subway, New York City)

TWIGGY (1949–   )

Twiggy is a Metrecal junkie.
(Subway)

Twiggy is an android.

Twiggy is the deflated British pound.

U

UNICORN TAPESTRY

The Unicorn Tapestry eats paisley pears.

Unicorn Tapestry for President.

The Unicorn Tapestry forever.

(Wall, New York City)

The Unicorn Tapestry is really news.

(On the side of a newsstand, New York City)

The Unicorn Tapestry smokes pot.

(Washington Square Arch, New York City)

You can bank on the Unicorn Tapestry.

(Savings bank on West 4th Street, New York City)

UNIDENTIFIED FLYING OBJECTS, *see* FLYING SAUCERS

UNITED NATIONS

The only difference between an unclear war and a nuclear war is the way you use the UN.

(University of Michigan)

UNITED STATES CONGRESS

If pro means for and con means against, what is the opposite of progress? The answer is Congress.

(IRT subway, Hunter College stop, New York City, 1971)

The inclination to turn on, like the inclination to make love, is unlikely to be affected by the will of Congress.

A plague on both your houses.
(Public washroom, U.S. Capitol)

Send your congressman a candygram.

Whack HUAC.

UNITED STATES—FOREIGN RELATIONS

If you like Vietnam and Cambodia you'll love Jordan.
(Men's room, Princeton University, 1970)

Stop sending planes to Israel—Equality for the Arabs.
(Ladies' room, Hunter College, New York City)

Yankee go home!!
UNDERNEATH
and take me with you.

Yankee go home!
UNDERNEATH
via Pan Am.

UNITED STATES OF AMERICA

America good country, the people no good.
(Grand Central Station, New York City)

America has a frog in its throat.

America: love it or improve it.
(On a construction worker's hard hat, Detroit, 1971)

America, love it or leave it.
" " sell it or rent it.
" " bend it or peel it.
" " steal it or change it.
" " stuff it or puff it.
" " hire it or fire it.
" " comb it or clip it.
" " fold it or spindle it.
" " rape it or pillage it.
" " cook it or freeze it.
" " import it or deport it.
" " sink it or float it.
" " chew it or swallow it.
" " shoot it or sniff it.

(Cited by Howard Smith, The Village Voice, *December 31, 1970)*

America, rich and arrogant, founded on racism and theft. You'll get yours this summer, 1966.

(Engagé Coffee House, New York City)

America! We're up your ass. ☮

(Tortilla Flat Restaurant, New York City)

An American's a person who isn't afraid to criticize the President—but is always polite to traffic cops.

(Construction fence, Midtown, New York City)

Amerika, save it or screw it.

(University of California at Los Angeles, 1970—use of "k" is a reference to Fascism, i.e. Ku Klux Klan)

The bald eagle wears a hair piece.

(University of Michigan)

Don't think, follow! Don't talk, shoot! It's the American way.

Horray for the Apollo 11 Eagle! To hell with you degenerated mentally sick bathroom scrawlers, negro worshipers, beatniks, misc. decadent souls. Up America. Up the glorious romantic fire of the QUEST!

UNDERNEATH

Up the ass of the ruling class.

(Men's room, New York University, 1969)

Is the U.S. ready for self-government?

(Robert Saffron found this title for his book in the subway, scrawled on a wall)

Just as with communist tyranny, to hell with U.S. Government tyranny; Travel ban, HUAC, Support of South Africa and Franco, Failure to send troops to the South, bombing of civilians in N and Central Vietnam. Sustaining S. Amer. oppressive autocracy. And more!!

UNDERNEATH

Fuck this.

UNDERNEATH

says chicken-shit right wing.

UNDERNEATH

Fuck you, Bitch.

UNDERNEATH

usual Fascist far-rightest intellectual approach—brilliant, logical, fair.

UNDERNEATH

Your ideas are as wet as your piss.

(Walls, bathroom, New School for Social Research, April, 1965)

Motherhood, apple pie, and the American way WILL NO DOUBT LEAD US DOWN THE PRIMROSE PATH TO WORLD WAR III.

(Florida State University)

This is the home of the free and the brave. The free are in Canada, the brave are in jail.

(Ladies' room, University of California at Berkeley, 1971)

U.S.A. entered World War II after Stalingrad, El Alemain, Pearl Harbor.

UNDERNEATH

To make profits.

(Stockholm official graffiti wall [Kotterplank], *November 7, 1968)*

USA is a mist.

U.S. has the answer.

UNDERNEATH

What was the question?

U.S. is the more ignorant nation on earth.

(The Dom, St. Mark's Place, New York City)

UNIVERSITIES AND COLLEGES, *see also* EDUCATION

As I slide down the bannister of life,
I will always remember Princeton as a splinter in my ass.

(Laundry room, Princeton University, 1971)

Avenge Kent State.

UNDERNEATH

Burn the protester. Light up a Kent.

(IRT subway, New York City, Mother's Day, 1970)

Crazed Columbia U remedies.

(Construction fence, Harvard University, 1972)

Q: Did you hear about the man'eating monster that got loose on the Bates Campus?
R: No—what happened?
A: It died of starvation.
R: I heard it gained weight.
A: You heard wrong—it's emaciated.
Moral of the story: No men on Bates Campus.

(Library stacks, Bates College, Lewiston, Me.)

That is, wipe out the fraternity system.

(Men's room, University of Colorado)

Getting an education at the University of Kansas is like having $50.00 shoved up your ass, a nickel at a time.

(University of Kansas)

God said "Shit" and then there was Alfred University.

(Fence, Alfred University, N.Y.)

Goddard College: Most faculty are in a perpetually arrested state of puberty.

(Goddard College, Plainfield, Vt., 1971)

Underneath an arrow pointing to toilet paper
Hunter College diploma.

(Ladies' room, Hunter College, New York City, 1972)

Join the N.Y.U. 4H club:
—Horns
—Hype
—Hysteria
—Hassling.

(New York University, 1969)

Remember Kent. Shut it down.

(University of California at Los Angeles, 1970)

Rutgers is a whore, you pay to get fucked.

(Men's room, Rutgers University)

Sorbonne, rue des Eagles = School of the street.
And if the Sorbonne were to be burned down?

(Sorbonne, May, 1968)

UPDIKE, JOHN (1932–)

Lesbians read John Updike.

URINATION

The attendant here gets $3 a day and all the piss he can drink.

Between the thighs
is the cunt,
out of which flows pure water.
—ha ha

(High school, Braunau, 1908; written in Latin)

Bulls with short horns stand close.

Come out you coward, you just have to piss.

Cuddle up a little closer, it's shorter than you think.

Did you ever see Sally make water?
She has a terrible stream;
She piss' three miles and a quarter,
You couldn't see Sally for steam.

(Cited in Anthropophyteia, *Vol. 4, 1907)*

Do like pa not like sis, raise the lid before you piss.

Do not throw cigarettes in the urinals, we do not piss in your ashtrays.

Don't be a star, use both hands.

Don't eat yellow snow.

(Men's toilet, bar, Alaska)

Don't forget to pull the chain for Waterloo needs the water.

(Electric Park, Waterloo, Iowa, September 9, 1932—cited in Lexical Evidence from Folk Epigraphy, *by Allen Water Read, Paris, 1935)*

Don't piddle on the seat, we'd rather you piddle on your feet.

(Toilet, London)

Flush hard, Tucson needs the water!

(Restaurant, Phoenix)

God bless all men who piss this way.

Here patrons drink piss, employees eat pussy.

(The Village Gate, New York City)

However hard you shake your peg
At least one drop runs down your leg.

(British version)

I hate to pee and leave.

(Ladies' room, The Dom, New York City)

If you are reading this you are probably pissing in your left shoe.

UNDERNEATH

No, my right shoe I'm cross-eyed.

(Lion's Head, New York City)

If you can piss this high join the fire dept.

(This legend is always written high on a wall)

If you can piss this high, you're baptizing the cat in the urinal on the other side.

(Men's room, New York University)

If you read this you are not aiming in the right direction.

If your hose is short and your pump is weak
You better stand close or you'll pee on your feet.

In case of air raid, duck under urinal, it hasn't been hit yet.

Is urinating a religious experience? No it is an expressive religion.

Is urinating a religious experience?

UNDERNEATH

Yes, it is giving of oneself.

UNDERNEATH

Only in groups.

(Ladies' room, Le Metro Caffe Espresso, New York City)

The Leaning Tower of Pisser.

(Engagé Coffee House, New York City)

Little drops of water
upon the toilet floor
uses lots of elbow grease
and makes the porter sore
So now kind friends remember
before the water flows
please adjust the distance
according to your hose.

(Madison River Camp, Yellowstone National Park, August 10, 1928)

The man who stands
With his prick in his hands
And pisses all over the seat
Is the man who should have
His ballicks smashed
And his ass kicked over the street.

(Two Medicine Camp, Glacier National Park, Mont., August 6, 1928)

Many a girl pisses here, oh how I could enjoy the juice.

(Men's room, Breslau—cited in Anthropophyteia, *Vol. 6, 1909)*

Men with short bats stand close to the plate.

My host, I've wet the bed. My sins I bare, but why? you ask. No pot was anywhere.

(Pompeii, 79 A.D.)

No matter how you dance and prance
The last two drops go down your pants.

Notice: Men with peckers too short to reach over the seat, please piss outside.

(Many Glacier Camp, Glacier National Park, Mont., August 4, 1928)

Oh! I wish I had the balls of a stallion
and a prick of a fellow I know
I would flee to the highest church steeple
and I would piss on the people below.

(Banff, Alberta, 1928)

Old rams with short horns please stand up close.

(Fort Lewis, Tacoma, Wash., c. 1945)

One masturbates, one pisses and craps until life's thread is cut.

(Men's room, Munich—cited in Anthropophyteia, *Vol. 5, 1908)*

One step from the nose is the water hose.
One step from the neck is the sausage factory.

(Breslau—cited in Anthropophyteia, *Vol. 5, 1908)*

Pilgrims with short muskets stand within firing range.

(Toilet, Boston)

Pilots with short engine mounts—please taxi up close.

(Men's toilet, Alberta)

Piss for poverty.

(Graffiti Restaurant, New York City)

Piss in bliss.

Piss on the floor Mr. Johnson can't swim.

(P.S. 161, Brooklyn)

Pisser, don't piss on my bones, I pray,
nor defecate, if you'd be yet more kind.
See the thick pile of nettle—turn away.
Here it's not safe to squat with bare behind.

(Pompeii, 79 A.D.*)*

Please flush the toilet, Regina needs the water!

(Biffy, Moose Jaw, Saskatchewan)

Puritans with short muskets step up to the firing line.

(Damiscotta, Me., c. *1950)*

Save water—do not flush until it's dark yellow.

Stags with short horns, please stand close!

Stand close, don't flatter yourself.

Stand closer, don't be so proud.

(Men's room, Greyhound bus station, New York City, 1940)

Stand closer, the monks have bare feet.

(Cited in Graffiti *by Richard Freeman, England)*

Stand up close. The next fellow may be a Southerner and be barefooted.

(Camp Maxey, Paris, Tex., 1945)

Stand up close. The next man might have holes in his shoes.

Stop me before I piss again.

(Men's room, Telephone Company, New York City, 1969)

Take a giant step, it's not as long as you think.

This is a urinal, not a rifle range, pee in it, not at it.

(Men's room, Sheppard Field, Wichita Falls, Tex.)

"To the beloved"
The dog pisses on 3 legs,
on all fours pisses the cow.
Everyone pisses with what he's got.
In my heart is only you.

(Men's room, Chemnitz—cited in Anthropophyteia, *Vol. 4, 1906; the humor consists of the pun on the words* bist *and* pisst*)*

Two hands for beginners.

The following was written on a sign that said, "Water unfit for drinking":
The urine is not too bad.

(Men's toilet, Statue of Liberty ferry, New York City, 1969)

Veni, vidi, wiwi.

(Harvard Club, New York City)

We aim to please, you aim too please.
The management. P.S. Our janitor can't swim.

(University of North Carolina, 1959)

We aim to please, your aim will help.

We don't swim in your toilet
Please don't piss in our pool.

What are you looking up here for? You're pissing on your shoes.

Written high on a wall and sideways:
While you are reading this you are peeing on the guy next to you.

You can shake and shake as much as you please.
But there'll still be a drop for your B.V.D.s.

You can wiggle, jiggle, jump or dance
But the last three drops go down your pants.

Young bucks with short horns step up close.

(Men's room, Wy.)

UTTERANCE

I have nothing to say.

(Paris, May, 1968)

I have something to say, but I don't know what it is.

(Paris, May, 1968)

It often shows a fine command of the English language to say nothing.

(University of Michigan)

It's better to die in silence than to start to say something and get cut off.

V

VAN GOGH, VINCENT (1853–1890)

Go, Van Gogh.

(On The Van Gogh Apartments, New York City)

VENEREAL DISEASES

Any lady who believes her mother about clap etc. from toilet seats should not be in bars.

(Ladies' room, "55" Bar, New York City)

Bright is my Silvia, when she' drest;
When naked, cloath'd with wond'rous Charms;
Her Mein has oft my Heart opprest;
Her Nakedness I have possest;
And by the last I am distrest,
By the Embraces of her Arms.
What can we Mortals say of Love?
Why? 'Tis the Pleasure of the Gods above:
But then if Cl–ps proceed from Love,
How hot are all the Gods and Godesses above!
A fine Reward for Love for Love!

UNDERNEATH

Avoid the Thunder-Cl–ps, and After-Cl–ps, says Jove.

(On a window, Merton College, Oxon, 18th century)

For V.D. cases only!

(In a stall, Madison High School, Brooklyn, 1953)

Here did I lay my Celia down;
I got the pox and she got half a crown.

(On a window in Chancery Lane, London, 1719)

Here I'd the luck a lovely girl to win.
Folk call her beautiful, she's filth within.

(Pompeii, 79 A.D.)

Here to the girl with the coal black eyes.
The soul of deceet the inventor of lies.
I hope in hell she will roast.
She sucked my dick with a hell of a dose.

(Merced, Cal., 1928)

I cannot relate to this environment.

UNDERNEATH

You don't have to relate—just fuck them.

UNDERNEATH

Suppose they have V.D.?

UNDERNEATH

Only 50% have V.D. the rest have T.B.

UNDERNEATH

Okay, just fuck the ones who cough.

(Vietnam, 1971)

I have had a clap
By a sad mishap;
But the doctor has cur'd it,
And I've endured it.
The bitch that gave it me,
She is gone over sea,
God damn her arse,
That fir'd my tarse.

(Pancras Wells, 18th century)

I suspect I have gonorrhea, what can I do about it?

UNDERNEATH

It doesn't always have symptoms in females, but it can make you sterile.

UNDERNEATH

Go to a free clinic and have a test done.

UNDERNEATH

What's the matter with sterility? Motherhood is a myth.

(Ladies' room, The Idler Coffee House, Cambridge, Mass., 1972)

Is grape-nuts a venereal disease?

Jenny has got a clap
Which was my mishap;
But Doctor R— set me right,
And I'm now in good plight.
Jan. 20, 1720. J.W.

(Bridge, The Crown, England)

Keep the clap out of Max's.

(Max's Kansas City Restaurant, New York City)

Merry syphilis and a happy gonorrhea.

Moby Dick is a venereal disease.

(Men's room, Queens College, N.Y.)

My maidenhead sold for a guinea,
A lac'd head with the money I bought;
In which I looked so bonny,
The heart of a gamester I caught;
A while he was fond, and brought gold to my box
But at last he robbed me, and left me the pox.

UNDERNEATH

When you balance accounts, it sure may be said,
You at a bad market sold your maidenhead.

(On a panel at the Faulcon, St. Neot's, England, 18th century)

Newark, N.J. is the syphilis capitol of the U.S.

(Ladies' room, Lion's Head, New York City)

Sing High Ding a Ding,
And Ho Ding a Ding,
I'm finely brought to Bed;
My Lord has stole that troublesome Thing,
That Folks call a Maidenhead.
Jane Hughs eighteen Years of Age.

Then sing High Ding a Ding,
And Ho Ding a Ding,
You're finely brought to Bed;
For something you've got for that troublesome Thing,
A Cl–p for a Maidenhead.
By my Lord's Gentleman.

(On a window, public house, near Tunbridge, England)

Sitting on yon bank of grass,
With a blooming buxom lass;
Warm with love, and with the day,
We to cool us went to play.
Soon the amorous fever fled,
But left a worse fire in its stead.
Alas! that love should cause such ills!
As doom to diet, drink and pills.

(On a window of a green house, near Tunbridge, England, 18th century)

Syphilis can be fun.

V.D. is nothing to clap about.

(Library, New York University, 1972)

W—: lay at the Angel in Marlborough Town,
And an angel lay with him all night;
He tipp'd her an angel before she lay down,
Which you know was but decent and right.
But an angel of darkness she proved to be sure;
For scarce twenty angels would pay for his cure.

(On a window, The Angel, Marlborough, England, 18th century)

Yesterday in a dark corner,
today it hurts urinating.
Yesterday on a soft pillow,
today it burns when pissing.

(Men's room, Germany)

VERDI, GIUSEPPE (1813–1901)

Who says that women are fickle?

UNDERNEATH

Verdi.

(Takeoff on a hairspray ad)

VIETNAM WAR

America lost her virginity in Vietnam
And she caught the clap, too
That's nothing so did I
I did too, but now I watch who I go out with
So should America.

(Vietnam, 1971)

As I slide down the
bannister of life,
I'll always remember
Vietnam as a splinter
in my ass.

(Vietnam, 1971)

Be free, go Canada.

The big damn Americans can't beat the small Vietnamese.

Black peoples should support our Vietnamese brothers!

(Watts, Los Angeles, 1971)

Bomb Haiphong

UNDERNEATH

Better yet, get bombed.

UNDERNEATH

Only lifers get bombed

UNDERNEATH

Then bomb Haiphong with lifers

(Vietnam, 1971)

Bomb Hanoi Now!

Bomb Saigon!

Bombing can end the war—bomb the Pentagon.

Bring the war home—Oct. 8, Chicago.

(On various walls all over New York City, Sept., 1969)

Coitus interruptus in the rape of Vietnam now!!!

(Fence, Yale University, 1970)

Con Ed. is the chemical branch of the Viet Cong.

Dubček, get out of Viet-Nam.

(Wall, Helsinki, 1970. Alexander Dubček was the leader of the 1968 Czech uprising to liberalize the country)

8965 days to go
how come?
I'm Vietnamese.

(Vietnam, 1971)

End the boys in Vietnam; bring the war home.

(1966)

End the war.

UNDERNEATH

In here or out there?

(Ladies' room, Top of the Gate, New York City)

End the world in Vietnam.

Escalate the war.

Fuck the war, please.

(University of California at Los Angeles, 1970)

Get the fuck out of Vietnam.

UNDERNEATH

There is no fuck in Vietnam not even a suck.

(Men's room, Slugs', New York City)

Girl Scouts wear the green beret.

Give Nixon time with his withdrawal program.

UNDERNEATH

Withdrawal is something Nixon's father should have done 58 years ago.

UNDERNEATH

You shithouse philosophers have all the answers.

UNDERNEATH

BETTER THAN YOU NON THINKING LIFERS.

(Vietnam, 1971)

God in the form of a white dove, came before the Americans and said kill, kill, kill all unfree, undemocratic people in my name.

A green beret is a Girl Scout hat, especially if you're a Brownie.

(Ladies' room, Lion's Head, New York City)

Hooray for the Green Bidets!

(Vietnam, 1971)

I cannot relate to this environment

UNDERNEATH

You don't have to relate—just fuck them

UNDERNEATH

Suppose they have V.D.?

UNDERNEATH

Only 50% have V.D.

UNDERNEATH

The rest have T.B.

UNDERNEATH

Okay, just fuck the ones who cough

(Vietnam, 1971)

I can't relate to my environment.

(Roadside shelter, Saigon)

I gotta get out of here.

UNDERNEATH

The shithouse or Nam?

UNDERNEATH

The army, you shithead.

(Men's room, Vietnam, 1972)

I killed in V.N. Hang me too!! Free Calley.

(Fort Benning, 1971)

I won't go!

UNDERNEATH

You're already here stupid.

(Men's room, Vietnam, 1972)

I'd rather have my country die for me.

(Men's room, Princeton University)

In Vietnam the wind doesn't blow, it sucks.

Join the Campus Crusade for Cong.

(Toilet, Humanities building, University of Minnesota)

Keep Vietnam out of U.S. politics.

(The Riviera, New York City)

Kill for peace, kill for freedom, kill Vietnamese, kill! kill!

Le May's wet dream—Vietnam.

(Boston University)

Let's bomb them all and let God sort it out.

Let's help our boys in Vietnam come.

(Lion's Head, New York City)

The liberals got us into Vietnam, Nixon will get us out.

(Wall near Union Square, New York City, June 1971)

Moishe Dayan should run our war in Viet-Nam.

UNDERNEATH

We will even give him 7 days.

(Wall, Boston)

Napalm is a figment of the collective imagination of the commie pinko hippie yippie leftist queers.
—Agnew.

(Vietnam, 1971)

Only 364 days to go—seems like I got here yesterday.

UNDERNEATH

You did, you stupid shit.

(Vietnam, 1971)

Remember Song My!

UNDERNEATH

No, how does it go?

UNDERNEATH

Yeah, it seems I heard that song before.

(Men's room, New York City, 1970)

Richie, Akron, Ohio, 112 days to go in the 'Nam!
Boot! 4 days to go.
Boot! 1 day left.
Boot! Only 12 hours left.
Boot! I'm leaving as soon as I finish this shit.
Boot! I haven't got time to take a shit.
Boot! I left last week.

(Men's toilet, Post Exchange, Hill 327, Da-Nang, Vietnam, February, 1967—"Boot" is Marine Corps slang for recruit)

I'm so short I can fit under the door
I'm so short,
I left yesterday—this is a recording.

(Vietnam, 1971)

Stop communism emperialistic (sic) aggression in S. Vietnam. Support U.S. Policy in Vietnam.

(Subway, New York City)

Stop demonstrations by ending the war in Vietnam.

UNDERNEATH

What kind of idiot thinks that foreign policy can be made by throwing temper tantrums in the streets of big cities?

(IRT subway, New York City)

Stop flim-flamming and get down to business—give a damn. End the economic war in Vietnam—Free Huey and the 21.

UNDERNEATH

This won't help.

(Men's room, Brooklyn College)

Stop murdering the Vietnamese people.

Stop the war! I want to get off!

Stop the war.

UNDERNEATH

On poverty.

CHANGED TO

Stop the war on puberty.

Stop the world . . . I want to get back on!

A sucking chest wound is nature's way of telling you you've been in a fire fight.

(Men's room, Vietnam)

Support our boys in Canada.

Take a VC to dinner tonight.

UNDERNEATH

Okay, but what restaurant serves dog meat?

Take a Viet Cong to lunch this week.

(University of Southern California at Los Angeles, 1966)

This is a way of the unwilling led by the unqualified dying for the ungrateful.

U.S. get out of Vietnam.

UNDERNEATH

U.S. get out of Berkeley.

(University of California at Berkeley)

The U.S. will win over the Marines.

(Nanterre, May, 1968)

A Viet Cong rebel sat here.

The Vietcong are the good guys.

Vietnam is a Bob Hope joke.

Vietnam; love it or leave it.

Vietnam—love it or leave it
or fuck it.

Vietnam: The Edsel of Foreign policy.

We'll bring peace to this land if we have to kill them all.
—Custer

Why me?

(Vietnam, 1971)

Why should the U.S. Gov't fight for fascism in Vietnam?

UNDERNEATH

To fight for the interests of the capitalists.

UNDERNEATH

End the war in Vietnam.

UNDERNEATH

How?

UNDERNEATH

By killing all commies and reactionaries like you.

(Bathroom walls, New School for Social Research, April, 1965)

Will the last GI out of Vietnam please turn out the light at the end of the tunnel.

(On the side of a bunker, Danang, Vietnam, 1972—cited by Herb Caen, columnist, San Francisco Chronicle*)*

With more people like me on our side, we woulda lost the war.

(IRT subway, New York City)

VIOLENCE

. . . And who is to define the nature of violence?

(Wall, Cambridge University, 1971)

A cop sleeps within each of us, he must be killed.

(France, May, 1968)

Don't shoot, I don't want to be President.

Free yourself from the Sorbonne. (By burning it.)

(Sorbonne, May, 1968)

If all men expect wisdom tomorrow from violence today; then who can expect a tomorrow.

(Engineering Society of Detroit, 1971)

Kill, rape, burn, pilage [*sic*]

UNDERNEATH

My Mommy won't let me.

(IND subway, New York City, 1971)

Legalize private murder, why should the government have all the fun?

Long live Rape and Violence.

(Nanterre, May, 1968)

Mace the nation.
Beat the press.

(Men's room, Conrad Hilton Hotel, Chicago, August 28, 1968—during Democratic Convention)

The pen is mightier than the switchblade.

(Long Island Courthouse, Mineola, 1970)

Violence in the defense of liberty is art in action.

(University of California at Los Angeles, 1970)

VIRGINITY, see CHASTITY

VIRTUE

Penelope rejected the suitors—not in stereo but in living high fidelity.

(Ladies' room, Bennington College)

Written at the Request of a Lady who on her Wedding-Day entreated an old Lover to write something upon her in the Window:

This glittering Diamond, and this worthless Glass,
Celia, display thy Virtue and thy Face;
Bright as the Brilliant while thy Beauty shows,
Ev'n Glass itself's less brittle than thy Vows.

VIVALDI, ANTONIO (c. 1675–1741)

Viva Vivaldi.

VOLTAIRE, FRANCOIS-MARIE AROUET DE (1694–1778)

God is dead.
—Voltaire
Voltaire is dead.
—God

(Métro, Paris)

VOYEURISM

God is a voyeur.

O girl, what did you do!
In jumping you fell,
you showed everything and
all the other parts.

(Bathroom, railroad station, Binz auf Rügen, 1903—this is high school prose and is found throughout Germany, earliest example 1892)

Upon the Ground he spread his Cloak;
The Nymph she was not shy, Sir;
And there they fairly did the Joke,
Whilst through this Crack peep'd I, Sir.
Oct. 27, 1722.

UNDERNEATH

Mr. Pimp, had I known your Worship was there,
Which I no more dreamt of, than sleeping,
When once I'd dispatch'd my Affair with the Fair,
By G—d, you'd paid dear for your Peeping.
Dec. 1722.

(On a wainscot, Sun Tavern, Billingsgate, England)

W

WALL WRITERS, *see also* GRAFFITI

All of us are sitting in the toilet but some of us are writing on the walls.

(Variation on the lines of Oscar Wilde: "All of us are lying in the gutter but some of us are looking at the stars)

All shithouse poets when they die,
Should have erected in the sky,
A fitting tribute to their wit,
A monument of solid shit.

(Public lavatory, Scotland)

And those who write on walls—Do they really know it?

(Old Spaghetti Factory, San Francisco, 1967)

Anybody who writes here hasn't got a good pussy to fuck.

UNDERNEATH

I've got a good pussy to fuck but not to write on.

Bewitched by a wall.

(Ladies' room, Brooklyn College, 1969)

Both mine and Women's Fate you'll judge from hence ill,
That we are pierc'd by every Coxcomb's Pencil.

(On a window, The King's Arms Tavern, Fleet Street, London)

By the funny display of wit
It looks like Shakespeare had
been here to shit.

Coming soon to this wall: St. Louis Fats, world famed graffitist. Watch this space for his scrawled obscenities.

(Wall, Berkeley, Cal., 1972

Do not write on walls!

UNDERNEATH

You want we should type maybe?

(Forum Coffee House, New York City)

Don't think everyone who comes in here is clever! Actually the owners write all this to pretend this is an "IN" bar—Good try!

(Lion's Head, New York City)

Don't write dirty things (like chastity) on the fucking walls.

(Ladies' room, Le Metro Caffe Espresso, New York City)

Don't write on our walls
We don't shit in your notebooks.
—The Regents

UNDERNEATH

What's found in our notebooks is shit anyway.
—The Students

(Main Library, University of California at Berkeley, 1965)

Eat your Wheaties and you'll write better graffitis!

Everybody writes here on the walls but me.

(Pompeii, 79 A.D.*)*

Everything is dirt. He who doesn't believe it should leave his inscription here.

(Men's room, Vienna—
cited in Anthropophyteia, *Vol. 5, 1908)*

Fools names are like their faces,
always seen in public places.

(Tourist Park, El Centro, Cal., June 27, 1928)

The 'garbage' on these walls means a point in history where students gain the freedom to determine their own destinies.

(University of California at Los Angeles, 1970)

Good Folks, sh–t and write, and mend honest Bog's Trade,
For when you sh–t Rhymes you help him to Bread:
He'el feed on a Jest, that is broke with your Wind,
And fatten on what you here leave behind.

(Playhouse boghouse, England)

He who wrote this is a tail licker.

(Pompeii, 79 A.D.)

He with aspirations small
Writes his name on the shithouse wall.

NEXT TO IT

Who wrote this shit?

Hey, I wonder if girls write similar shit in their johns?

UNDERNEATH

No we come here to write.

UNDERNEATH

Liberate Women!

(Men's room, University of Michigan)

Hither I came in haste to shit,
But found such excrements of wit,
That I had to show my skill in verse,
Had scarcely time to wipe my asse.

UNDERNEATH

Damn your writing,
Mind your shiting.

(Boghouse, Pancras-Wells, England—cited in: The Merry Thought, *London, 1731)*

How come there's nothing intellectual on these walls?

UNDERNEATH

$E = mc^2$

UNDERNEATH

Prove it.

(Macomb County Community College, Warren, Mich., 1972)

I didn't gain a very flattering judgment of students. On all sides one draws symbolic depravity.

(Men's room, Vienna—cited in Anthropophyteia, *Vol. 5, 1908; written in Croatian)*

I do believe with all my wit,
That Shakespeare's ghost comes here to shit.

(Picatinny Arsenal, Dover, N.J.)

I like not to write on walls.

(Nanterre, May, 1968)

I like to rite in fonetics.

(Paris, May, 1968)

I think that people who write in latrine stalls are immature and troubled and need psychological treatment.

If anyone write here may he waste away and his name be lost. May the man who damages property rouse up the Pompeian Venus against him. May the man committing a nuisance here wake up the Wrath of God Almighty.

(Pompeii, 79 A.D.)

If billies had brains as big as their balls,
They wouldn't write on shithouse walls.

(Men's room, Hillbilly Tavern, Chicago)

If man's brains were as big as his balls,
There'd be less writing on shithouse walls.

(Men's room, National Park, 1957)

If smell of t—d makes wit to flow,
Laud! what would eating it do.

(Pancras boghouse, London, 1731)

If you have been reading these, you are stupider than most of the writers.

UNDERNEATH

Then why have you written this?

(Construction wall, Philadelphia, 1969)

I'm a woman who doesn't need to copy men's lack of social behavior.

(Ladies' room, State University of New York at Stony Brook, 1971)

I'm proud to say this crapper has less vulgar poet*** in it than the past dozen I've been in. It shows only people with brains use this crapper.

(Bryce Canyon National Monument, Utah, August 20, 1928)

I'm witty, I'll Write,
I'm valiant, I'll Fight,
And take all that's said in my own Sense:
In Liquor I'm sunk,
And confoundedly drunk,
So there is the Source of this Nonsense.

(The White Lyon, Bristol)

Is writing on the wall basically a destructive act?

UNDERNEATH

It depends on what you have to say.

UNDERNEATH

Ask the person who has to clean this wall.

(Ladies' room, Barney's Restaurant, Cambridge, Mass., 1972)

It is characteristic of mirrors to reflect the faces of men and it is a vanity of jerks to write their names here.

(Men's room, bus terminal, Laredo, Tex.)

It's the Lover who writes, the Sod who reads it, it's clear.
The Listener twitches and itches, and he who goes by is a Queer.
And me, I'm a Bear's-dinner, I'm the twerp who stands reading here.

(Pompeii, 79 A.D.)

Join the Graffiti Guild of America.

(Co-ed toilet, Engagé Coffee House, New York City)

The literature here is what publishers reject—Halleluyah!

(The Exit Coffee House, New York City)

Men have more respect for your name and don't write it down in a shit house.

(Germany, 1904)

A man's a fool, and he should know it
Who makes himself a lavatory poet.

(Cited in Graffiti, *by Richard Freeman, London, 1966)*

A man's ambition must be small to write on a lavatory wall.

Moby Dick is a venereal disease.
George Eliot is a dyke.
Oedipus loves his mother.
I'm afraid of Virginia Woolf.

UNDERNEATH

Why don't all you lit majors go home and leave some room for us pornographers.

Never had Mortal greater Wit
Than I who ever wanted it;
But now my Wants have made me scrawl,
And rhyme and write the Devil and all.
J. Forbes, 1720.

The next person found writing on these walls will be forced to eat in this restaurant.

—The management

(Men's Room, Blum's Restaurant, New York City, 1972)

Of all the poets
under the sun the shit house
poet is worse than none
I wish the one that first
wrote in this place
was lying where I could
shit in his face.

(Norris Junction Camp, Yellowstone National Park, August 14, 1928)

The Wish:

Oh! may our Senate, learn'd and great,
(In order to perpetuate
The tuneful Strains and witty Flights,
Of him that Studies while he sh—ts)
Decree all Landlords, thro' the Nation,
Shall lay (on Pain of Flagellation)
In some meet Corner of their Dark Hole
A cuspidated Piece of Charcoal;
Or, where the Walls are cas'd with Wainscot,
A Piece of Chalk with equal Pains cut;

That those who labour at both Ends,
To ease themselves, and serve their Friends,
May not, reluctant, go from Sh–t,
And leave no Relict of their Wit,
For want of necessary Tools
To impart the *Proles* of their Stools:
Then *Cibber's* Odes, and *Tindal's* Sense,
Caleb and *Henley's* Eloquence,
Woolston, and all such learned Sophi's,
Would be cut down in House-of-Office:
Oxford and *Cambridge* too would join
Their Puns, to make the Boghouse shine:
Each learn'd Society would try all
(From lowest Club, to that call'd Royal,)
To furnish something might improve
Religion, Politicks, or Love:
Grand *Keyber,* Gormogons, Free Masons,
And *Heydeger,* with all his gay Sons,
Would find to suit, with Lectures there,
Their Intellectuals to a Hair;
Bodens might pick up Wit from thence, and lay
The *Drama* of another Modish Play.
So wise a Law would doubtless tend
To prove our Senate, Learning's Friend;
Whilst Trade, and such like fond Chimeras,
Might wait more fit and leisure *Aera's.*

(Boghouse near Lincoln's-Inn-Fields, England)

Oh wall, so many come here to scrawl, I wonder your burdened sides don't fall.

(Pompeii, 79 A.D.)

OK so you're taking my deathless power off the wall.

(Ladies' room, Limelight Restaurant, New York City)

One might think from this flow of wit
That Shakespeare's ghost had come here to shit—
Or Byron with his flaming tongue
Had stopped in here to drop his dung!

(Wall, outhouse, 1916)

One should not write in public places.

UNDERNEATH

There are no private places.

(Ladies' room, Brooklyn College, 1969)

One would judge from all this wit
That Shakespeare had been to shit
And this my friend may well be true
For Shakespeare had to do it too.

(Cited in Graffiti, *by Richard Freeman, London, 1966)*

One would think
By all this writing
That Shakespeare himself
Had been here shiting.

(By the cathedral at Ripon, England, August 11, 1929)

People probably chipped these things on the walls of Egyptian bathrooms 2000 years ago. So progress is a ball point pen.

(The Florentine, Berkeley, Cal.)

People who write on shit house walls
Should roll their shit in little balls,
And those who read these lines of wit,
Should have to eat those balls of shit.

Please help me stop writing on bathroom walls.

(Men's room, Princeton University, 1970)

Privies are now Receptacles of Wit,
And every Fool that hither comes to sh–t,
Affects to write what other Fools have writ.

(Boghouse, Epsom-Wells, England)

See on these walls sexual repression and the denial of the self. (Down with obscurantism.)

(Paris, May, 1968)

Sick people write on walls.

UNDERNEATH

This exploits walls.

(Goddard College, Plainfield, Vt., 1971)

Some come here to shit and stink
and scratch their itchie balls
But I come here to stand and think
and write upon the walls.

(Norris Junction Camp, Yellowstone National Park, August 14, 1928)

Some people are poor
While others are rich
But a shithouse
Poet is a Son of a Bitch.

(Men's room, Artesian Park, Ogden, Utah, August 16, 1928)

Soon the sun will come and dry these words from the earth.
Or the rains or snow will leave no trace of their birth.
And for those who read, some may soon forget,
And in their hearts there will be no regret.
There are some who will pass this place before the words of chalk are gone.
And some will remember not the writer of the word for unimportant is his name.
But scribbled on the wall:
WE ARE ALL THE SAME.

(Band shell in Central Park, New York City, December 28, 1971)

Stop vandalism—don't scribble on walls.

(On a freshly painted wall—cited by Norton Mockridge, columnist, Boston Herald, *December 2, 1966)*

There's Nothing foul that we commit,
But what we write, and what we sh–t.

(Boghouse, Hampstead, England)

They're writing equations on Moscow subway signs.

(Construction fence, New York City)

A thing that never should be done at all
Is to write your name on the backhouse wall.

(Kicking Horse Auto Camp, Yoho National Park, British Columbia, 1928)

This is the first time I ever wrote on a wall.

UNDERNEATH

Couldn't you be more creative for your 1st time?

(Ladies' room, Goddard College, Plainfield, Vt., 1971)

In a toilet which had nothing but obscenities written on the wall, someone wrote:

This is why we may be second to the moon.

This wall is ready for any budding scatologist.

(Men's room, Rutgers University, 1969)

This wall would be really good if people were not so inhibited and afraid of saying what they really thought for fear that others would condemn them for it.

UNDERNEATH

Shut up.

(On wall in which people were invited to express themselves, Hallmark Gallery, New York City, 1972)

Those who write on shithouse walls
Roll their shit in little balls
Those who read those words of wit
Eat the little balls of shit.

Very kindly you are requested—this goes for everyone of you smearers—one should not use the wall. Yet if the joke oppresses you too much and is worthy of being preserved, don't put it here. Just think, there is still writing paper on earth.

(Elberfeld, 1907)

Warning! If patrons do not stop writing on the walls, the walls will be removed. The Management.

(IRT subway, New York City, 1972)

We don't have time to write.

(Nanterre, May, 1968)

We the wallwriters of this place called Philly
Will try our best to beauty the city.
So we're trying to put an end to all graffiti
We're doing our part by doing constructive art
We won't let you down
So give us some space to write around town.

(Wall, Philadelphia, 1971)

Well sung of Yore, a Bard of Wit,
That some Folks read, but all Folks sh–t;
But now the Cafe is alter'd quite,
Since all who come to Boghouse write.

(Boghouse, Middle Temple, England)

Because they cannot eat, some Authors write:
And some, it seems, because they cannot sh–te.

(Boghouse, Middle Temple, England)

Who scribbles on the Wall when he's at sh—,
May sure be said to have a Flux of Wit.

(In pencil in the Vault at Chelsea College, England)

Whoever writes his name in a shithouse is an ass and will ever remain so.

(Men's room, Langenau in Silesia—cited in Anthropophyteia, *Vol. 6, 1909)*

Why write jokes on the wall when you're holding one in your hand?

Why write on a wall?

UNDERNEATH

Because it's there.

Write everywhere!

UNDERNEATH

But before writing learn to think.

(Paris, May, 1968)

You who instead of Fodder, Fingers use,
Pray lick 'em clean, and don't this Wall abuse.

UNDERNEATH

These House-of-Office Poets, by the L—d,
Instead of Laurel, should be crown'd with T—d.

(Boghouse, Trinity College, Dublin)

The young make love.
The old make obscene gestures.
Who are the pigs who dare write on walls?

(Paris, May, 1968)

WALLACE, GEORGE (1919–   )

George Wallace is passing.

George Wallace uses hair straightener.

A hill billy farmer named Hollis,
Used possums and snakes for his solace.
The children had scales and prehensile tails,
And voted for Governor Wallace.

(Men's room, Princeton University, 1970)

A honky ain't shit, especially Wallace.

(Men's room, Gitlitz Delicatessen & Bar, New York City, 1969)

McGovern cannot govern,
Nixon cannot cope,
Wallace in a wheel chair,
Is still the nation's hope.

(Construction fence, Trenton, N.J., 1972)

WALLACE, LURLEEN (1926–1968)

The Governor of Alabama is a Mother.

(Lexington avenue subway, New York City—during governorship of Lurleen Wallace, wife of George Wallace)

WAR, *see also* VIETNAM WAR

Ban the bomb, save the world for conventional warfare.

Dow—better murder through chemistry.

(Men's room, Harvard University—variation on slogan: "Dow, better living through chemistry")

How many are there like myself, especially innocent ones, who will continue to fall under the bullets. I still have a few hours left in this life but I hope to be avenged by the Reds.—A student teacher

(Prison, Dijon, 1942—during German occupation of France)

I am Marc Boillet. I am a sniper. Tomorrow the first of July 1944, I will be shot. May God receive my soul.

(Prison, Dijon, 1944—during German Occupation of France)

Is there a life before death?

(Written on a wall in large white letters after a 10-hour gun battle, Whiterock section of Belfast, 1972)

Let's win the war!

UNDERNEATH

Let's win the war, to hell with Hitler!

UNDERNEATH

The war is over, the hell with everything!

(Commuter's Bar, San Francisco, October, 1945)

Make love and if you want to make war, enjoy yourself.

(IND subway, New York City)

The only difference between an unclear war and a nuclear war is the way you use the UN.

(University of Michigan)

War causes chromosome damage.

(Men's room, Rutger's University)

War is good business—invest your sons.

(Lamont Library, Harvard, also on a button)

War is insane.
—Nat'l Institute of Mental Health

(On seat of crosstown bus, New York City, 1969)

The world rejected God and it became mad. The Japanese make coal with rubber, the Germans make rubber with coal and we have to buy ersatz tires for 2000 francs and they last only one month.

(Prison, Dijon, 1943—during German occupation of France)

WARHOL, ANDY (1931–)

Andy Warhol stencils.

*(Prophetic graffito—*Time *reported his girl friends now paint his pictures)*

Warhol traces.

(University of Florida)

WASHINGTON, GEORGE (1732–1799)

George Washington shat here.

(George Washington Hotel, New York City)

WATER CLOSET

And they say Pepsi is the pause that refreshes.

Another fine product by MBP abrasives.

(Over toilet paper, physics building, University of Minnesota)

Are these facilities beneath you?
UNDERNEATH
They won't do the job if they're not.
UNDERNEATH
Yes, too low for a high-class girl like me.

(Ladies' room, Brooklyn College, New York, 1970)

At ease.

(Men's room, U.S. Naval base, Newport, Rhode Island, 1961)

Attention hillbillies—the rock candy in the urinals is not for you.

(Greenwich Village coffee house, 1962)

The Boghouse Lament
Oh their shifting grandpa's grave to build a shit house,
Oh! Their shifting it at very great expense,
Their bringing in some drains, and making way for change to satisfy the local residents.

Now whats the use of having a religion if when you're dead you cannot be at ease.
Just because some rich nit-wit wants a pipe-line for his shit.
They wouldn't let poor old grandpa be at peace,
Now dear old grandpa ne'er was he a quitter and I'm bloody sure he ain't no quitter now,
So all dressed up in his sheets, he will haunt those shit house seats,
And he'll only let them bog when he'll allow.
Oh! won't there be such pangs of constipation,
And won't those brass-bound bastards rant and rave,
But it will serve them right, they sure deserve their plight for fucking around with an Aussie workman's grave.

(Popular toilet graffito with Australian soldiers during World War II)

Democracy: ten cents to take a shit and a dollar won't get you anywhere.

(Men's room, New Orleans airport, Louisiana, 1972)

Do not throw cigarettes in the urinal as they become soggy and hard to light.

Do you feel the need to unwind?

(Written above toilet-paper holder, men's room, Lansdale, Pennsylvania, 1972)

Face it—this is the most worthwhile thing you've done all day.

(Ladies' room, Graffiti Restaurant, New York City)

A flush is better than a full house.

(Men's room, Indiana University, 1940)

Flush hard, it's a long way to the kitchen.

(Phoenix restaurant)

For those in a hurry with no time to sit
Please lift the lid for a more direct hit.

(Ladies' room, Berkeley, California, 1963)

Girls:
I promise to support your cause for sex and marijuana, etc., if you keep the sink clean and throw papers and such in the waste basket.
—Thank you, Le Metro.
(Ladies' room, Le Metro Caffe Espresso, New York City)

God bless the toilet—It takes our sins away.
(Men's room, The Jabberwock, Berkeley, California)

Happiness is getting here on time.
(Men's room, Beer Hall, Berkeley, California)

He who never with sweaty face,
gasped toward the can, he knows
not the feeling of voluptuous relief
when you reach it.
(Elberfeld, Germany, 1905)

Here every man has to pull the shorter one (or get the short end of the stick).
(Breslau, Germany, cited in Anthropophyteia, *Vol. 5, 1908)*

Here everyone grabs his end.
(Breslau, Germany, cited in Anthropophyteia, *Vol. 5, 1908)*

I would have answered sooner but someone was in this stall for three straight days.
(Men's room, Grumman Aviation Company, Bethpage, New York, 1966)

If you come to deposit money in this bank, don't leave change on the counter.
(Ladies' room, Mexico City bank, Mexico)

In the grave and in this big hall
all men are equal.
In the grave all are rotting
and here rich and poor stink.
(Germany, 1906)

J.P. Sanchez sat here.

UNDERNEATH

Thanks for warning me.

(Men's room, Wayne University, Detroit, Michigan)

Kilroy wouldn't dare come in here.

(University of North Carolina, 1959)

Occupancy by more than 401 persons is dangerous, unlawful and somewhat unsanitary.

—Dr. Equi Excrementi Civilis

Please flush twice the Hudson River is at a low level.

(Men's room, Columbia Presbyterian Medical Center, New York)

Pray for towel.

(Written on empty towel machine, Paradox Restaurant, New York City)

Pull for joy.

(Written next to chain, Paradox Restaurant, New York City)

Remember the Maine,
To hell with Spain,
Don't forget to pull the chain.

(Popular toilet-wall inscription during and several years after the Spanish-American War)

Save water, don't be a four-flusher.

Smile, You're on Candid Camera.

(One of the most popular toilet-wall one-liners)

Stamp out pay toilets.

(Horn and Hardart, New York City; also on a button)

Take the four-letter word out of the classroom and restore it to its rightful place. Here.

(Men's room, Greyhound bus depot)

This urinal will self-destruct in 5 seconds.

(Men's room, Under the Stairs Bar and Restaurant, New York City, 1969)

Toilet paper compliments of Acme sand and gravel company.

(American Academy of Dramatic Arts, New York City, 1969)

The water closet like the harp is essentially—a solo instrument.

(Ladies' room, Blind Lemon Pub, Berkeley, California)

Whoever heard of a toilet seat as a substitute for a psychrists [*sic*] couch?

(Toilet, men's faculty lounge, Hunter College, New York City)

WAYNE, JOHN (1907–)

John Wayne for Secretary of Defense.

(On various walls, also on a button)

WELCH, ROBERT (1899–)

(Note: Founder of the John Birch Society)
I'm for Robert Welch.

(On various walls, also on a button)

WEST, MAE (1892–)

Thanks, I enjoyed every inch of it.
—Mae West

WHIMSY

Absurd is Nothing.

(Wall near People's Park, Berkeley, Cal.)

All life is sacred except flies and mosquitos.

(Ladies' room, University of California at Berkeley, 1971)

Anne fell here.

(Federal building on Foley Square, New York City—cited in The New Yorker, *1937)*

Arm the vagrants.

UNDERNEATH

Arm the cockroaches.

(Co-ed toilet, East Village Other, *1970)*

Letter to Will S—rs, Esq;
Dear *Will,*
I ever will
Be at your will,
Whene'er you will,
And where you will;
So that your Will
Be Good-Will,
I never will
Dispute your Will;
But give you Will
For Will.
At this Time,
At all Times,
Or any Time,
But such Times
As bad Times:
For Lemon Thyme,
Or Common Time,
Or Tripple Time,
Are not Times
Like your Times
And my Times
For Pastimes.
Then betimes
Suit your Time
To my Time;
Or my Time
Is lost Time.
I wish you well,
And I hope you're well,
As I am well;
So all's well
That ends well;
Then farewell.
R.B. April 17. 1714.

(On a window, Star-Inn, Coventry, England)

Death to the penis invasion.

(Julius Restaurant, New York City, 1950—the meaning of this phrase puzzled people for years)

Down with Emperor Ming.

Easternize the Midwest.

Eat, drink and bite Mary.

(Men's toilet, Newport Jazz Festival, 1967)

Eat me, I'm a pregnant jelly bean.

(Men's room, University of New Hampshire)

F**K
*You see?

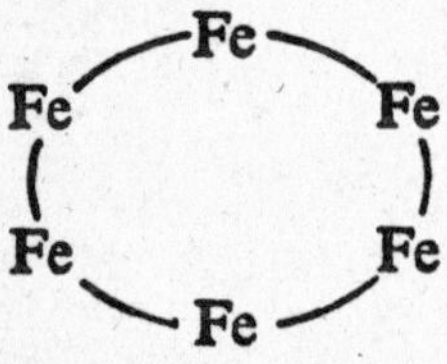

Ferrous Wheel!

(Laundry room, Princeton University, 1971)

Free the gypsies.

Get the Greeks out of Ilium.

After Dutch elm disease struck one of two beautiful trees which stood together on the Cornell campus, the following graffiti appeared almost simultaneously on the stripped stump of the dead one:

Is Euthanasia in the case of Dutch Elm disease justified?

This tree died for our sins.

This is the Math tree, it has ordered pairs and square roots.

That tree over there [*arrow pointing to the other tree*] is very angry. Would you like somebody to write all over your dead brother?

This tree is a dorm
For deep in the elm
Is dwelling a worm
Whose name is Anselm.

Please stop scratching on my walls.
—Anselm

Où sont les graffiti d'antan?

Graffiti space for dogs.

Help send a girl to Boy's Town.

Help stamp out and abolish redundancy.

Help stamp out quicksand.

Help stamp out red ants!

Help stamp out Whooping Cranes.

Horse power.

I, C, U, B
Y Y for me. J.S.

*(Summer house near Farnham, England—
"I see you be Two wise for me.")*

I love grils.

UNDERNEATH

It's spelled girls

UNDERNEATH

What about us grils.

I once had a grunch, but my eggplant ate it.

(Florida State University)

I was not here.

I'll cut you in Zen pieces.

I'm a Marxist, Grouch type.

(Nanterre, May, 1968)

Independence for Lapland!

*J. Jackson currit plenum sed
Et laefit meum magum ad.*
The English Translation, Word for Word.
J. Jackson run full-but,
And hurt my Great Toe.

*(Wall at a school in Norwich, England—
written in Dog Latin)*

Keep the baby.
—Faith

Let me tickle your fancy

A lion is loose from the zoo.

Little Mary from Boston, Mass.
Stepped into water up to her ankles.
It doesn't rhyme now,
But wait till the tide comes in.

Magic is a foot.

UNDERNEATH

Left or right.

(Men's room, Lansdale, Pa., 1972)

Many are cold but few are frozen.

Miasma!

Mira! Mira! on the wall.

Nomads of the world unite!

North Dakota is a hoax.

Paracelsus Parimutual.

(Paradox Restaurant, New York City—what the famous Swiss physician's name means in this context is a mystery)

The pen is mightier than the pencil.

Pigs ate my roses.

Plaid power.

(Lion's Head, New York City)

Power to the polyethylene.

(Princeton University, 1972)

Promotion is nice but it rots the teeth.

(Free Library of Philadelphia, 1968)

Saxons go home.

(Cited in Graffiti *by Richard Freeman, London, 1966)*

SDRAWKCAB is backwards spelled backwards.

(Men's toilet, Telephone Company, New York City)

Seltzer Power!

Sleep quickly we need the pillows.

Stamp out distemper, but don't step in it.

(Cited by Norton Mockridge, columnist)

Stamp out philately!

(Library staff lounge, Fort Belvoir, Va.—cited in American Library Association Bulletin, *April, 1969)*

TVA levitates . . . . .

Take a turtle home for din-din.

(IND subway, New York City)

Think Dog!

The tongue is mightier than the toe!

(Florida State University)

Up with down.

Up your lazy river.

(The Village Gate, New York City)

We like Vitamin C.

(Paris, May, 1968)

Welcome to the Wrinkle Room.

(The Pilgrim Restaurant, New York City)

What about a date?

UNDERNEATH

July 3, 1776.

Whatever happened to Harry's hair?

UNDERNEATH

It turned pubic.

UNDERNEATH

On which exchange?

UNDERNEATH

Your mother's moustache.

(Limelight Restaurant, New York City)

Write anything that comes: trains, lovers, snow.

(IRT subway, New York City, 1970)

WHISTLER, JAMES McNEILL (1834–1903)

Whistler's mother is off her rocker.

WHITMAN, WALT (1819–1892)

Walt Whitman gets emotionally involved with his patients.

(Cited by Jim Moran, columnist, Chicago Daily News, *May 27, 1967)*

WILDE, OSCAR (1854–1900)

Oscar Wilde and Lord Douglas are more than just friends.

(Cited by Jim Moran, columnist, Chicago Daily News, *May 27, 1967)*

Oscar Wilde for Homecoming Queen.

(Wall, Berkeley, Cal., 1972)

Release Oscar Wilde.

(Ladies' room, Limelight Restaurant, New York City, 1965)

WIT AND HUMOR

More things are wrought by laughter,
Than tears about your late disaster.

More things are wrought by laughter
Than by threats of hereafter.

(Lion's Head, New York City)

Puns have two evil Ends:
Sometimes they gain us Foes,
Sometimes they make us lose
our Friends.

(The Crown, Uxbridge, England)

WOMAN

Death and Marriage are by Destiny,
And both these Things become a Maiden's Fee,
Whether they die between a Pair of Sheets,
Or live to marry, they will lose their Wits;
So is it destin'd by the Gods above,
They'll live and die by what they love.

(The Crown at Harlow, England)

The Nature of Women:
Fair and foolish, little and loud,
Long and Lazy, black and proud;
Fat and merry, lean and sad,
Pale and peevish, red and bad.

(Summer house near Richmond, England)

Sent by an unknown Hand.
O ye Powers above!
Who of Mortals take Care
Make Women less cruel,
More fond, or less fair.
Was *Helen* half so fair, so form'd for Joy,
Well fought the *Trojan*, and well burnt was Troy.

Woman is a temple built on a sewer.

(Men's room, Princeton University, 1970)

Woman is like a pig,
All the parts are good,
It goes well with all sauces.

(Café, St. Germain, Paris, 1966)

A Wretch, whom Fortune has been pleas'd to rowl.
From the Tip-top of her enchanted Bowl,
Sate musing on his Fate, but could not guess,
Nor give a Reason for his Fickleness:
Such Thoughts as these would ne'er his Brain perplex,
Did he but once reflect upon her Sex:
For how could he expect, or hope to see,
In Woman either Truth or Constancy.

(The White Lyon, Bristol)

WOMEN'S LIBERATION

Be kind to your sisters, only they understand.

(Ladies' room, Boston, 1972)

Burn your bra!

(Girls' room, elementary school, New York City—cited by Lindsy Van Gelder in New York Post, *March 28, 1972)*

A cock will ruin your life in 5 seconds.

(Ladies' room, New Hope, Pa.)

Don't cook tonight—starve a rat today.

Don't you get the feeling you should be home cleaning instead of fucking around?

(Ladies' room, Limelight Restaurant, New York City)

Down with phallic imperialism.

Eliminate sexism. Free all the sisters.

(Wall, Berkeley, Cal., 1970)

Eve got a bum rap.

Fewer men—fair admissions.

(Yale University, 1970)

Girls who use men sexually for power are really abusing themselves.

UNDERNEATH

Groovy abuse.

(Ladies' room, New York University)

Hey, I wonder if girls write similar shit in their johns?

UNDERNEATH

No we come *here* to write.

UNDERNEATH

Liberate Women!

(Men's room, University of Michigan)

I am a woman—I am a human being. I will achieve more than this.

(Ladies' room, West End Bar near Columbia University, 1972)

If we all work together we can put a woman in the White House.

(Ladies' room, Bernard Baruch College, New York City, 1970)

Ladies—Don't let society rule you. We're all under wraps.

UNDERNEATH

Wraps? Well it's cold outside.

(Ladies' room, New York University, 1969)

Marriage legalizes rape.

My father was open minded. He gave my mother permission to vote for liberals.

(Wall, Helsinki, 1969)

Princeton women are just men who worked their balls off!

UNDERNEATH

This is just another case of P.U. male chauvinism.

UNDERNEATH

Typical co-ed reaction.

(Laundry room, Princeton University, 1971)

Sisterhood is powerful.

(Ladies' room, Boston, 1972)

Vasectomy [*sic*] not pills.

We believe in Woman's Liberation.

(Written in chalk on the wall at the Woman's House of Detention, Greenwich Village, New York City, 1971)

Wives are unpaid labor.

Woman power.

(Ladies' room, Boston, 1972)

Women of the world wake up! Fight for all you should have had since the beginning of the world. Be second to no man.

(Ladies' room, Limelight Restaurant, New York City)

Woman's Lib? Put them behind bras.

(Long Acre Pub, London, 1971)

Women's Liberation
Right On!

The following was written on a Virginia Slims cigarette ad that said, "You've come a long way, baby!":

You took a long time to come.
—Vagina Slims

(New York City, 1972)

WOOLF, VIRGINIA (1882–1941)

Who's afraid of Virginia Woolf?

(Found by Edward Albee on a toilet wall)

WORK, see LABOR

WYETH, ANDREW (1917–)

Andrew Wyeth paints by #.

(Billboard, Chaddesford, Pa., 1967)

Y

YOUTH, *see also* PUBERTY

Join the teen-age rebellion.

(On various walls, also on a button)

McDougal teeny boppers evaporate! (please)

(Engagé Coffee House, New York City)

Pimples are wasted on adolescents.

(Men's room, New School for Social Research, New York City)

Student power.

(Sorbonne, May, 1968, also on various walls in U.S. and on a button)

Support the breakfast programs.

(East Harlem, New York City, 1970—slogan of Young Lords advocating subsidies for food for underprivileged children)

S.W.I.N.E.

(University of California at Los Angeles, 1970—acronym, said to be the work of cartoonist Al Capp, that stands for "Students Wildly Indignant about Nearly Everything")

The teeny boppers shall inherit the earth.

The young are a country.

(Wall, Santiago, Chile, 1970)

Z

ZOOERASTY

He who never fucked a horse, does not know the true value of the animal.

(Men's room, Breslau—cited in Anthropophyteia, *Vol. 6, 1909)*

I fuck all vaginas in women, goats and cats.

(Men's room, Breslau—cited in Anthropophyteia, *Vol. 6, 1909)*

I screwed my old father in the ass because my black tom cat had run away.

(Men's room, Prussia-Silesia, 1910)

Montana—where men are men and women are sheep.

(Bar-Cafe Service Station, State Highway, Mont.)

My husband fucks only his sheep, sometimes he fucks the cow, therefore I cannot sleep at night. My cunt won't give me any peace.

(Ladies' room, Breslau—cited in Anthropophyteia, *Vol. 6, 1909)*

My wife now has her fourth child, soon I will fuck only cats and cows.

(Men's room, Prussia-Silesia—cited in Anthropophyteia, *Vol. 7, 1910)*

The softest and most beautiful cunts are found among cats. Therefore anyone who fucks anything else is crazy.

The following was written on a street sign that said, "Yield to Horses."

If you dig 'em.

(San Francisco Mill Valley, 1971)

Zoophiliacs unite! The farmlands of Bavaria are stricken with zoophilia.

(Men's room, library, University of Maryland, 1972)

SELECTED BIBLIOGRAPHY

Brassai. *Graffiti.* Stuttgart: Belser Verlag, 1960.

Freeman, Richard. *Graffiti.* London: Hutchinson, 1966.

Kohl, Herbert. *Golden Boy As Anthony Cool.* New York: The Dial Press, 1972.

Pritchard, V. *English Medieval Graffiti.* London: Cambridge University Press, 1967.

Reisner, Robert. *Selected Scrawls from Bathroom Walls.* New York: Parallax, 1967.

—— *Graffiti, Two Thousand Years of Wall Writing.* New York: Cowles, 1971.

Tanzer, Helen H. "The Common People of Pompeii." Baltimore: Johns Hopkins Press, *The JHU Studies in Archeology* #29, 1939.